# Shooter's Bible GUIDE TO CONCEALED CARRY

## 2nd Edition

## A Beginner's Guide to Armed Defense

**BRAD FITZPATRICK**
Foreword by J. Scott Rupp

SKYHORSE PUBLISHING

Skyhorse Publishing books may be purchased in bulk at special discounts for sales promotion, corporate gifts, fund-raising, or educational purposes. Special editions can also be created to specifications. For details, contact the Special Sales Department, Skyhorse Publishing, 307 West 36th Street, 11th Floor, New York, NY 10018 or info@skyhorsepublishing.com.

Skyhorse® and Skyhorse Publishing® are registered trademarks of Skyhorse Publishing, Inc.®, a Delaware corporation.

Visit our website at www.skyhorsepublishing.com.

10 9 8 7 6 5 4 3 2

Library of Congress Cataloging-in-Publication Data

Cover design by Adam Bozarth

Print ISBN: 978-1-5107-3602-3
Ebook ISBN: 978-1-5107-3603-0

Printed in China

**DISCLAIMER**

Check your state and local laws before carrying a handgun, concealed or otherwise. Laws vary widely from state to state. Some states allow concealed carry without a permit, some require a permit, and some states do not allow concealed handgun carry at all. All states put restrictions on where and how handguns can be carried legally. In addition, several states outlaw particular modes of concealed carry. Your local law enforcement department or district attorney's office should know the details.

This book is not designed to take the place of a qualified and competent instructor; rather, it is a resource designed to supplement quality training.

# CONTENTS

# Foreword

*C*oncealed carry is nothing new. People have been toting "hideout guns" since the 1850s to defend themselves and those dear to them from criminal attack. But what has changed, at least in the United States, is the sheer prevalence of concealed carry. Efforts by the National Rifle Association and state gun-rights groups have significantly expanded the number of states where it's possible to carry concealed. The scope and pace of these efforts are impressive. In 1995, there were only about half a dozen states with a "shall issue" policy for concealed-carry permits whereby state law requires permit-issuing agencies—typically police departments and sheriff's offices—to furnish a permit to any applicant who met the qualifications instead of having to show cause why he or she needed one.

By 2012, that number had climbed to thirty-seven. Four other states require no permitting process whatsoever; if you're legally allowed to own a handgun, you're legally allowed to carry concealed anywhere in the state where such carry is not prohibited. Only one state, Illinois, prohibits concealed carry outright, and at press time a federal circuit court had ruled that ban to be unconstitutional. If the ruling stands, all fifty U.S. states will permit concealed carry in some form.

That's a big reason why today more and more people are availing themselves of the opportunity to defend themselves wherever they may be. Why a firearm? Because, for one, it's the great equalizer. A gun gives a slight woman, an old man, a person with physical limitations—everyone, really—a fighting chance against a bigger, stronger attacker. Forget knives, baseball bats, martial arts training, and the like; the only real defense in a battle of unequals is a firearm. Not that a handgun is the end-all in any fight. There is no such thing as a handgun cartridge that will always stop every attack from every attacker instantly, but you're a heck of a lot better off with one than without one.

While the world may not be a whole lot more dangerous than it's ever been, the police can't be everywhere. Even if you had the chance to call 911, if you get jumped in a parking lot at night or find yourself in the middle of a convenience store robbery that's going from bad to worse, there's almost no chance the cavalry is going to show up in time to save you. In the end, you're responsible for your own safety.

Infamous mass public shootings by deranged criminals—such as recent high-profile incidents involving committed active shooters targeting innocent civilians—would give anyone pause as well. Incidents such as these certainly have moved some people to consider concealed carry who otherwise may not have given the practice any thought or perhaps were even opposed to it. Would a legally armed citizen on the scene have reduced the carnage in these and other instances? No one can say for sure. But ask yourself this: If you had been there, would you have felt more or less safe if you'd had a gun? It's hard to see how the answer could be anything other than "more."

On the flip side, cases such as the Florida incident involving Trayvon Martin and George Zimmerman point to how any shooting—even one that may be held to be legally justifiable—can land the shooter in hot water. There's an old saying, "It's better to be judged by twelve than carried by six." It's hard to argue with that, but at the same time, the vagaries of the legal system and the very real possibility of criminal and civil repercussions of self-defense firearms use can't be dismissed.

What it boils down to is this: Carrying a concealed handgun involves much more than buying a gun, a holster, and some ammunition. While these are important, the biggest thing to remember is that concealed carry is not merely a practice; it's a way of life. It affects—or should affect—the way you dress, the way you behave, the way you think. At the root of concealed carry is this maxim: No one is supposed to know you have a gun. No longer can you just throw on jeans and a shirt to go to the store or be careless about how you pick up something from the ground. No longer can you accept a hug from a casual acquaintance at a party. No longer can you go about your daily routine without being observant, vigilant.

It's a serious responsibility, this business of carrying a gun. And while Hollywood makes it seem "oh so easy" to get the drop on a bad guy and save the day, the fact is—as any firearms expert will tell you—you will not "rise to the occasion"; you will default to your training. And if you haven't taken the time to get any training, to diligently practice the skills involved in concealed carry, to understand the laws of your state and the laws of human behavior . . . well, good luck with that.

But since you're holding this book in your hands, whether you are ready to begin to carry concealed or are just considering it, you've already taken the first step. Brad's done an excellent job of delivering the information you need to know to be a responsible gun-carrying citizen. This book builds a foundation for a lifetime of responsible gun ownership by teaching you how a gun works, how to handle it, and so much more—moving the first-time gun owner (or longtime gun "possessor" whose firearm has resided in a dresser drawer from Day One) from tentative newcomer to comfortable, competent gun handler.

Forget all the high-speed "tactical" stuff you see on TV. It's far more important simply to be able to load/reload, draw, and fire your gun surely and safely and to understand the common-sense practices necessary to keep your gun hidden, secure, and ready to use for defense.

By the time you're done reading Brad's book, you'll have the confidence not only to buy a gun but to shoot it regularly, maintain it, and carry it in a safe and responsible manner. But don't stop there. Whether you're a longtime gun person or new to firearms, you can never have enough training. One of the most knowledgeable defensive handgun experts I know, a man with decades of law enforcement experience and countless hours of training, still avails himself of every combat handgun class he can afford to attend. Because he knows that we should never stop learning and never believe we're truly ready to face a life-or-death defensive situation.

You owe it to yourself, to your loved ones, and to your fellow citizens to be the most skilled and sensible practitioner of concealed carry you can be. You've taken an excellent first step with this book.

**J. Scott Rupp**
**Editor in Chief, *Handguns* magazine**

# Preface to the Second Edition

*I*t's been five years since I wrote the original version of *The Shooter's Bible Guide to Concealed Carry*, and a great deal has changed during that period of time. Some of the changes have been good; I now have two small children, and they've changed my perspective on almost everything—including personal defense. However, not all recent events have been good. The original version of this book went to print not long after the murders at Sandy Hook Elementary School, and as badly as I wish I could say that was the latest incident where innocent people were killed, I cannot. The Mandalay Bay shooting, Charleston church shooting, and the recent events at Marjory Stoneman Douglas High School remind us that the we live in a dangerous world.

I don't write this with the intention of scaring you into buying this book, nor do I choose to delve into politics. This book is, as it was in 2013, designed to be a manual to help new gun owners—and there are a lot of them—become safer and more proficient with their firearms. I learned to shoot from my father, and he was safe and skilled with a firearm. When I had questions about guns, and I had many, he was my go-to source of information. But, I realize, not everyone has that in their life. Over the course of the years leading up to the publication of the first edition of this book, and more commonly in the years that followed its release, I've been asked to help new shooters master the basics of firearm handling. There are few things I enjoy more! Unlike so many people who only associate firearms with violence, I grew up in a time and a place where guns were a tool. They were used to fill our freezers, to protect our homes, but primarily for recreation. We shot for fun, and I still do that (and get paid for it, which is even more exciting). I spent hours and hours at the range as a kid breaking clays and shooting tin cans. I enjoyed guns, and I still enjoy teaching others how to shoot.

Somewhere down the line I came to the realization that not everyone has access to a firearms expert who is willing to take the time to teach them to shoot properly. My father demanded that I learn the basic tenets

▲ As of 2018 there were roughly 16 million CCW permit holders in the United States, and the number continues to grow. The increase in concealed carry permits has coincided with a nationwide decline in violent crime.

of firearms safety before I ever touched a real gun, and I still remember the pride I felt when I got to accompany my dad on a deer hunt when I was in the first grade. I took a toy firearm and it became my training tool in the field. Dad would ensure that I understood and demonstrated proper firearms handling techniques before I was ever allowed to touch a firearm that actually fired projectiles. But what would have happened to me if I hadn't grown up in a house where firearms were present and respected? It's hard to imagine how different my opinion on guns might be if I'd never been around them.

What this book is designed to offer readers is a thorough examination of the primary principles of concealed carry. You see, one other thing that I realized

▲ With so many Americans taking responsibility for their own protection, more and more companies are offerings products designed with concealed carry in mind. Kahr's new CT380 Tungsten semiauto pistol is compact, reliable, and accurate. And it has to be—there's never been a more competitive field of carry handguns from which to choose.

during the writing of the first edition of the book is that gun writers write for gun enthusiasts. There was—and still is—a limited amount of information about the most basic elements of firearm ownership. There are exceptions to this, of course—the National Shooting Sports Foundation and National Rifle Association have worked to provide a variety of resources to shooters about safe firearm handling and proper shooting, but rarely has that information been assembled in one text in a straightforward, easy-to-read format that provides answers to the most basic questions.

Lastly, I'd like to share an experience I had while writing an article after the publication of the original *Shooter's Bible Guide to Concealed Carry.* Two years ago, *Handguns Magazine* editor Scott Rupp gave me the go-ahead to write a feature article discussing carry options for runners (which provided some valuable information that was not in the original text but does appear in this most recent version). During the course of my research for that article, I sought the opinion of runners and, with a little digging, I found a running forum where someone had asked the same question I was posing. The thread started out with a young male runner asking what type of holster setup other runners used when they carried.

The initial response to this young man's inquiry was something along the lines of, "If you're running in an area where you think you need a gun, then maybe you should choose another place to run." Several other comments followed, many haranguing the person who had posted the initial question. Most respondents cheered on the "find somewhere else to run" theory.

I was appalled.

There are two major problems with the "if you need a gun, find somewhere else to run" notion. First, this advice implies that *we know exactly where crime will occur.* It implies that violence will never happen in our *homes,* in our *churches,* at our *schools,* or at the grocery store in a safe part of town in broad daylight. But guess what? Crime happens in all those areas. It may not happen every day, but it happens. And what do victims always seem to say when asked about violent attacks that occur in those places? *I just didn't think it would ever happen here.* Crime rates do indeed vary by location and hour of day, and some places are statistically safer than other, but the notion that you can predict where a crime will happen with complete

▲ As you learn about personal defense you'll be better equipped to make good buying decisions and find the right firearm and accessories for personal defense. Here, gun shop owner Jeff Steele of Ohio discusses purchasing options with a new shooter.

certainty and eliminate all risk of being attacked by simply avoiding those areas is simply false. Criminals take advantage of victims who are unaware and unsuspecting. A violent attack can happen at home, at work, on the street, at the carwash, or at the dog park. When I'm asked where I carry my sidearm, my response is that I carry everywhere I'm legally allowed to do so. If you're serious about personal defense, then you need to understand a critical concept that very few civilians grasp—location does not equal protection. I'm sure that most runners assume that the trail or route they choose is safe and crime-free. Only a fool would seek out a high-risk area to exercise. But you're alone, you're tired, and you're an easy target. I'm a runner myself, and I don't want to go through life looking over my shoulder every few steps. I'm also aware, however, that I'm vulnerable, and so I am armed when I am on the trail. Do I expect anything will happen? No, but if it does, I'm ready to defend myself against violence.

I don't think my house will burn down, but there are functioning smoke detectors in every room and fire extinguishers on every floor.

There's one more issue with the "find somewhere else to run" argument, and it's more philosophical. The idea that we must seek out the safest location to run (or bike, or picnic, or hike) places, at least to some degree, blame on the victims of crime. Would you tell a jogger that had just been assaulted that they brought the attack on themselves by running in the wrong neighborhood? I'd like to think not, and if you would, perhaps you should swap this book for one of the many self-help manuals that have been published in recent decades. Of *course* you wouldn't blame the victim. It's not their fault, is it? Well, according to the "find a safe place to run" mantra, the victim is, at least partially, at fault when they are attacked. I say that's nonsense, and I'll never believe for one moment that a crime such as that is the fault of anyone but the criminal.

▲ Shooting is about more than personal defense—it's also fun. As you become more proficient with a firearm your group sizes will shrink and you'll grow more comfortable and confident. Do not, however, overlook safety.

We're fortunate that our founding fathers believed so deeply in the concepts of life and liberty that they felt that all law-abiding citizens should have the right to bear arms. Those who take matters of personal protection into their own hands, who defend their lives and the lives of loved ones when criminals attack, should not be blamed. I hope that this book helps you to be a safer, more confident, and more prepared shooter.

▲ Several new guns have come on the market since the original *Shooter's Bible Guide to Concealed Carry* was published. Some of the most exciting new carry firearms include (from the top) Ruger's 7-shot GP100, Kimber's K6s revolver, and Springfield Armory's XD-S Mod 2.0 .45 ACP.

# I. An Introduction to Concealed Carry

*E*ach year millions of Americans make the decision to carry concealed firearms to protect themselves, their families, and their property. Despite claims from anti-gun factions that increasing numbers of armed citizens would lead to an increase in shooting and violence, the passage of legislation allowing lawful Americans to carry concealed weapons has caused a decrease in the number of violent crimes, and the number of concealed weapons permits continues to rise annually in this country. As of 2017, roughly sixteen million CCW permits had been issued.

Perhaps you've considered obtaining a concealed carry permit yourself. Perhaps you've read the newspaper or watched the news and shaken your head in disgust at the latest unwarranted and malicious attack on a defenseless citizen. Maybe you decide you should carry a concealed firearm.

But carrying a *gun*?

As I've prepared to write this book, I've spent considerable time interviewing people about concealed carry laws, violence in America, and their opinions on firearms. I've spent time on the range with individuals who have made the decision to exercise their rights to carry a gun, many of whom had little or no previous experience with firearms. Most of the people I met in these concealed carry classes had the same goal in mind: All of them wanted to protect themselves and their loved ones from violence. However, the students in these classes came with varying amounts of knowledge and experience with firearms. Many of them shrugged off our suggestions while they were shooting, confident that they knew all there was to know about shooting and firearms. Some of them were even slightly afraid of guns, and one told me she was *terrified* of firearms as she stood at the range, a Smith

▲ Learning to shoot a firearm can be rewarding and exciting, but you must understand the basics to be both safe and proficient.
Photo courtesy of the National Shooting Sports Foundation.

basic information about firearms is glossed over or ignored altogether. Such books include chapters on all sorts of tactical skills, training the reader to shoot around stationary objects, clear a house, or win in a knife fight.

That's not what this book is about. I sat down with the intention to write a book for the people who want to learn to carry concealed firearms but who have little or no experience in the safe handling, use, and maintenance of firearms. This book is written for people who may not even *like* guns but feel the need to learn enough about them to be responsible and safe. Perhaps you've considered taking a concealed carry course, but you just feel overwhelmed at the thought of having to line up on the range and shoot a pistol. Maybe you've already taken the class, but you still don't feel that you have learned all the skills necessary to carry a loaded firearm with the intention of using it under the worst of circumstances.

Most writers can tell you about the events that inspired them to write a book. I can tell you the exact moment that the idea for this one came about. I helped a very good crew of instructors in Ohio as they conducted concealed carry classes, spending most of my time on the range to help talk the students through the live fire portion of the test and make sure that they didn't do anything careless with a gun in their hands. We had a running joke (though there was a good deal of truth in it) that one of us would be responsible for separating the husbands and wives because husbands that accompanied their wives to class were, without fail, the absolute worst instructors. The husband-wife

& Wesson revolver on the table in front of her, faced with passing the shooting portion of her twelve-hour concealed carry class.

If you know all there is to know about shooting and firearms, then this book isn't for you; though if you *do* believe that, I challenge you to read it anyway. I think you'll find something here that you weren't aware of and you might even pick up some simple, practical advice. However, if you are one of the millions of Americans who want to carry concealed, but you feel intimidated or uneducated in regards to firearms, this is the book for you. Much of the literature about firearms is written for an audience that has some understanding of the basics of firearms. Much of the most pairing would almost invariably end in a fight, so we tried to step in and intervene, offering an objective voice and plenty of support.

On the day I decided to write this book, I was in the midst of helping a woman who was taking the class with her husband. The husband, a longtime shooter, kept giving orders and correcting her, and all the while she became more and more frustrated until she was in tears and completely overwhelmed. We took a break from shooting and stepped away from the range. We spent some time talking about her background, her career, and her family. She had three kids between the ages of five and nine, worked as a legal assistant, and she was horrified of guns.

"He loves shooting and he just expects me to like it too," she said as she waved her hand toward her husband. "The truth is I didn't grow up around guns like he did. I'm scared of them. I know it makes sense to carry just in case I ever need a gun, but they just make me nervous." She shook her head and put her face in her hands.

At that moment I decided this woman would become my model for a book about concealed carry. I began speaking to people who had taken concealed carry courses and asking them about their experiences. Many of those permit holders I spoke with said they enjoyed their classes and that they felt confident and capable in regards to carrying a loaded firearm. There were others, however, that felt they weren't "gun savvy," and even though they'd passed the course and were licensed to carry guns, they didn't feel competent with a gun. I also spoke with individuals who had never taken a concealed carry course because they didn't feel comfortable shooting guns. Some didn't even want to be in the same *room* as a firearm.

▼ Learning to shoot properly requires two basic steps: First, you must learn how to safely handle guns, and secondly, you must commit to practicing often enough that you are comfortable with the process of firing. The goal of this book is to provide you with the necessary information to safely handle firearms and the practice drills needed to make you a better shooter. Photo courtesy of the National Shooting Sports Foundation.

▲ Students at one of the National Shooting Sports Foundation's (NSSF) "First Shots" seminars, where beginning shooters learn how to safely handle firearms and receive instruction on the basics of shooting. Photo courtesy of the National Shooting Sports Foundation.

This book was conceived as a textbook for anyone who is serious about learning to handle firearms. Before you can become comfortable shooting guns you must be comfortable around guns, which means you must be familiar with guns and feel safe and confident when handling them. So, how do we become safe and confident with firearms? Accomplishing this requires a basic understanding of how firearms work and how to handle them. This book is designed to be a technical guide to firearms as well as a coaching manual designed to help you feel not only familiar with guns but comfortable with them as well. It is also intended to help you learn the rules of gun safety and how to correctly handle firearms. When you have the basic knowledge required to safely handle guns, you will be better prepared to become a competent shooter.

So, why do you want to obtain a concealed carry permit? If you are like the majority of applicants, you want to be able to protect yourself and others against violent crime, which is a very compelling and logical reason. I'm not going to try and scare you with statistics about violence in America. If you feel compelled to carry concealed, you probably already have a basic understanding that, while the majority of people we come into contact with each day do not pose a serious threat to us, there are dangerous people out there. We picture them in back alleys, in the shadows of big cities, and a dozen other dark and dangerous places. But what if we encounter them in our homes? What if they find us on the way to work one day, on the familiar and comfortable path we follow that has become a part of our daily routine? Violent crime happens at any moment of the day or night, at home or at work, in dark alleys and brilliantly lit public places. And it's terrifying. But if you are terrified of the attacker *and* the gun you carry to defend yourself, you stand little chance.

## Familiarity with Firearms

This book will never prevent anyone from attacking you. So what can be accomplished by reading this book and practicing the techniques presented here? You will have a basic knowledge of firearms, and you will be familiar enough with the firearm you choose to carry to defend yourself if the need arises. The first step in this process is familiarizing yourself with firearms. In the next chapter I'm going to examine some of the reasons, either intentional or accidental, that we have been trained to fear firearms.

For those of us that grew up around firearms and were taught at an early age to handle them safely and enjoy them in a responsible manner, guns aren't terrifying or things to be viewed as instruments of death. I can remember shooting with my dad as a kid, practicing the skills I'd later take to the field while hunting. Later, I shot competitively in college and then began assisting at gun safety courses. Once you become familiar with firearms and feel comfortable handling them, you will not only be a safer shooter but you will also be better prepared to carry a gun with the intent of protecting yourself.

I've designed this book to help you understand firearms, starting with the most basic premises and working up to more complex ones. In the next chapter, I will examine the truth about guns, crime, and criminals. Following that, I will cover basic firearms terminology so that you feel comfortable and confident speaking the language of firearms. This glossary will serve as a guide for the rest of the book. One of the problems with concealed carry classes and instruction books is that there is little emphasis on learning common gun terms. In your career field there is probably a standard vocabulary of words, abbreviations, and acronyms required for competency in that field. Likewise, there are a host of firearms terms that can be confusing. What is a clip? Is it the same as a magazine? What is a bullet, and how is it different from a cartridge? What is a semiautomatic gun? What do DA, SA, and DAO stand for? These terms are often taken for granted by experienced shooters. That's why the glossary chapter in this book is designed to help explain these terms in plain English. Refer to this section anytime you find a word that you do not understand.

One of the most difficult steps in purchasing a firearm is determining which caliber is right for you. The good news is that there are quite a few different calibers of gun that will work for you. Once you've learned basic firearms terminology, we'll spend some time examining the dozens of calibers available and we'll then discuss the major calibers in depth to help you better understand which caliber meets your needs as a shooter.

Following this I've dedicated a chapter to each of the main handgun types: semiautomatics and revolvers. Which type is right for you? That depends on a variety of factors, from your experience level to how you plan to carry the gun and how much time you have to practice shooting. These chapters also include safe handling procedures for both types of firearms and detailed images that explain loading, unloading, and safe storage for both semiautomatics and revolvers.

Safety is paramount when handling firearms, and in Chapter VII you will find basic principles for safe gun handling. Always focus on safety when you are around firearms and practice basic safety rules at all times.

If you are ever going to be confident and comfortable enough with a firearm to use it in a life-or-death situation, you'll need to spend some time at the range. However, before you put your first round (or bullet) downrange, you need to understand how to safely handle guns. Chapter VII examines the universal rules of safe gun handling. It will also discuss the rules of range safety, range commands, and so forth.

Learning how to properly handle firearms is essential. Later in the book I will look at how to practice correctly so that you become a more confident shooter. The goal of this shooting program is to give you the confidence to shoot safely and correctly, but before you can reach that level of proficiency with a firearm you must spend time practicing the basic skills necessary for becoming a better shooter. This section examines grip, stance, eye dominance, sighting, and all the other aspects of proper shooting. Each step will be presented in a simple, straightforward manner.

Finally, I will discuss how to carry your loaded firearm and how to store it safely in your home. Deciding how you are going to carry your firearm is critical, and almost every professional has a different opinion regarding the best way to carry a firearm. If you are going to carry concealed, it is important for you to find a way that is safe and comfortable and that doesn't show the firearm. There are a variety of ways to accomplish this, and I will examine several different methods of carry. It's also critical to store your gun safely when you are not carrying. Despite what certain media outlets would have you believe, it is possible to keep a loaded gun safely and securely stored in the home for personal protection.

## Three Simple Goals

Despite a relatively long chapter list, this book only has three main goals. First, it is essential that you learn

▲ The author taking aim with a pistol. Successful shooters practice frequently, and when you are carrying a gun to defend your life, it is important not only to know the basic functions of your firearm but also to practice these skills until they become automatic.

the skills necessary to handle firearms in a safe manner, from knowing how to properly store your gun to selecting the correct ammo and understanding range safety. It is essential that you understand that guns *can* be handled in a safe manner, and that if you follow the rules of gun safety, accidents with firearms are exceedingly rare.

After you have learned the rules of gun safety and you can handle a firearm in a manner that doesn't endanger yourself or others, you will begin to develop confidence as a shooter. Gaining confidence, which is the second goal of this book, will encourage you to shoot more often. Confident shooters feel secure in their ability to correctly handle firearms, and they learn to enjoy shooting.

Lastly, I will discuss practice methods to make you a better shooter. Once you feel safe and confident, you must spend time on the range familiarizing yourself with your firearm. This book will teach you how to shoot correctly. The most essential element for your success in becoming a good shooter is practicing

proper shooting technique until it becomes second nature. If you are ever faced with an attacker and you need to shoot to stay alive, it is essential that you have developed the muscle memory necessary to shoot without thinking your way through every step of the process. The only way to achieve this level of muscle memory is by understanding the basic steps involved in firing a handgun and repeatedly practicing those steps until shooting becomes second nature.

So, the goal of this book is to make you a *safe* and *confident* shooter and to teach you the basic skills that will allow you to *practice* with your gun until shooting becomes second nature. And odds are that if you feel safe and comfortable around firearms and practice frequently, you may begin to enjoy firearms, shooting for recreation and perhaps even shooting competitively. I hope at the very least that this book offers you a new perspective on firearms, helping you to better understand the reality of guns in America and to rethink some of the media-driven biases against guns and gun owners. The founding fathers thought that the right to bear arms was pivotal in the development and preservation of a free republic. Shooting is not only an exciting pastime but it is also one of our constitutional rights as Americans. And, when done safely and correctly, shooting is fun.

New shooters often worry that they have no experience with guns. Don't let that concern you. In fact, in many cases people who have never shot a gun in their lives become better shooters more quickly than those who have been improperly trained, because it takes so much time to correct mistakes and bad habits shooters have learned over a lifetime of practicing bad technique and form. New shooters oftentimes learn the proper skills very quickly. Sometimes, as an instructor, I find it almost impossible to break poor shooting habits because they have become part of muscle memory, and over the years, the shooter has developed such a set routine of shooting the wrong way that they virtually have to start from scratch to learn to shoot properly.

Despite your previous experience with guns, follow along with this book and learn the basic knowledge and skills required to make you a safe and competent shooter. The book is broken down into several chapters that give you basic information about carrying concealed and learning to shoot. No tactical stuff, nothing fancy, just practical knowledge delivered in an easy-to-follow format.

Now, let's begin learning the basics of concealed carry.

▼ A student at an NSSF "First Shots" seminar learns the basics from a professional. Shooting instructors can help build confidence in shooters and ensure that they handle their guns safely and correctly.

# II. Guns in America

hile I was in college I shot for Northern Kentucky University's trap and skeet team, which meant that every Wednesday and Sunday afternoon I traveled to the shooting range in Crittenden, Kentucky, to break clays in preparation for our next match. On one particularly cold, breezy afternoon in December, I met my friend and teammate Eric Nordman at the range.

"Where's Mike?" I asked, inquiring about another teammate who was absent during our usual Sunday shooting session.

"Mike?" Eric said as we headed toward the shooting range. "Mike won't be here for a while. He broke his leg."

"Broke his leg?" I asked.

"Yeah," Eric said. "He went skiing in Indiana. Took a bad fall and broke his leg."

We put our guns in the rack and began loading our vests with shotgun shells.

"I'm glad I don't do anything dangerous like that," Eric said.

I looked at him for a moment.

"Eric, we shoot guns all week. Some people probably think that's dangerous."

"Think about it," he said. "How many people do you know that ever got hurt shooting shotguns?"

It was true. Eric and I, along with the rest of our teammates, shot thousands of times each week, and none of us had ever been injured. To many, perhaps most, people, shooting seems far more dangerous than going skiing. Statistically, however, it is not, and

▲ In the United States we enjoy the right to protect ourselves with firearms, but our rights are under constant attack. The truth is that the vast majority of Americans enjoy shooting responsibly and all of us have the constitutional right to defend ourselves.

www.skyhorsepublishing.com

▲ A competitive shooter takes aim on a pistol course. There are a variety of handgun competitions that help hone the shooter's skills, from the most basic target matches to complex tactical courses. For more information, see Appendix A in the back of the book. Photo courtesy of Yamil Sued.

although Eric's statement was true, it shocked even me. Of the dozens of shotgun shooters I knew, I couldn't think of one that had ever been injured by a gun. I knew two that had been in major automobile accidents, and after Mike's spill on the slopes, one who'd been sidelined while skiing.

If you are ever going to feel comfortable shooting a gun, which is the ultimate goal of this book, you must first understand that the media has done a very good or very bad (depending on which side of the fence you are standing on) job of associating guns with violence. Guns certainly *can* be dangerous if handled in an irresponsible manner, and they *do* have the potential to kill. The same could, of course, be said of motor vehicles and knives. The difference is that cars and kitchenware are part of our daily lives. We pack our children into the car each morning and drive them to school, not once thinking that another car could careen across the center line and strike us head on, completely forgetting the fact that we are riding overtop of a tank filled with highly volatile gasoline vapors. Nor do we

fear for our lives when we walk into a deli and see an employee wielding a ten-inch butcher knife. Why not? Because we have not learned to associate those items with injury and death, despite the capabilities of automobiles and knives to harm or even kill us.

The same cannot be said of firearms. What was your first experience with firearms? For me, like so many other kids who grew up in a rural farming community, guns were a way of life. I learned at a very young age to appreciate the capabilities of firearms and to handle them in a safe and responsible manner. I was not alone in this; it wasn't uncommon to see neighbors walking along the road with firearms in hand (some shudder as they read that), heading out for an afternoon's hunt or perhaps traveling to a shared shooting range. Guns were part of my culture and I felt comfortable around firearms.

For many others, however, guns represent something entirely different. For people who were introduced to guns by the media in print and on television, the gun represented something far more sinister. Guns were a symbol of death, killing machines designed to end lives and destroy things. Have you ever seen a gun in a movie or television that was not being fired at someone?

Millions of Americans were introduced to guns this way and naturally learned to associate guns with terror and death. What other option did they have? The media's link between firearms and violence slowly trained the American public to view guns as evil and dangerous.

For those of us who were raised in households with firearms and were trained in their proper use, guns represented something very different. For us, guns represented recreational time, afternoons with our mothers and fathers spent target shooting in the back yard. This is where I learned how to shoot trap, practicing first by breaking clay targets my father threw from a steel machine he fabricated himself in the metal shop (he taught industrial arts at the local high school). Guns didn't represent violence and death, didn't conjure up images of pain or suffering, any more than the sight of the family sedan conjured images of the twisted metal and shattered glass that result from a car crash. As a child did I understand that guns could be dangerous? Sure, if used incorrectly or irresponsibly, the same as hand tools or the electric sockets in the walls of our home.

## A Perspective on Guns

Fear and risk are not directly proportional, and statistics bear out the fact that we humans have a pretty poor perspective on the true risks we face in our daily lives. When we enter the ocean we fear shark attacks, though we are twice as likely to be killed by a riptide. We fear flying in an airplane, though we are ten times as likely to fall out of our own beds and die as we are to be killed in a plane crash. We fear grizzly bears, but we are more likely to be killed by a domestic dog than a bear.

Bees, in turn, kill more people than dogs, and the most likely animal to kill you worldwide is the diminutive *Anopheles* mosquito, vector of such terrible diseases as malaria.

Guns are treated in much the same manner in the United States. The term "gun violence" has become commonplace, a catch-all term used so frequently in the media that the uninformed reader might imagine that homicides were the leading cause of death in this country. If we assume, as many anti-gun groups do, that fewer guns equal less violence, then we could safely assume that more guns would result in more violence. Such is not the case. Gun ownership increases by about 4.5 million per year according to the NRA Institute for Legislative Action, which compiles statistics on firearms. The NRA-ILA study shows that as firearms sales continue to increase, firearm accident death rates continue to decrease, which contradicts the notion that guns in the house are inherently dangerous. In fact, accidental deaths by firearms represent about one-half of 1 percent of all accidental deaths per year, far below the incidence of deaths from car accidents (comprising almost 40 percent of accidental deaths annually), fires, drowning, falls, and suffocation. Poisoning accounts for over forty times as many deaths in the United States

▶ Learning to properly and safely carry a firearm will help protect you under the worst of circumstances. It is essential, however, that you learn to carry safely and practice often. Thankfully, gun accidents are exceedingly rare. Photo courtesy of Galco Gunleather.

◄ The NSSF hosts a "Don't Lie" press conference to share the truth about firearms with the public. The media's treatment of firearms and firearm owners is often lopsided and unfair, so it is important to learn the truth about guns in America. Photo courtesy of the National Shooting Sports Foundation.

as firearms accidents. The odds of being killed in a car accident are far greater than the odds of dying from a gunshot wound (either homicidal or intentional), yet we still wake up each morning and drive ourselves to work despite the obvious risk associated with motor vehicles. Are we all ignorant?

According to facts released in a 2011 study conducted by the National Safety Council, cases of unintentional firearms fatalities dropped 60 percent between 1989 and 2009, the highest twenty-year decline among principle types of accidental injuries like fires, motor vehicle accidents, and choking (National Safety Council Injury Facts, 2011 edition). In that same year accidental shootings accounted for only 0.6 percent of unintentional fatalities in the home, far below poisonings (which accounted for 52.6 percent of unintentional fatalities), falls (25.9 percent), fire (4.5 percent), choking (3.5 percent), and overheating/freezing to death (which accounted for 25 percent more accidental deaths in 2009 than firearms). More recently, a National Safety Council report released in 2017 found that fatal firearms injuries dropped 17 percent from 2014 to 2015. The total number of accidental firearm deaths was 489, the lowest number since record keeping began in 1903. Of the more than

146,000 accidental deaths reported during that same period, accidental shootings accounted for just three-tenths of one percent of all fatalities. Perhaps more importantly, that record drop in fatal firearm injuries happened at a time when more Americans than ever own and carry guns.

Hunting, oftentimes viewed as a dangerous sport, is actually one of the safest outdoor activities. According to a US Fish and Wildlife report, hunting resulted in .05 injuries per 100 participants, and most of these injuries did not involve firearms but were the result of falls and other accidents. To add some perspective to this, hunting is slightly more dangerous than billiards (which accounts for .02 injuries per 100 participants) and is safer than bowling. Water skiing is about three times as dangerous as hunting, and tennis is almost four times as dangerous. Compare these activities with other activities like softball (1.11 injuries per 100) and skateboarding (1.70 injuries per 100), and you quickly see that hunting is one of the safest outdoor activities despite the fact that it involves a gun, which many people automatically assume increases inherent risk dramatically.

It is difficult to say with absolute certainty what has caused the dramatic drop in firearms injuries over the

past two decades, but the availability of information regarding safe gun handling has almost certainly had a significant impact on the decline in accidental shootings. Today's gun owners have more resources available in the form of books, classes, seminars, and gun safety programs developed by the National Rifle Association and the National Shooting Sports Foundation. These two organizations have been at the forefront of educating Americans about safe gun handling, and their combined efforts, along with the work of other organizations like them, have resulted in fewer gun deaths.

It is important to remember that this reduction in accidental firearms deaths occurred in spite of nationwide accep-

▲ With proper training, target shooting is a safe and exciting pastime. This Kimber .22 produces very little recoil, and ammunition is cheap. Learning to shoot this gun will also prepare you to fire one of the company's larger 9mm or .45 Auto handguns in a self-defense situation. Photo courtesy of Kimber America.

▼ Comparatively speaking, target shooting is safer than skateboarding or volleyball. Each year millions of Americans spend time on the range without accident or injury. The key is learning how to safely handle firearms and always adhering to safety protocols. Photo courtesy of the National Shooting Sports Foundation.

tance of concealed carry laws. There are statistically far fewer shooting injuries today than there were twenty years ago despite the fact that there are far *more* firearms!

## Guns and You

I don't know what your own experiences with firearms have been. Perhaps they have been positive like mine and you enjoy shooting. Perhaps the total sum of your experiences comes from years spent listening to the nightly news. Maybe you've even been the victim of a violent crime in your life, and you want to protect yourself against reliving that awful experience. The goal for everyone reading this book is the same: You will learn to safely handle, load, unload, clean, maintain, store, and shoot a firearm. You'll become comfortable with guns, or at least you will have the ability to handle guns safely without the risk of injury.

The key to being a successful and safe shooter is to first understand the reality, abide by the rules, and practice the regimen. I've touched on the reality of guns here, and as you read through this book you will learn more about firearms in general and be able to choose the correct gun for your shooting needs. You will also learn the safety rules that dictate correct gun handling, helping you prevent injury or death that results from ignorance about the capabilities and operation of firearms. Lastly, you must practice the techniques listed in this book until you become comfortable shooting the gun you are going to carry.

Statistics show that educated firearm owners are safer firearms owners, and the aim of this book is to provide you with the fundamental tools necessary to be a safe shooter. By learning how to safely handle firearms, you are decreasing the risks of an accidental shooting.

## Guns and Kids

Should you purchase a firearm if you have children in your home? Maybe the reason you want to obtain your concealed carry permit is to protect them and to be certain that you can defend your family. But perhaps you are also hesitant to have a gun in the same house as your children. Rest assured that you can safely keep a firearm in the house safely while children are

there and that having a gun in the home with children doesn't make you a bad parent. That nonsensical attitude is akin to saying that you shouldn't drive with your children in a car because they might not be restrained and you'll get into an accident. Irresponsible parenting is irresponsible parenting regardless of whether it is manifested by improperly handling a gun or driving drunk while your kids are standing on the back seat of the car.

There is nothing irresponsible about teaching children to shoot and handle guns safely from a young age. Although kids should always be carefully supervised and must be taught the rules of safe gun handling before they ever fire their first shot, children can enjoy shooting guns the same way they enjoy learning to play the guitar or hit a baseball. Statistically speaking, your child is less likely to be injured while out hunting than while playing volleyball, according to the National Shooting Sports Foundation. Other sports are even more dangerous, like snowboarding (nineteen times more likely to result in injury), cheerleading (twenty-five times more likely to cause injury), and football, which is over a hundred times as likely to result in injury than going hunting.

The results are similar in the home. According to the 2008 CDC WISQARS Injury Mortality Report, the risk of a child under the age of fourteen dying from drowning, suffocation, or motor vehicle accidents are all much higher than the odds of being killed by an accidental shooting. Firearms can be dangerous, but pools, plastic trash bags, ladders, and household poisons like Drano are all more likely, statistically speaking, to result in the death of a child in the home than accidental shootings.

Parents who educate their children about firearms and help them to understand that guns can be dangerous if handled irresponsibly help prevent injuries from occurring. Adult supervision is always required when children are handling firearms, though.

## The Myth of the Exploding Firearm

One of the prevailing notions about guns is that they simply "go off" unexpectedly, like explosive devices. The reality is that firearms failures (particularly spontaneous firing) are extremely rare, as evidenced by the decrease in accidental shootings. Modern firearms

▲ Carrying a firearm doesn't automatically protect you from crime. To become proficient with a gun, you must learn the fundamentals of carrying, shooting, and storing a firearm. Photo courtesy of Kimber America.

manufacturers have gone to great lengths to ensure that their products are functional and reliable. Despite what is published about guns going off accidentally or accidents that occur while cleaning firearms (no one should ever be cleaning a loaded firearm anyway), actual mechanical failures in firearms that result in shootings are extremely rare.

Inexperienced or irresponsible shooters tend to blame the firearm in accidental and intentional shootings. However, there is no validity to the argument that mechanical failure on the part of the firearm caused injury or death; in reality, it was a negligent shooter. Safety devices like transfer bars in revolvers (to prevent a dropped hammer from causing a gun to accidentally fire) and trigger and grip safeties help protect us against accidental discharges to a certain degree, but it is up to the shooter to become educated on how to safely handle firearms to prevent injury.

Ignorance also leads to a percentage of firearms-related injuries each year. Improper handling of guns and ignorance or neglect concerning the rules of gun safety can result in injury or death, so it is important to understand how to properly handle guns and to always comply with firearms safety rules.

## The Key to Success with Firearms

Knowledge and proper training can make you a safe shooter. Even though the odds of being injured while shooting are low, ignorant shooters are dangerous. Firearms are powerful and should be respected, but it is possible to enjoy a lifetime of shooting without injury.

# III. Basic Firearms Terminology

ew shooters are often overwhelmed by the terminology or "gun words" that they hear when speaking to shooters or classroom instructors. In fact, this was one of the major reasons cited by people I interviewed for not getting the most out of their concealed carry class.

This is a list of terms associated with firearms that will be helpful for you to know. You can read through the terms or use them as a reference, returning to them each time you find unfamiliar vocabulary in the text.

**+P:** These cartridges are loaded to higher pressures than standard cartridges. Examples include the 9mm Luger+P, the .38 Special+P, and the .45 ACP+P. Guns must be rated for these higher pressure loads to fire them safely. For instance, many carry revolvers are chambered for .38 Special+P rounds (this should be stamped on the barrel) and can fire both high-pressure .38 Special+P rounds as well as standard .38 Special rounds. +P ammo is labeled accordingly on the original manufacturer's box.

**+P+:** Rarely seen today, +P+ ammunition produce pressure levels above standard +P loads. +P+ guns and ammunition were originally designed for police and military work. Though it is unlikely you'll ever come across +P+ guns or ammo, these loads produce pressures higher than what is required for concealed carry.

**Accessory Rail:** A fixed rail, usually on the underside of the barrel or slide on a handgun. Also known as a tactical rail, the accessory rail is where lights and lasers can be mounted on defense pistols.

**ACP:** Abbreviation for "Automatic Colt Pistol," ACP cartridges were designed by engineer John Browning for use in semiautomatic handguns. They include the .25 ACP, the .32 ACP, the .38 ACP (rare), the .380 ACP, and the .45 ACP. Guns chambered in .380 ACP and .45 ACP are very common for concealed carry, while the .32 ACP and .25 ACP are less popular because of the lower energy levels they produce. Sometimes ACP rounds are referred to as "auto" cartridges, as in the case of someone who says they have a gun chambered for ".380 Auto."

**Action:** The action is a group of moving parts responsible for loading, firing, and unloading the handgun.

**Adjustable Sights:** Sights that can be adjusted manually to shoot to a different point of impact. Adjustable sights are common on long-barreled target handguns, but they are less common on small concealed carry guns because adjustable sights are more fragile than fixed sights and can become caught up in clothing and holster material as the gun is drawn in self-defense situations. See **Elevation**, **Gutter Sights**, **Patridge Sights**, **U-Notch Sights**, and **Windage**.

**Ambidextrous:** Control lever that can be operated by both left- and right-handed shooters without modification. Typically applies to the safety, slide stop, and magazine release.

**Appendix Carry:** Carry position where the gun is placed in the front of the waist between the pants pocket and the belt buckle. Appendix carry offers a high level of concealment.

**Auto-loading:** Auto-loading handguns, also called **Semiautomatics**, use the movement of the action to extract and eject spent cartridges and to chamber the next cartridge from the magazine. Thus, the shooter can simply pull the trigger for each shot until the magazine runs empty.

**Back Strap:** Rear portion of the grip, or handle, of the gun. Also written "backstrap."

**Back Stop:** Dirt or similar material that stops bullets behind the targets at a range.

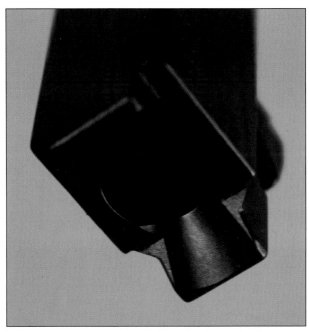

▲ The feed ramp is a piece of metal that guides the cartridge from the magazine into the chamber. Feed ramps that are burred or fouled can cause feeding problems and may potentially jam a semiautomatic handgun.

**Barrel:** The tube that the bullet travels down when fired. Modern barrels contain rifling, which causes the bullet to twist in the air to stabilize itself. The muzzle is the terminal point of the barrel where the bullet exits the gun. See also **Chamber**, **Muzzle**, and **Rifling**.

**Biometric:** Some gun safes are equipped with biometric sensors that identify your fingerprint. These safes open automatically when a stored fingerprint appears on the touch pad and combines firearm security with rapid access.

**BlueGuns:** Plastic replicas of firearms that are used for training purposes. BlueGuns are available from different retailers and allow you to go through the motions of drawing, gripping, aiming, and firing without handling a real firearm. BlueGuns are common tools for beginning shooters.

**Blued:** A common finish applied to the metal parts of many firearms. "Bluing" guns actually makes the metal appear blue/black. This process provides some level of corrosion protection, but blued steel can still rust and must be maintained. Bluing is the most common metal treatment for firearms.

**Bonded Bullet:** Bullets that have their copper jacket and lead core electrochemically or electrically bonded together. This bonding process makes the components of the bullet (the copper jacket and lead core) remain attached when fired into an object, providing uniform and dependable expansion for self-defense bullets. When the lead core and jacket separate when striking an object, this separation causes erratic bullet performance.

**Bore:** Interior of the barrel. The projectile travels down the bore when fired, and rifling inside the bore causes the bullet to spin. "Big Bore" is a generic term for large caliber handguns and rifles.

**Brass:** Cartridge cases are generally referred to as "brass." Some shooters collect fired brass to reload.

**Break-In Period:** Newly manufactured firearms "break-in" over time as shots are fired and metal parts move more freely. Mechanical problems are less likely after the break-in period, which is typically 250–500 shots. This is one of the reasons it is critical that you practice with your carry gun.

**Caliber:** The diameter measurement of a bullet. American manufacturers typically give caliber designations in terms of inches. For instance, a .327 Federal Magnum has a bullet diameter (or caliber) of .327

▼ The anatomy of a cartridge: The cartridge case holds the primer, powder, and bullet in place. When the firing pin strikes the primer, it ignites the powder, which forces the bullet down the barrel. Photo courtesy of Winchester Ammunition.

inches, and a .41 Remington Magnum fires a .410-inch bullet. Metric cartridges measure bullet diameter in millimeters, such as the 9mm Luger.

**Capacity:** The number of cartridges that a firearm will hold. Capacity in revolvers refers to the number of chambers in the cylinder, and magazine capacity in semiautos typically refers to the number of cartridges that can be loaded into the magazine.

**Cartridge:** Loaded ammunition for use in firearms. Cartridges contain a primer, a cartridge case, powder, and a bullet. Some people mistakenly refer to cartridges as "bullets." In reality, the bullet is only the projectile that exits the barrel. When the gun is fired, the firing pin strikes the hammer, causing it to ignite. This, in turn, causes the powder to burn, and the resulting energy propels the bullet down the barrel. The empty cartridge case remains inside the chambers in revolvers. In semiauto guns the cartridge case is extracted from the gun and ejected.

**Cartridge Case:** A tube, usually made of brass, that holds the bullet, powder, and primer (centerfires only). After firing, the cartridge case is either ejected (semi-autos) or held in the chambers in the cylinder (revolvers). Cartridge cases typically have a head stamp that tells the original manufacturer or the ammunition and the caliber. See also **Brass** and **Head Stamp**.

**Ceasefire:** Command on the shooting range that requires all shooters to stop firing, make their guns safe, and put their guns down in a safe place. Anyone on the range can call ceasefire for any reason and at any time.

**Center of Mass:** Aiming point for most self-defense shooting situations. The center of mass on human targets is in the center of the chest.

**Centerfire:** Cartridges that contain a primer, identifiable by the ring on the base of the cartridge. Rimfires do not contain a primer; priming material is located within the rim, so the hammer simply has to strike any portion of the rim to ignite the cartridge. Most of the cartridges suitable for concealed carry are centerfire cartridges. Examples of rimfire cartridges are .22 Long Rifle cartridges.

**Cerakote:** Ceramic-based firearm finishes that protect the gun from damage.

**Chamber:** Where the cartridge is located when firing takes place. Revolvers have several chambers in the cylinder. Semiautomatic firearms have a single chamber. When the slide is pulled back and released on a semiauto, the forward motion pushes a cartridge from the magazine into the chamber and the gun is ready to fire. Allowing the slide to move forward on a semiauto is referred to as "chambering a cartridge." Chamber also refers to the cartridges that can be fired in a particular gun, as when someone says they have a handgun that is "chambered in 9mm Luger."

**Checkering:** Pattern in a handgun grip that prevents the grip from slipping in the shooter's hand.

**Cock the Hammer:** The hammer of a gun is a piece of metal that swings on an axis at the rear of the gun and strikes the firing pin, initiating the shot. Cocking the hammer, or simply "cocking," involves moving the hammer into a rearward position so that the gun is ready to fire. On a single-action

revolver you must cock the hammer with your thumb before each shot. Double-action revolvers and pistols allow you to cock the hammer by pulling the trigger.

**Compact Ready Position:** When the gun is held in both hands near the chest with the muzzle pointed forward and the finger off the trigger. Useful defensive position that keeps the gun out of reach of attackers at close range.

**Controlled Expansion Bullets:** Bullets that are engineered to open in a reliable fashion when fired into an object. Bonded bullets, which have their jacket and core fused together, are controlled expansion bullets, because when they strike an object they expand in a consistent manner. Lead bullets and full metal jacket bullets are examples of bullets that are not designed for controlled expansion. Lead bullets flatten when they strike a target, and full metal jackets do not expand when they strike an object under normal conditions.

**Cross-Dominance:** Shooters that have different strong hands and dominant eyes are referred to as "cross-dominant." An example would be a left-handed shooter whose right eye is dominant. For more information about cross-dominance see Chapter X, "Taking Your First Shots."

This photo shows checkering on the grip of a handgun. Also, notice that the magazine is extended below the bottom of the grip. Extended magazines provide extra gripping surfaces for larger hands and additional space for rounds. Photos courtesy of Kimber America.

**Cylinder:** The round, rotating portion of a revolver that contains the cylinders. Different revolvers have different numbers of chambers depending on the caliber of the bullet and the diameter of the cylinder. The cylinder rotates in either a clockwise or counterclockwise direction (depending on the model) and lines each chamber up with the bore for firing. The cylinder is rotated by pulling the trigger (on double action and double action–only revolvers) or by cocking the hammer. On most double action and double action–only revolvers you can push a button and swing the cylinder out of the frame for loading, unloading, and cleaning.

**Cylinder Release Button/Cylinder Latch:** The metal button that must be pressed to swing the

Finish: The outer protective coating on the exterior of a firearm

▲ Firearms are available with a variety of finishes, including specialized finishes like this striking blue. This is a single action Kimber Sapphire based on the Colt 1911 platform. Photo courtesy of Kimber America.

cylinder of a double action or double action–only revolver out of the frame for cleaning, loading, and unloading.

**Decocker:** Some double action semiautomatic handguns have a decocker lever that allows you to safely lower the hammer on a cocked firearm. This button is usually located with or near the safety, but check the manual that accompanies your particular firearm to determine if the gun has a decocker and where it is located.

**Double Action (DA):** Double action pistols and revolvers have triggers capable of performing two functions (hence the name). Pulling the trigger cocks the hammer and fires the gun, so double action revolvers allow you to keep pulling the trigger and the gun will continue to fire until empty. Double action guns can also be fired in single action mode, where the shooter manually cocks the hammer and the trigger is then pulled to fire the gun.

**Double Action–Only (DAO):** Double action–only guns, or DAO, are similar to double action guns in that the trigger serves two functions each time you pull it: Each pull of the trigger first cocks the hammer and then fires the gun. Usually the hammer is located internally, so DAO pistols and revolvers do not typically have visible hammers; therefore, the shooter cannot shoot the gun in single action mode. DAO guns are simple to operate.

**Double Feed:** A type of malfunction in which a cartridge is fed from the magazine before the previous cartridge is removed from the chamber. Generally, it is the result of a failure to extract. Double feeds must be cleared safely to operate the firearm.

**Double Tap:** Term for rapidly firing two shots at a target. For concealed carry a "double tap" means that you raise the gun, take aim, and fire two quick shots at the center of mass. Double tapping gets the shooter into the habit of delivering two shots at a target very quickly, increasing the odds of stopping an attacker.

**Dry Fire:** Firing a gun with no ammunition. Dry firing is a good way to practice trigger pull and pistol function. Some guns (most new guns) are not harmed by occasional dry firing, but it is always best to consult your owner's manual.

**Ejection:** The process of expelling spent cartridges

▲ With the slide pulled back on this semiauto, you can see a cartridge resting in the top of the magazine. When the slide is released the cartridge will be pushed forward and will travel up the feed ramp into the chamber. "Chambering" a cartridge readies the semiautomatic to fire. Photo courtesy of Kimber America.

from the firearm. Semiautomatics have ejectors that automatically push the empty cartridge case out of the ejection port when each shot is fired. Revolvers require the shooter to press an ejection rod to remove spent cartridge cases.

**Ejection port:** The opening in a semiautomatic handgun where spent cartridge cases are expelled after firing.

**Ejector:** Mechanical device that expels spent cartridge cases. See also **Extractor**.

**Ejector Rod:** Manual device used to remove cartridge cases and unfired cartridges from the chambers in the cylinder of a revolver. After all of the chambers have been fired, the shooter presses the cylinder release button, swings out the cylinder, and pushes the ejector rod at the front of the cylinder. The ejector rod then pushes the spent cartridges from the cylinder. Because of the swelling that occurs during firing (see **Obturation**) spent cartridge cases are sometimes difficult to remove. Do not strike the ejection rod with hard objects to remove spent cases, as this can cause damage to the ejector rod.

**Elevation:** Term used to describe vertical sight adjustments. Elevation adjustments cause the gun to shoot higher or lower on the target. Lowering the rear sight will lower point of impact, and raising the rear sight will raise point of impact.

**Extractor:** Mechanical device that extracts the cartridge from the chamber. See also **Ejector**.

**Failure Drill:** Also known as the "Mozambique Drill," this procedure involves firing two shots to the chest and a third shot to the head portion of a target.

**Failure to Extract/Failure to Eject:** When a semiautomatic firearm does not properly remove (extract)

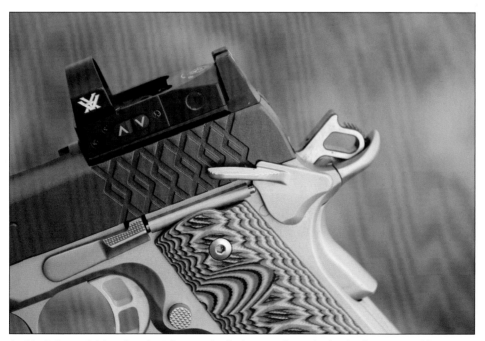

▲ This Kimber Aegis is based on the Colt 1911. It has both a grip safety and a thumb safety, so guns of this type can be carried "cocked and locked" with the hammer cocked and the safety engaged (in the up position).

brass from the chamber or when spent brass is not completely thrown clear (ejected) from the firearm. Failures to extract and failure to eject cause semiautomatic firearms to jam.

**Failure to Load:** When a semiautomatic firearm doesn't properly load the cartridge from the feed ramp into the chamber.

**Feet Per Second (FPS):** The units of measure of a bullet's velocity. Most defense bullets travel between 900 and 1,300 feet per second.

**Fixed Sight:** Iron sights that cannot be adjusted.

**Fouling:** The accumulation of debris in the gun after firing. Barrel fouling specifically refers to materials such as powder debris and heated copper that line the gun barrel after use. Regular maintenance and cleaning removes this fouling and ensures proper function of the firearm.

**Frame:** The frame is the fixed (nonmoving) portion of the firearm. In a revolver, the frame is the metal surrounding the revolving cylinder. In semiauto hand-

guns, the frame is below the slide, mainspring, and barrel and is the fixed portion of the gun that the slide moves along during firing.

**Front Strap:** Front of the grip, particularly in semiautos. Sometimes the front strap is checkered to prevent the gun slipping in the hand.

**Full-Length Underlug:** A piece of metal located under the barrel of a revolver that runs the full length of the barrel. Full-length underlugs help balance the revolver and improve accuracy.

**Full Metal Jacket (FMJ):** A bullet with a core that is completely covered (or jacketed) in copper. The base of FMJ bullets is not typically jacketed because it does not come into contact with the target. The full copper jacket prevents expansion of the soft lead inside the bullet and the bullet retains its shape after entering an object. FMJ bullets provide outstanding penetration, but because they do not expand they do not provide the hydrostatic shock that other bullets generate. Bullets with full metal jackets also penetrate much deeper than

▼ The head stamp is located on the bottom of the cartridge and tells the shooter both the caliber and the manufacturer. In this case, the cartridge is a .38 Special and the manufacturer is Remington-Peters.

expanding bullets, and in residential areas this can create dangerous bullet pass-through. For these reasons FMJs are not typically used in self-defense situations.

**Gas-Operated Semiautomatic:** A semiautomatic that uses the gases produced by the fired cartridge to work the action.

**Grip:** Commonly called a handle, the grip on a handgun is the portion of the gun you hold on to while firing. Most handguns have grips that can be changed, and there are many aftermarket grips to comfortably fit your hand.

**Grip Safety:** Certain handguns, like the Colt 1911 and most of its clones, have a grip safety, which is located on the back of the grip. Because this grip must be pressed before the gun can fire it represents another measure of safety when carrying a loaded gun.

**Grooves:** The deepest portion of the rifling twist in a barrel. See also **Lands**.

**Group:** A series of shots on a target. A "tight group" or "good group" means that all the bullets fired struck close to the same point on the target.

**Gutter Sights:** The most simplistic of all handgun sights, gutter sights include a rear sight that is cut into the slide or frame (usually a U-notch) and a low-profile front sight, usually a short, simple post. Though these sights are small and nonadjustable, they won't get hung up as the gun is drawn and they work fine for close defensive shots.

**Half-Cocked:** Generally refers to single action revolvers, which require that the hammer be pulled partly back to load and unload the gun. The trigger will not allow the hammer to fall when it is half-cocked.

**Half-Moon Clip:** A device that aids in the reloading of a revolver cylinder. The name is derived from the semicircular or crescent shape of the clip, which holds cartridges so that they can be quickly reloaded into a revolver.

**Hammer:** The mechanical device that propels the firing pin into the primer, beginning the firing process. Some guns have exposed hammers, while others do not. Cocking the hammer with your thumb allows for lighter trigger pull in double actions.

**Hangfire:** A dangerous situation wherein there is a delay between the hammer falling and the gun firing. When you pull the trigger and nothing happens, keep the muzzle pointed in a safe direction for at least thirty seconds in case of hangfire.

**Headstamp:** Information about the cartridge that is stamped into the base (head) of the cartridge case. Generally, headstamps tell the caliber and manufacturer of the cartridge.

**High Ready Position:** When the handgun is held in both hands about a foot in front of the shooter's face with the muzzle canted roughly 70 degrees up and away from the shooter.

**Holster:** A device that secures a firearm for carry.

**Hot:** In reference to the firing range, hot means that you may begin firing. Always be sure you are wearing eye and ear protection when the range master calls the range "hot." Hot can also refer to powerful cartridges that produce higher levels of recoil and energy than average loads.

**Hydrostatic Shock:** The rapid movement of fluids caused by a bullet and the subsequent tissue damage that results. Hydrostatic shock levels tend to be higher when firing bullets designed for self-defense.

**In Battery:** A firearm that is ready to fire. For instance, if your semiautomatic jams and you clear the jam so that the gun is once again ready to fire, the handgun is "back in battery" once it can be fired again.

**Indexing:** The act of keeping your trigger finger *outside* the trigger guard along the frame of the gun. Your finger should remain indexed anytime the gun is in your hand, unless you are actively firing.

**Isosceles Stance/Isosceles Position:** Shooting position in which the shooter's shoulders and arms form a triangle when viewed from above.

**IWB:** Holsters that ride inside the waistband.

**Jacket:** The outer core of a bullet. Jackets are typically made of copper and slow the expansion of lead in the core of the bullet. Bullets with full metal jackets typically do not expand. See also **Jacketed Hollow Point**.

**Jacketed Hollow Point:** A lead core bullet with a copper jacket that has a hollow nose channel. As the bullet strikes, the hollow cavity causes the lead to expand, but the copper jacket prevents the bullet from opening quickly and splattering. This ability to expand reliably and consistently means that jacketed hollow point bullets are often used for self-defense.

**Kinetic Energy:** The amount of energy a bullet possesses as measured in foot-pounds (ft-lbs) of pressure. Kinetic energy is based on bullet weight and velocity, with heavier bullets and higher velocities producing increased kinetic energy. For example, a 9mm Luger Hornady Critical Defense bullet travels at 1140 fps and produces 332 ft-lbs of kinetic energy. The larger .40 S&W Critical Defense load pushes a 165 grain bullet at 1175 fps, generating 506 ft-lbs of kinetic energy.

**Kydex:** A thermoplastic material that is widely used in the production of holsters. Kydex is lightweight, nearly indestructible, and affordable. Plus, moisture does not affect Kydex holsters as it can leather holsters.

**Lands:** The raised portion of the rifling in a pistol barrel.

**Laser Sight:** Projects a laser light on an object to assist in aiming a firearm. Lasers are effective for close-range shooting under most lighting conditions. Many concealed carry guns come from the factory with laser sights.

**Loaded Chamber Indicator (LCI):** A visible warning on a semiautomatic handgun that lets the shooter know that there is a loaded cartridge in the chamber. Most LCIs consist of metal pieces that rise up from the top or side of the firearm when a cartridge is loaded into the chamber.

**Loading Gate:** A portion of the frame at the rear of the cylinder in single action revolvers that swings open to allow for loading and unloading.

**Locking Notch:** Indents on the cylinder of a revolver that serve as anchor points to ensure that the cylinder properly aligns the chamber and barrel when firing the revolver. The locking notch is typically rectangular in shape and is located on the rear portion of the cylinder. Many locking notches have arrows notched into them that indicate whether the cylinder travels clockwise or counterclockwise during firing.

**Low Ready Position:** At the range, the low ready position means having the gun gripped properly and pointed at the ground in front of you with the finger indexed. Some instructors teach their shooters to swing upwards to shoot. A better method is to bend the elbows and keep the gun held slightly closer to the body, then extend the arms out toward the target.

**Magazine:** Storage device for ammunition in a semi-automatic handgun. The magazine is often incorrectly referred to as a "clip." A spring inside the magazine pushes the ammunition up toward the chamber so each return stroke of the slide of a semiauto picks up another cartridge and pushes it into the chamber. The total number of cartridges that a magazine holds is referred to as "magazine capacity."

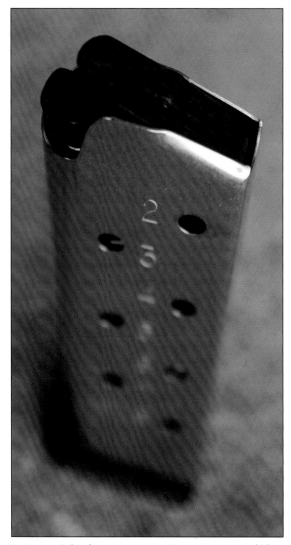

▲ Semiautomatic handguns store ammunition in a magazine, which is shown here. Often mistakenly called a "clip," the magazine is a metal or plastic housing where cartridges are stored and are pushed upward into the chamber by a spring. The magazine follower, which is located at the top of the magazine spring, presses cartridges upward and keeps feeding ammunition into the chamber as the gun is fired.

**Magazine Release Button (MRB):** Located near the front portion of the grip on most semiautos, pressing the magazine release button drops the magazine from the gun. Locating the MRB is key to safely handling a semiautomatic handgun.

**Mainspring:** Metal portion of the firearm that is responsible for making the gun fire.

**Misfire:** When ammunition fails to fire, due to a problem with either the ammunition or the firearm.

**Muzzle:** Point where the bullet exits the barrel.

**Muzzle Blast:** The concussion produced as a result of gases escaping the barrel of a gun during firing. Guns with higher velocities produce more muzzle blast. Muzzle blast can be unpleasant, and shooters should always wear hearing and eye protection while shooting a firearm. It is important to keep the muzzle pointed downrange and never fire a gun near anyone else because of the concussive effects of muzzle blast and the possibility of injury resulting from escaping gases and powder.

**Muzzle Flip:** The sharp upwards thrust of a handgun when fired. Muzzle flip depends upon the size and weight of the gun and the caliber being fired. For instance, large-framed, heavy .357 Magnum revolvers have moderate muzzle flip in most cases. Lighter, shorter-barreled .357 carry revolvers have much more muzzle flip. Muzzle flip is a result of the recoil generated by the shot.

**Muzzle Velocity:** The velocity of a bullet as it passes from the muzzle of a firearm. Muzzle velocity is measured in feet per second.

**Night Sights:** Sights that are visible in complete darkness. Most use tritium, a radioactive isotope of hydrogen.

▲ This is the Yaqui Paddle Holster made by Galco Gunleather. Holsters hold a firearm in place, and paddle holsters like the Yaqui have a wide plastic piece that supports the firearm and allows it to be quickly removed without the shooter having to remove his or her belt. Photo courtesy of Galco Gunleather.

**Obturation:** The swelling of a cartridge after firing. Obturation can make it difficult to remove spent cartridge cases from revolvers and semiautos.

**Off-Body Carry:** Carrying a concealed firearm in a manner such that it is not physically attached to your person. This is sometimes necessary, but on-body carry is preferred so that the firearm is physically attached to you at all times. Carrying a gun in a purse is an example of off-body carry.

**Ogive:** Sloping portion of the bullet that runs from from the tip to the point of widest diameter (the anterior portion of the bullet shank). This slope increases aerodynamics and decreases wind resistance and can be seen on the nose of missiles and fighter jets. See also **Shank**.

**On-Body Carry:** A method of carry where the firearm is always attached to your body, such as in an ankle or shoulder holster. This is the most common and preferred method of carrying a firearm for self-defense because the gun is always with you.

**OWB:** Holsters that ride outside the waistband.

**Paddle Holster:** A holster with a wide, curved piece of leather or plastic that is designed to fit in the waistband and can be removed quickly without unbuckling the belt.

**Patridge Sights:** A common sighting system found on modern firearms that consists of a rear sight with a square notch and a square front sight. To correctly align Patridge sights, the eye should align the front sight in the notch of the rear sight.

**Plink:** Informal shooting practice. Shooting cans and stumps in the backyard are examples of plinking.

**Point of Impact (POI):** Location where the bullet strikes the target. Sometimes the point of impact of a group of shots on the target is an indicator of shooter error, such as when a shooter bends the wrist downward in anticipation of the shot. This "breaking of the wrist" will result in shots that are consistently low as a result of movement of the shooter's hand. On guns with adjustable sights it is possible to manipulate the point of impact.

**Polymer Tip:** Bullets with traditional hollow point construction and the addition of a tip made of polymer. Polymer tips are aerodynamic and are usually designed for controlled expansion. Many premium defense bullets have polymer tips.

**Porting:** Holes on the barrel of a firearm that allow for the lateral release of gases when the gun is fired. Porting reduces felt recoil and muzzle flip but increases muzzle blast.

**Powder/Smokeless Powder:** The propellant that, when ignited, forces the bullet down the barrel. Smokeless gun powder (which is used today) is ignited when the firing pin strikes the primer, causing an ignition that causes the powder to burn. Powder is highly flammable and explosive.

**Primer:** When struck by the firing pin, the primer provides the ignition necessary to light the powder inside the cartridge case. Centerfire cartridges have a primer that is located in the center of the head of the cartridge. Rimfire cartridges, like the .22 Long Rifle, lack a visible primer; instead, the entire head of the cartridge acts as a primer, and striking the cartridge head at any location will ignite the powder. The primer sits in a depression in the head of the cartridge known as a primer cup.

**Print:** Printing refers to the ability to identify a firearm under clothes when the gun is being carried concealed. Hammers, grips, and cylinders that are large and obvious make a gun more likely to print, and thus to be visible through clothing.

**Projectile:** The object that leaves the barrel of the gun when fired. For most pistols, the bullet is the projectile that is fired.

**Propellant:** Material that, when burned, creates an explosion that moves another object (projectile). In the case of most handguns, the propellant is smokeless powder and the projectile is the bullet.

**Range Bag:** A compact carrying case that allow you to easily transport four firearm, ammunition, holster, cleaning accessories and other items to the range.

▼ Close-up of a double action revolver with a stainless finish. This Ruger SP101 .22 revolver has an exposed hammer and adjustable sights. Note the fiber optic front sight, which provides increased visibility. Photo courtesy of Benjamin Gettinger.

▲ The muzzle is the point where the bullet exits the barrel. One key to gun safety is to remain aware of the location of the muzzle. It should always remain pointed downrange. Photo courtesy of Benjamin Gettinger.

**Recoil:** Also called "kick," recoil is the rearward force generated by a gun when it is fired. Larger guns firing heavier bullets generate more recoil. It is important for the new shooter to find a gun that produces manageable recoil in order to shoot well. Some guns, such as the .44 Remington Magnum, .454 Casull, and the .460 Smith & Wesson Magnum produce excessive amounts of recoil for all but the most experienced shooters. For recoil-sensitive shooters, guns like the .380 Auto and .32 H&R Magnum produce low levels of recoil. In addition, ammunition companies produce low-recoiling loads as well.

**Recoil-Operated Semiautomatic:** Semiautomatic that functions using the energy generated by the recoil of the gun. The recoil from a fired shot causes the slide to move backward, pick up another cartridge from the magazine, and slide forward. The cycle is repeated with each pull of the trigger.

**Recoil Reducer:** A device that helps minimize effects of recoil.

**Recoil Shield:** Located at the rear of the cylinder in revolvers, the recoil shield deflects escaping gases away from the shooter.

**Reload:** Ammunition that was not loaded in a fac-tory. Many experienced shooters reload their own ammunition to save money. Reloading requires resizing and cleaning spent cartridge cases, replacing the spent primer, and adding powder and a bullet. Reloading should only be attempted by knowledgeable individuals, and it is not advisable to shoot other people's reloads, as you cannot be sure about the quality of the work.

**Revolver:** A handgun with a revolving cylinder. This cylinder contains multiple chambers, and as each chamber rotates into alignment with the barrel, the firing pin strikes the primer and ignites the powder, firing the gun. After the shot, the cylinder rotates again, aligning another chamber with the barrel and being held in place by a locking pin in the frame that fits into a locking notch in the cylinder. For more information, see Chapter V, "The Revolver."

**RFID:** Radio-frequency identification, or RFID technology, is found on many gun safes. Using a key tag, the gun safe can be opened using electromagnetic frequencies.

**Ricochet:** When a bullet strikes an object and, instead of entering the object, travels elsewhere. Ricochets can be very dangerous and every effort should be made to avoid them. Don't shoot any object with a hard surface or water.

**Rifling:** Spiral grooves cut into the interior of the barrel. These metal spirals cause the bullet to spin as it exits the barrel, increasing accuracy and range. The highest point of the rifling is referred to as "lands," and the deepest portion is referred to as the "grooves."

**Rimfire:** Cartridge where the entire rim (base) of the cartridge acts as a primer. The most common rimfires are the .17 and .22.

**Round:** Another name for a cartridge. In common terminology, shooters refer to "chambering a round," which means pulling back and releasing the slide to load a cartridge from the magazine into the chamber for firing. Magazines with a "ten-round capacity" are capable of holding a maximum of ten cartridges. See also **Cartridge**.

**Semiautomatic:** Handgun that automatically loads another round from the magazine after firing. Semiautomatics rely on the slide to move backward, extract and eject the spent cartridge case, and slide forward to pick up a new cartridge from the magazine. Semiautomatics require the shooter to release the trigger between each shot, as opposed to automatic guns that continue to fire rounds with a single pull of the trigger. Automatic guns are limited to military applications and are not used for concealed carry.

**Shank:** The portion of a bullet between the base (bottom) and the ogive (where the bullet starts to narrow toward the tip to increase aerodynamics). The shank is the same diameter throughout. See **Ogive**.

**Sight Picture:** The alignment of the front and rear sights with the target. Since the eye cannot focus on all three elements of the sight picture (rear sight, front sight, and target), the eye should be trained to focus on the front sight.

**Sights:** Devices used to properly align the muzzle of the firearm so that when the gun is fired the bullet strikes where intended.

**Single Action:** Firearm with a trigger that serves only one (single) function: firing the gun. In the case of single action revolvers, the shooter must manually cock the hammer before a shot can be fired.

▲ This CZ 9mm semiauto is a double action, which means that the trigger can be used to cock the hammer and fire the gun (hence the "double action" title). The magazine release button is located just behind the trigger. The safety is located just under the slide, and in front of the safety is the slide release that allows for disassembly of the gun for cleaning purposes. Photo Courtesy of CZ-USA.

**Slicing the Pie:** Refers to shooting from behind cover. In most instances, shooters want to "slice the pie" as they lean around cover, engaging each target as they come into view.

**Slide:** The top portion of a semiautomatic handgun that moves with each shot. As the slide moves backward after the shot, it removes the spent cartridge case from the chamber, cocks the hammer, and picks up another cartridge (round) from the top of the magazine. As the slide moves back into place, it shoves the new cartridge into the chamber, and the gun is ready to fire once more. This process continues as the shooter continues to pull the trigger.

**Slide Stop:** A lever on the frame of a semiautomatic firearm that holds the slide back. This lever keeps the action open, meaning that the gun cannot be fired. Pressing the slide stop down releases the slide and allows it to slide forward. If there is a full magazine in the gun a cartridge will be chambered and the gun is ready to fire. The slide stop usually locks automatically when the last shot is fired. Use caution when pressing the slide stop lever, since the slide will close and could pinch the finger or hands.

**Speed Loader:** Mechanical device that assists in loading magazines, thus reducing strain on the hands.

**Squib Load:** Load that is underpowered and doesn't fire correctly.

**Striker Fire:** Double action–only semiautos which have an internal "striker" that acts as the firing pin. Glock pistols are examples of striker fire guns.

**String:** One series of shots on target. The shooter with a six-shot revolver will shoot a string of six rounds. They may shoot several strings to form a group on the target.

**Stringing:** A group of bullets fired that forms a line on the target. Stringing is the result of incorrect shooting. Vertical strings (bullet holes in a vertical line on the target) indicate inconsistency in the height of

the shots fired, while horizontal strings indicate inconsistency in the horizontal hold. For more information about assessing groups, see Chapter XI, "Range Etiquette and Proper Practice."

**Sul Position:** A firearm position where the gun is held muzzle down close to the chest (with the muzzle pointed ahead of the shooter's feet). The non-shooting hand rides between the gun and the chest. Useful for moving and checking surroundings.

**Suppressor:** Also known as a silencer (though they don't truly "silence" a firearm), suppressors are muzzle devices that allow gasses traveling behind the bullet to expand to reduce muzzle blast and noise.

**Swing Gate:** A hinged gate that must be moved away from the rear of the frame to load and unload single action revolvers.

**Tactical:** Usually refers to military or police tactics used in combat. Oftentimes anything to do with defensive shooting is referred to as "tactical," because the objective is shooting to engage an attacker and not recreational or sport shooting. Much of the equipment designed for concealed carry is referred to as "tactical gear."

**Tactical Rail:** Also known as an accessory rail, the tactical rail is usually located on the underside of the frame in semiautos and serves as an anchor point for mounting accessories such as flashlights and lasers on the gun.

**Take Down Lever:** Mechanical device that allows the gun to be disassembled, particularly on semiautos. Understanding the location of the take down lever is the first step in learning to disassemble a firearm.

**Tap-Rack Drill:** The most common solution to clear a jammed semiautomatic firearm is

◀ Located just behind the cylinder of a revolver is the cylinder release button. With most revolvers, like this Taurus Judge, you push the cylinder release button forward and simultaneously press on the right side of the cylinder to load and unload the revolver. Photo courtesy of Taurus International.

the tap-rack drill, which involves keeping the muzzle downrange, tapping on the magazine with the heel of the hand, turning the gun 90 degrees (to facilitate removal of the jammed cartridge case), and "racking" the slide.

**Target:** Object used to determine the accuracy of a firearm. By firing a series of shots at a target, the experienced shooter can determine point of impact of a firearm.

**Threaded Barrel/Threaded Muzzle:** A barrel with threads cut at the muzzle to accept a muzzle device such as a suppressor.

**Trigger:** Mechanical device that initiates the firing process in firearms. Double action triggers perform two functions: The initial portion of the trigger pull cocks the gun and the final portion of the trigger pull fires the gun. Single action triggers perform only one function—firing the gun. See also **Double Action**, **Single Action**, and **Double Action–Only**.

**Trigger Control:** The shooter's ability to control the trigger pull. The front joint of the shooting finger should be used to pull the trigger, and the rearward pressure should remain consistent until the gun fires. Heavy triggers and bad trigger control lead to poor accuracy.

**Trigger Guard:** A loop of metal or plastic that surrounds the trigger and prevents the shooter from accidentally contacting the trigger and firing the gun. Your finger should remain outside the trigger guard at all times until you are prepared to fire.

**Trigger Lock:** Device used to secure the trigger of a firearm so that the firearm cannot be fired. Most trigger locks require a key to remove.

◄ This photo shows the rear portion of a Kimber single action semiautomatic handgun that is cocked and ready to fire. These high-visibility sights are by Meprolight. The safety, seen here on the left side of the receiver, must be pressed downward to make the gun fire. In addition, this gun also has a grip safety located on the rear of the grip.
Photo courtesy of Kimber America.

**Tuckable Holster:** An inside-waistband (IWB) holster with a clip design that allows the holster to be fastened to the pants or belt and allows a shirt to be tucked into the space between the clip and the holster, effectively concealing the firearm.

**U-Notch Sights:** Sights on a handgun that consist of a rear sight that is rounded at the bottom (hence the name "U-notch") and a fixed front sight.

**Velocity:** Rate at which a bullet travels. Ballistics charts usually give velocity as a measure of the number of feet that the bullet travels in one second, or feet per second. Velocity, coupled with the mass of the bullet, determines kinetic energy levels. Typical velocities for defensive bullets range from 900 fps to 1,400 fps.

**Wadcutter:** Lead, flat-nosed bullets designed for target practice (not self-defense). Wadcutters are so named because they leave round holes with clear edges in paper targets.

**Weaver Stance/Weaver Position:** One of the two main shooting stances, the Weaver stance was developed by California pistol shooter Jack Weaver in the 1950s.

**Windage:** Term used to describe horizontal sight adjustment, though wind has no appreciable effect on close-range shooting in defensive situations. Most iron sights are "adjustable for windage and elevation," which means the sights can be adjusted horizontally and vertically to change the point of impact. See also **Elevation**.

# IV. Cartridges and Cartridge Selection

One of the first questions that most concealed carry students ask instructors is which caliber handgun they should purchase. On the surface this seems like a simple question, but there are a wide variety of choices available, and even shooting experts do not agree on which caliber is "best." That's fine; there are several good choices for beginning shooters. There are also, however, a few bad choices, especially for a beginner.

In this chapter, we will examine virtually every cartridge available in modern concealed carry guns. Deciding on a cartridge will depend somewhat on what characteristics you are looking for in a carry gun. If you want a revolver, you won't be able to find one in .357 SIG, and if you want a subcompact gun then a .45 ACP will probably be out of the question. You will see trends as you begin shopping for a carry gun. Many of the smallest, lightest semiautos are chambered in .380 Auto, which is a fine choice, and the majority of revolvers designed for concealed carry are chambered in .38 Special, which is another successful self-defense cartridge. In this section, I'm going to give a brief rundown of each of the major cartridges, discussing key components like energy, recoil, and what

type of handgun that particular cartridge is most often chambered in.

Even though experienced shooters and gun writers continue to argue about which cartridge is best, the key element in cartridge selection is choosing a gun and cartridge with which *you are comfortable*. Does the .45 ACP produce more kinetic energy than the .380 Auto? Absolutely, but you must understand that the extra power is of little value if you are afraid of the recoil generated by a .45 ACP. So, is the .45 ACP a good carry gun? Certainly, but only if the shooter is capable of shooting it well. You need to find a cartridge that suits your needs and that you are not afraid to shoot. The good news is there are plenty of relatively mild-recoiling cartridges that make excellent self-defense rounds.

## Bullet Selection

Proper bullet selection is as important, if not *more* important, than caliber selection. Shooters often refer to "knockdown power," a generic term for energy or the perceived impact on a target. The bullet diameter is only one aspect of the damage a bullet does when it strikes an object. The ability of a bullet to stop an attacker depends largely upon the amount of damage that occurs after it enters the body (provided, of course, that the bullet reaches the body cavity before breaking up or being stopped by heavy clothing), and this internal disruption is largely a result of the bullet's reaction with body tissue. Bullets generate varying levels of *hydrostatic shock* depending upon how they react with liquids in the body. Self-defense bullets expand as they enter the body, transferring hydraulic force on the water in the body and creating what is, in essence, a major shock wave. This hydrostatic shock destroys body tissue, providing the energy necessary to stop an attacker. Bullets that do not expand (like full metal jackets) do not provide the same level of hydrostatic shock that controlled expansion bullets (bullets that expand in a reliable manner when they enter the target) generate.

There are a variety of very high-quality expanding bullets designed specifically for self-defense, and no matter what type of handgun you choose or what caliber you select, I believe it is extremely important to choose a bullet that is engineered and designed specifically for self-defense. There are a host of cartridges available today that are loaded with very good

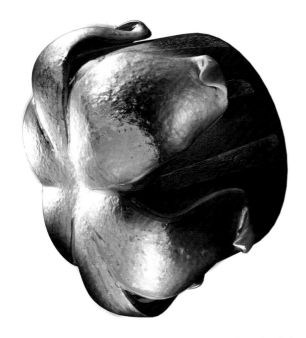

▲ This 9mm bullet is expanding properly. The copper jacket is bonded to the lead core and provides controlled expansion. This is why purchasing premium ammunition is at least as important as finding the right caliber for concealed carry. Photo courtesy of Winchester Ammunition.

▼ This cutaway shows the interior parts of the PDX-1 Defensive cartridge. The primer is ignited and the powder burns, forcing the bullet down the barrel. The spent cartridge case is then removed from the gun so that new ammunition can be fired. Quality ammunition is key for self-defense shooting. Photo courtesy of Winchester Ammunition.

is one of the fundamental keys to preparing yourself to survive a dangerous encounter.

### Bullet Weight and Energy

Bullet weight is measured in grains, an antiquated unit that was originally the equivalent of a single seed of barley. Because bullet weight was originally classed in grains, the unit has remained. It takes 437.5 grains to equal an ounce.

Since most of us don't have a solid understanding of the weight of a handful of barley, I'll try and simplify by giving you a general rundown of what several popular bullets of varying calibers weigh. The .32 Auto cartridge is typically loaded with a bullet that weighs between 55 and 75 grains, and .22 LR rimfires typically fire a bullet that weighs between 30 and 40 grains. 9mm Luger ammunition weighs somewhere from 115 to 158 grains, and the big .45 ACP traditionally fires bullets that weigh between 185 and 230 grains. Grain weight is proportional to caliber, as seen by these examples. The grain weight of bullets is typically listed on the ammunition box.

Bullet weight and bullet velocity both play a role in the amount of kinetic energy a bullet produces. For example, Hornady's Critical Defense 9mm Luger ammunition, which is specifically designed for concealed carry applications, fires a 115-grain bullet at a muzzle velocity of 1,000 fps and produces 411 ft-lbs of energy. The company's XTP 9mm ammunition drives a 147-grain bullet at 975 fps with an energy level of 310 ft-lbs, so even though the XTP bullet is heavier, it is traveling at a lower velocity and thus produces less energy.

### Bullet Design

It is vitally important to load your carry gun with ammunition that uses bullets that are designed for self-defense. These bullets have been designed to perform in defensive situations, and I highly recommend carrying your concealed gun with ammo that is engineered to stop an attacker. All bullets are not created equal, and ammunition that is engineered for defensive purposes has been designed and tested to perform as intended. As I've previously stated, choosing the right bullet may be as important as choosing the right caliber.

Thankfully, ammunition companies have made this relatively easy. There are several ammunition

self-defense bullets (and more being introduced to the market all the time), but some examples are Winchester PDX-1, Hornady Critical Defense, SIG Sauer's V-Crown, and Black Hills' Honey Badger loads.

It is not necessary, or economical, to practice with these defensive cartridges. While all of the bullets listed above are highly effective and well engineered, they are also expensive. Premium ammunition costs more than regular ammunition. While it is always a good idea to practice with the ammunition you plan to carry, by shooting less expensive bulk ammunition you can save money and practice more often, which

▲ Even though these are both .380 Auto cartridges, they will react very differently when they strike a target. The Federal cartridge on the left is designed for self-defense and will expand, creating hydrostatic shock and stopping an attacker. The .380 on the right has a full metal jacket and will not expand, reducing hydrostatic shock. The cartridge on the left is a better choice for concealed carry.

companies that have designed ammunition that is loaded with bullets that will serve well in defensive situations, so choosing the right one is really a matter of testing different ammunition in your gun and deciding which brand you want to use. You may want to purchase different brands of self-defense ammunition and test them in your gun to see which ones shoot best, but by and large the current offerings from companies like Winchester, Nosler, SIG, Black Hills, Hornady, Browning, Federal, and others will perform much better than non-defensive target ammo. These companies have thoroughly tested their ammo to ensure that it will perform as intended when called upon. Most defensive ammunition has a hollow point (sometimes referred to as jacketed hollow point, or JHP) design that offers reliable expansion and energy transfer.

Bullet selection for target practice is much simpler and more economical. Bulk ammunition can oftentimes be purchased at reduced rates, which offers more economical target practice, and having plenty of ammo encourages you to shoot more often, which is key to being prepared to defend your life. Most shoot-

ers choose inexpensive full metal jacket ammunition for personal defense, and companies like American Eagle, Hornady, Winchester, Browning, and others offer affordable training ammunition at a reasonable price.

### Reloaded Ammunition

Many experienced shooters reload their own ammunition. Reloading is fun and economical, allowing the loader to build custom ammunition at home. However, it is not legal for the reloader to sell ammunition unless he or she is licensed to do so. While proper reloads perform well (oftentimes better than factory ammo), not everyone who reloads ammunition does it correctly. The consequences could be dire if you shoot ammunition that is improperly loaded. Factory ammunition from licensed companies undergoes strict control measures to ensure that the cartridges are safe and functional. For the new shooter, it is advisable not to shoot reloads because you don't know the quality of loaded ammo, even if the person who reloaded claims that his or her ammunition can be trusted. Most experienced shooters avoid shooting someone else's reloads, though many of us reload for ourselves. At the beginning, it is best to stick to factory ammunition.

### Identifying Which Type of Ammunition Your Gun Shoots

It is important to understand what type of ammunition your gun shoots. On modern pistols, the caliber is listed on the barrel of revolvers and on the slide of semiautos. In addition, most magazines for semiautos also designate the caliber. Firing cartridges that are not designed for your gun can be dangerous or even fatal.

If you purchase a gun and do not know which type of ammunition can safely be fired in it, consult a professional or contact the manufacturer. Ammunition has a headstamp, which tells caliber and manufacturer, punched into the bottom of the cartridge case. The list below gives a brief description of the most common handgun cartridges on the market.

### A Brief Rundown of Popular Handgun Calibers

**Author's Note:** Cartridges frequently carry the name of the company that developed them. For instance, the .44 Remington Magnum was originally introduced by

▼ Purchase ammunition that is specifically designed for self-defense. Even though it is more expensive than standard target ammo, premium defense ammunition is engineered to perform in defensive situations. This box of Winchester PDX-1 Defender ammunition is designed for .40 Smith & Wesson (.40 S&W) semiautomatics, and the bullet weighs 180 grains. Photo courtesy of Winchester Ammunition.

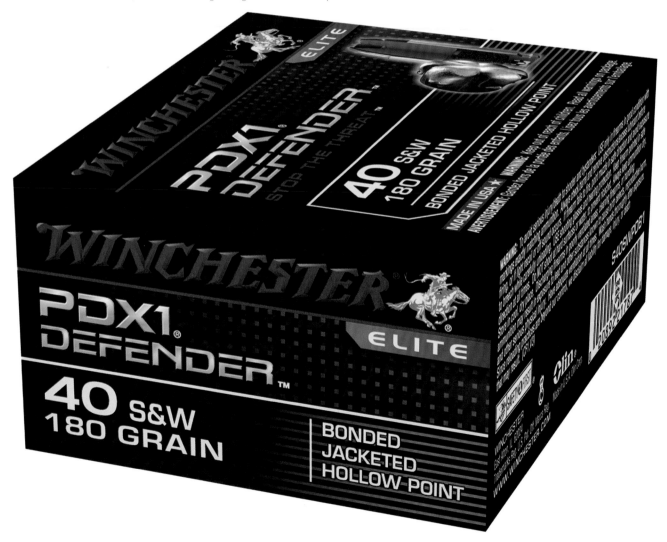

the Remington Arms Company. Common cartridges often have multiple common names. The .45 ACP is oftentimes referred to as the .45 Auto as well. The official title of each cartridge is listed below, and any additional common names for that same cartridge are listed. This is not a complete list of all of the handgun cartridges available, but this list covers all of the major self-defense cartridges currently on the market.

## .22s

**.22 Long Rifle:** The .22 Long Rifle is also referred to as the .22 LR, or, simply, the "22" (not to be confused with the .22 Winchester Magnum). The .22 LR has been around for well over a hundred years and is the gun beginning shooters most often learn to shoot because it generates very little noise, muzzle blast, and recoil. In addition, ammunition is widely available and inexpensive. Many shooting instructors start their students off with .22s. However, the .22 LR is considered to be underpowered for concealed carry. The .22 LR certainly can kill an attacker, and there have been many instances when homeowners and victims of violent crime have stopped assailants with .22s. One issue that prevents the .22 from being considered a suitable self-defense gun is the lack of bullets designed specifically for defensive purposes. .22s are great practice guns, fun, and economical, but they are largely regarded as too small for self-defense. The .22 LR is a "rimfire," meaning there's no circular primer in the base of the cartridge that the firing pin strikes to ignite powder. Rather, .22s ignite when a firing pin strikes the rim (flat base on the bottom of the cartridge), which ignites the gunpowder.

**.22 Winchester Rimfire Magnum:** Like the .22 LR, the .22 Winchester Rimfire Magnum (also known as the .22 Magnum) ignites when the firing pin strikes the rim, and it lacks a primer in the center of the base of the cartridge. However, the .22 Magnum generates considerably more power than the .22 LR and is more suitable for concealed carry than the smaller .22. Compact revolvers are sometimes chambered in the .22 Magnum, and these revolvers often hold many more cartridges than larger revolvers, like .38s. The .22 Magnum produces considerable noise and muzzle blast compared to the .22 LR, but recoil is not excessive with this cartridge.

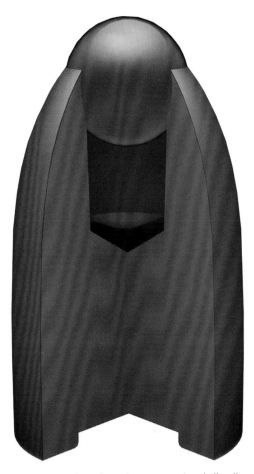

▲ The unique design of Winchester's Super-X .25 Auto bullet allows the bullet to penetrate and then expand thanks to a hollow cavity in the center of the bullet. Photo courtesy of Winchester Ammunition.

**.25 ACP (aka .25 Auto):** The .25 ACP is another cartridge that, although it is carried for defense and can kill, is on the low end of the energy spectrum for concealed carry. Most of the guns chambered in .25 ACP are compact semiautos that are easy to carry and conceal. They generally fire a bullet of about 40 grains that generates less than 100 pounds of energy, which limits its effective range to all but the closest shots.

## .32s

**.32 ACP (aka .32 Auto):** The .32 ACP was developed in 1903 by John Browning, designer of many of today's most popular semiauto cartridges. Colt chambered many of their small "pocket pistols" in .32 ACP, and the cartridge was the standard at the turn of the twentieth century for compact self-defense. The .32 ACP

▲ The .357 SIG is a powerful semiautomatic handgun cartridge that is recognizable by the "shoulder" on the cartridge case. The .357 SIG is not as common as other cartridges, but it is a favorite load for law enforcement and military applications. It also makes an excellent concealed carry cartridge for those who can handle the recoil. NOTE: All .357 SIG cartridges must be fired in guns chambered for that cartridge. It will not function safely in other .357 handguns. Photo courtesy Winchester Ammunition.

is certainly at the low end of the power spectrum for concealed carry guns, but it worked in 1903 and it can still work today at close range. Most .32s are very small subcompact guns that are easily concealed and lightweight. Very few .32s have anything but simple gutter sights, and accuracy and power limit range.

**.32 Smith & Wesson Long:** The .32 S&W Long is virtually extinct today, as there are no commercial concealed carry guns chambered for this round. However, .32 S&W Long ammo can still be found on store shelves and can be fired in guns chambered for .32 S&W Long, .32 H&R Magnum, and .327 Federal Magnum. The .32 S&W Long will work for

self-defense, but the .32 H&R Magnum and the .327 Federal generate more power, and ammunition is available for the latter two cartridges that is specifically designed for defense. However, if you have a .32 H&R Magnum or .327 Federal revolver and you want low-power practice loads that don't recoil, you can shoot .32 S&W Longs in your gun without discomfort.

**.32 Harrington & Richardson Magnum (aka .32 H&R, .32 H&R Magnum):** The .32 H&R Magnum is a relatively new creation, having been developed in 1983 as a joint effort between Harrington & Richardson Arms and Federal Cartridge. The .32 H&R Magnum was designed to generate more power than the .32 S&W Long, and gun companies such as Ruger, Charter Arms, and Smith & Wesson have chambered pistols for the ".32 Mag." Today there are still compact revolvers chambered in .32 H&R Magnum that work well for concealed carry. These revolvers will fire the less powerful .32 S&W Long cartridges, but the more powerful .327 Federal cartridge cannot safely be fired in .32 H&R Magnum revolvers. Black Hills Ammunition, Federal, and Hornady currently offer .32 H&R Magnum ammunition. Most .32 H&R Magnum ammunition generates about 200–250 ft-lbs of kinetic energy. The .32 H&R Magnum is a revolver cartridge.

**.327 Federal Magnum:** The .327 Federal Magnum was developed in 2007 as a joint venture between Federal Cartridge Company and firearms company Sturm, Ruger & Co. The .327 Federal is based on a lengthened .32 H&R Magnum cartridge and generates over 400 ft-lbs of kinetic energy, providing plenty of energy for concealed carry. In addition, guns chambered in .327 Federal Magnum will also shoot .32 H&R Magnum loads and .32 S&W Long loads, but will not fire .32 Auto loads. This is exclusively a revolver cartridge.

### .38s

**.380 ACP (aka .380 Auto):** The .380 ACP is one of the most popular cartridges for compact, semiautomatic concealed carry guns. Originally designed by John Browning in the early 1900s, the .380 was engineered for use in "pocket pistols." The .380 ACP was an immediate success and became a favorite carry gun back then. The cartridge generates far more power than smaller guns like the .22 LR, the .25 ACP, and the .32 ACP, yet it is a small enough cartridge that lends itself well to compact carry guns and doesn't generate painful recoil.

**9mm Luger (aka 9mm):** The 9mm Luger is one of the most popular handgun cartridges in the world, and guns chambered in 9mm Luger have served law enforcement and military duty around the world since the early 1900s, when it became the official cartridge of the German military forces. In the 1950s, firearms chambered for 9mm Luger became popular in the United States, and the cartridge is currently used by the US military and law enforcement. It is also a very popular cartridge for concealed carry, and many compact semiautos are chambered in 9mm. Also known as the 9mm Parabellum or the 9x19mm, the 9mm Luger should *not* be confused with the 9mm Makarov, which is a different cartridge altogether. Thankfully, 9mm Makarov guns and ammunition are rarely seen in the United States, and the vast majority of American firearms are 9mm Luger. As a concealed carry gun, the 9mm has proven reliable and effective, capable of stopping assailants when loaded with proper bullets. Accuracy is good, recoil is moderate, and energy is sufficient. Anyone shopping for a concealed carry firearm should consider the 9mm Luger. The vast majority of 9mm handguns are semiautomatics.

**9mm Luger+P:** Certain 9mm Luger loads have increased pressure (+P). These high pressure loads generate more energy than standard 9mm loads, but they should only be fired in guns rated for 9mm+P ammunition. If you have any questions about whether or not your gun is capable of shooting 9mm+P ammo, take the gun to a local qualified gunsmith. Better yet, shoot standard 9mm Luger loads through your gun. Today's crop of 9mm Luger self-defense ammo contains plenty of reliable options, and the added pressure will generate more power but at the cost of increased muzzle blast and recoil. Standard 9mm Luger ammunition should be sufficient for concealed carry.

▼ The 9mm Luger, which is shown here with magazines from Kimber's Solo semiautomatic, is a favorite cartridge for law enforcement and personal defense. The compact Solo's extended magazine holds a total of eight 9mm Luger cartridges, which is quite a few for such a small firearm. Photo courtesy of Kimber America.

**.38 Special (aka .38):** The .38 Special is the most popular caliber for concealed carry revolvers, and virtually every manufacturer that produces compact, double action revolvers chambers their guns for the .38 Special. Originally developed in 1902, the .38 Special has been a successful cartridge since its inception. Just as the 9mm Luger has become the "norm" for semiautomatic handguns, the .38 Special is the most obvious choice for a new shooter capable of handling the recoil this cartridge generates, which is more than the .32 H&R but far less than the powerful .357 Magnum. There are a wide variety of quality self-defense loads available from various cartridge manufacturers. In addition, there are light loads available from Hornady and other manufacturers that generate less recoil than standard loads, which is nice when you are shooting very light, small revolvers that produce more recoil energy than larger, heavier guns. The .38 Special should be on the short list of anyone considering a concealed carry revolver, and the choices seem almost endless. You can choose between double action and double action–only guns, and many companies build .38 revolvers with light frames made of alloys or titanium. Most .38 specials produce about 200 ft-lbs of energy, and this cartridge is exclusively chambered in revolvers.

**.38 Special+P:** .38 Special+P ammo simply generates more power than standard .38 ammo. The +P variant also generates more muzzle blast and recoil. Many of the .38 Special self-defense loads are +P, meaning they generate more power than standard loads, and many carry revolvers are chambered for .38 Special+P. If you purchase a .38 Special+P revolver, you can practice with lower pressure, lower recoil .38 Special ammunition, and can carry .38 Special+P ammunition in the gun for defense, since .38 Special+P revolvers will fire standard .38 Special ammo without any problems. There are a wide variety of premium self-defense .38 Special+P loads available from companies like Hornady, Remington, Winchester, Federal, Nosler, and other ammunition manufacturers. The .38 Special+P is a revolver cartridge.

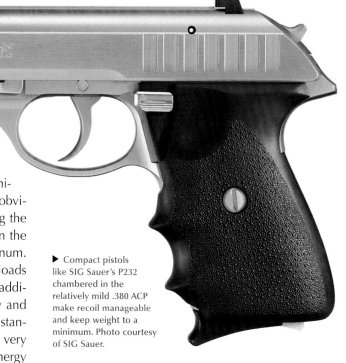

▶ Compact pistols like SIG Sauer's P232 chambered in the relatively mild .380 ACP make recoil manageable and keep weight to a minimum. Photo courtesy of SIG Sauer.

**.38 Super:** The .38 Super is less known than other midsize defense cartridges, and its name generates some confusion since guns chambered in .38 Super are semiautos and not to be confused with .38 Special revolvers. The .38 Super fires the same caliber bullet as the .380 ACP, the 9mm Luger, and the .357 SIG (all of which fire .355-inch diameter bullets). However, the .38 Super generates much more power than the 9mm and the .380 ACP (over 500 ft-lbs of energy). This level of power certainly leaves no doubt that the .38 Super is capable of stopping an assailant, but the noise and recoil is on the extreme end for inexperienced shooters. There are many +P versions of the .38 Super, so be sure to check with the manufacturer regarding whether or not your gun can handle +P loads before firing.

**.357 SIG:** The .357 SIG is another cartridge with a name that can confuse new shooters. While the .357 Magnum is primarily a revolver cartridge, the .357 SIG is designed for semiautomatic handguns and was originally developed in 1994 as a joint venture between SIG Sauer, who produced the handguns, and Federal, who produced ammunition. The .357 SIG cartridge is immediately recognizable, since it is a "bottleneck" cartridge, which does not have a cartridge case with a smooth tapered body but rather a sharp "neck" where the cartridge case narrows in diameter. The .357 SIG was developed by taking the .40 Smith & Wesson case and "necking it down" (narrowing the opening on the end of the case) to hold smaller .355-caliber bullets instead of larger .40-caliber bullets. This gives the .357 SIG its unique look. The .357 SIG is a favorite cartridge for law enforcement, and it continues to gain popularity. However, .357 SIG guns are still not common, and the power that this cartridge generates (over 500 ft-lbs) makes it hard to handle recoil and muzzle blast in compact guns. Full-size .357 SIG handguns generate plenty of power, but they are at the upper limit for most new shooters. The .357 SIG is strictly a semiauto cartridge.

**.357 Remington Magnum (aka .357 Magnum):** The .357 Magnum is one of the most popular handgun cartridges ever. Developed in the 1930s by Smith & Wesson, the .357 Magnum was designed to improve upon .38 Special ballistics. The .357 Magnum's case is .135 inches longer than the .38 Special, meaning that the .357 Magnum can hold more gunpowder and thus can produce more energy, since the bullet is traveling at a higher velocity. Revolvers chambered for .357 Magnum will also fire .38 Special and .38 Special+P cartridges without a problem, but .357 Magnum ammunition should never be loaded into revolvers chambered for .38 Special and .38 Special+P. Though the .357 Magnum produces plenty of power (like the .357 SIG and .38 Super, it is capable of generating more than 500 ft-lbs of energy), it isn't always the best choice for a new shooter. The .357 magnum produces noticeably more recoil and muzzle blast than the .38 Special or .38 Special+P. However, there are quite a few compact concealed carry revolvers chambered for the mighty .357 Magnum, and if you can handle the recoil and muzzle blast, there is no doubt that a well-constructed bullet fired from this gun will do considerable damage to an attacker. If you choose the .357 Magnum revolver for concealed carry, you can always practice with cheaper, milder .38 Special ammo. The .357 Magnum is a revolver cartridge.

### Larger Calibers

**.40 Smith & Wesson (aka .40 S&W):** In 1990, firearms giant Smith & Wesson announced that it had developed a semiautomatic handgun cartridge that filled the power gap between the 9mm Luger and the larger (too large for many) .45 ACP. This new cartridge was dubbed the .40 Smith & Wesson, and ammunition manufacturer Winchester simultaneously announced that it would begin producing .40 S&W ammo. The cartridge was an immediate success and remains so today, a favorite of law enforcement and a popular cartridge for concealed carry. This cartridge fires .40-inch diameter bullets weighing between 155 and 180 grains at velocities ranging from 900–1,200 fps, which generates between 400 and 500 ft-lbs of energy. There

▲ Cutaway view of the bullet: Most bullets have a lead core and a copper jacket. This image shows Winchester's PDX-1 defensive bullet, which is a hollow point bullet engineered to expand reliably when it strikes a target. Photo courtesy of Winchester Ammunition.

are several compact guns chambered in .40 S&W, and it is a popular choice for experienced shooters. However, the .40 S&W's biggest drawbacks are that it doesn't hold as many rounds as similar 9mm guns (because of its larger diameter) and the recoil, muzzle blast, and muzzle flip generated by the .40 S&W can be off-putting to novice shooters. Nevertheless, the .40 S&W remains popular, and many shooters believe the increase in power over the 9mm Luger is worth the lowered magazine capacity and recoil generated by the .40. The ultimate choice between these two cartridges can only be made by the shooter. The .40 S&W is typically chambered in semiautomatic pistols, though a few revolvers (like Charter Arms' Pitbull) have been chambered for this cartridge.

**10mm Auto:** The 10mm Auto was developed in 1983 and is one of the most powerful semiautomatic handgun cartridges on the market, capable of generating upwards of 750 ft-lbs of kinetic energy. That kind of power comes at a price, though; the 10mm Auto is a real handful and only experienced shooters will want to shoot this cartridge. In fact, the 10mm is carried by some hikers as an alternative to the larger .41 and .44 Magnums in bear country! This kind of power is impressive, but the new shooter should avoid a 10mm Auto handgun. This is primarily a cartridge for full-sized semiautos, and there are better options for new shooters.

**.41 Remington Magnum (aka .41 Mag):** The .41 Magnum is a handful for the experienced hunter, and it should be off the list for concealed carry unless you really want a revolver that can protect you from human attackers as well as grizzly bears. The .41 Magnum is a popular hunting cartridge, but revolvers chambered for this cartridge are big and bulky and the recoil and muzzle blast generated by the big .41 are far too great for most new shooters.

**.410 Shotshells:** Some revolvers, such as those by Taurus and Smith & Wesson, fire .410 shotshells. Unlike traditional handgun cartridges, .410 shotshell revolvers fire a cluster of pellets or disks, making them appropriate for close-range defensive situations. Be sure to check the information on the barrel of your .410 revolver to determine whether it can fire 2½" shotshells or 3" shotshells.

**.44 Smith & Wesson Special (aka .44 Special):** the .44 Special is actually gaining a bit of a following as a concealed carry/defensive gun, though most .44 Special revolvers are very large and bulky for concealed carry guns. There are plenty of people who choose to carry the .44 Special, and it certainly will do the job of stopping an assailant. The .44 Special generates between 300 and 400 ft-lbs of energy, and it generates moderate to heavy recoil, though it isn't out of the range of shooters that have gained a bit of experience with other handguns first. The .44 Special may not be the best choice, but it certainly isn't the worst choice, and it makes a fine defensive cartridge for the home. It will never be as popular as the smaller .38s and the .357 Magnum because of the increased size of

◀ Federal Premium's patented Guard Dog ammunition is unique. Although it is a full metal jacket, the bullet is filled with polymer to expand reliably and penetrate. Photo courtesy of Federal Premium Ammunition.

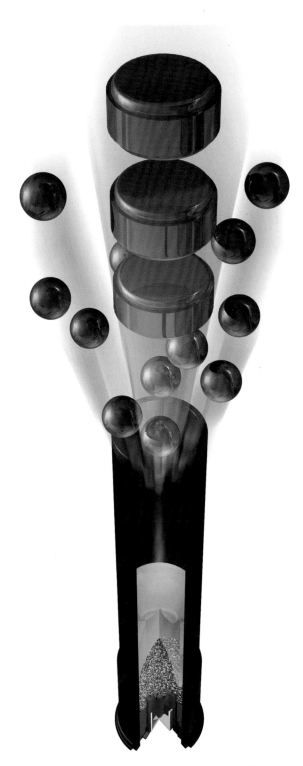

the gun, but the .44 Special will certainly work. It is a revolver cartridge.

**.44 Remington Magnum (aka .44 Magnum):** The .44 Magnum was made popular by Clint Eastwood's Dirty Harry Callahan character, who touted the .44 Magnum as the "most powerful handgun cartridge in the world." It isn't the most powerful cartridge today, but it is still popular. It is not, however, a concealed carry gun, especially for the new shooter. The .44 Magnum is designed for hunting big game and defending oneself against bears, not tucking into a purse to go out for a night on the town. The .44 Magnum generates far too much recoil and muzzle blast for the new shooter. You can fire .44 Special ammunition in guns chambered for .44 Magnum. This is a revolver cartridge, with the

▼ The impact of Winchester's PDX-1 Defender shotshell on a target. The impact of multiple projectiles can be seen here. Photo courtesy of Winchester Ammunition.

▲ Some revolvers, such as the Taurus Judge and the Smith & Wesson Governor, can fire .410 shotshells. In this case, the Winchester shotshell has three Defense Discs and twelve BB pellets that act as projectiles rather than a single bullet. Since .410 loads are available in 2½- and 3-inch lengths, be sure what length of shotshells your revolver is chambered for. Photo courtesy of Winchester Ammunition.

◄ This beautiful Kimber semiautomatic is chambered for the powerful .45 ACP cartridge, a favorite among concealed carry enthusiasts. The .45 ACP produces recoil levels that could intimidate new shooters, so although the .45 ACP is an effective cartridge, it is generally not the first choice for new shooters. Photo courtesy of Kimber America.

exception of extremely large frame semiautos like Magnum Research's Desert Eagle.

**.45 ACP (aka .45 Auto):** The .45 ACP may be the most storied handgun in American history, and it remains a favorite of law enforcement, military, competitive shooters, and concealed carry permit holders. One of the most popular .45 variants is the "1911" Model, which was designed after John Browning's original Colt .45 semiauto. The .45 ACP is a popular gun and fans of the cartridge seem to be among the most loyal, but the .45 ACP is at the upper limit of power for most new shooters. The .45 ACP is certainly a capable self-defense cartridge, and the recoil generated by this gun is heavy but not painful in most cases. The .45 generates about 400–500 ft-lbs of kinetic energy, which is ample for defensive situations. Every major ammunition manufacturer that produces self-defense ammo sells .45 ACP ammunition. Even small .45 Auto handguns are still larger than compact .380s and 9mms, so the .45 ACP is not the ideal choice for a shooter that is new to the game. The .45 ACP is primarily a semiautomatic handgun cartridge.

**.45 ACP+P:** This is the higher pressure load for the .45 ACP and should only be fired in guns capable of handling the increased pressure generated by this cartridge.

**.45 Colt:** The .45 Colt is an important piece of American history, and there are still companies chambering double action revolvers in .45 Colt. The .45 Colt is a fun cartridge to shoot, but it isn't ideal for concealed carry because it requires revolvers with large frames and generates more recoil than most new shooters care to put up with. However, there are those who choose the carry handguns chambered in .45 Colt, and it does perform well.

**.454 Casull, .480 Ruger, .460 Smith & Wesson, .500 Smith & Wesson:** These cartridges represent the extreme upper limit of handgun power and all of them are very bad choices for the new shooter. Revolvers chambered for these cartridges generate tremendous power, but that power comes with the price of a very large frame and excessive recoil. Stay away from these guns until you have lots of experience, and even then be ready to hold on tight!

# V. The Revolver

When Samuel Colt patented his newly designed revolver in 1836, it revolutionized firearms manufacturing. Colt's pistol was not the first revolver ever designed, but it was the first mass-produced, reliable revolver available in the world. The Colt revolver was carried by both Union and Confederate soldiers in the Civil War and is credited with playing a key role in westward expansion.

The Colt revolver was revolutionary. Two of the hallmarks of this firearm were reliability and simplicity. There were other revolver designs that predated Colt's gun, but none that could match the functionality of the Colt gun.

The revolver became an American icon, and "wheelguns," as they are sometimes called, not only played a role in our own bloody Civil War and our efforts to tame the West, but also in our cinema and early television. These were the guns the cowboys carried, like Wyatt Earp's Peacemaker and the guns that Roy Rogers and the Lone Ranger used to bring peace and justice to the innocent masses on Saturday television shows. An entire generation of American children grew up carrying cap pistols designed to mimic Colt's original creation. In later years, a snarling Clint Eastwood introduced the world to the Smith & Wesson Model 29 .44 Magnum, "the most powerful handgun in the world," in the cinematic role of "Dirty" Harry Callahan.

Today's revolvers have advanced far beyond anything Samuel Colt could have imagined when he was assembling his first prototypes of a revolving pistol in the nineteenth century, but the hallmarks of today's revolver are the same as they were when Colt set up shop: reliability and simplicity. Revolvers are simple to use; easy to load, unload, and maintain; and very dependable. It is for these reasons that revolvers are commonly used to introduce new shooters to the sport, and I maintain that every beginning handgunner should begin learning to shoot with a revolver. It has been my experience that most new shooters learn to shoot a revolver very quickly, and after a day on the range they are comfortable with the mechanics of the

▶ Revolvers like this Taurus 66SS make excellent guns for beginning shooters. And while this Taurus is a bit large for carry, that company and others make smaller revolvers that are easily concealed and provide plenty of power. Photo courtesy of Taurus International.

firearm. Semiautomatic pistols, because of their more complex designs, typically require more time to learn to shoot and maintain. Semiautos work very well for concealed carry, but they do require more range time to learn to shoot effectively.

The firing process in revolvers can be divided into two main steps. The first step is cocking the gun, and depending upon what type of revolver you have, you may have to cock the gun manually with your thumb or you may be able to cock the revolver by pulling the trigger back partially. The second step of the firing process involves releasing the hammer, which strikes the firing pin and ignites the primer. We therefore can divide the firing process into these two main steps: cocking the hammer and releasing the hammer.

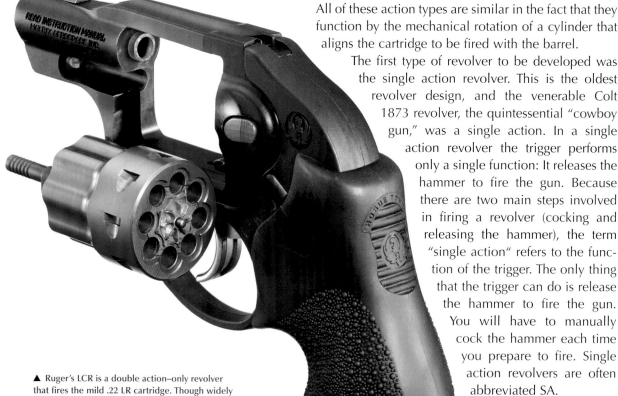

▲ Ruger's LCR is a double action–only revolver that fires the mild .22 LR cartridge. Though widely considered too light for defensive work, light recoil and reasonably priced ammunition make the .22 a favorite practice gun. In addition, Ruger chambers the LCR in .38 Special, which is a popular carry gun. Photo courtesy of Sturm, Ruger & Co.

The revolver gets its name from the movement of a round cylinder that sits within the frame of the gun. This round cylinder serves as the chamber and holds the loaded cartridges. The cylinder revolves when the gun is cocked, rotating until a new chamber is aligned with the barrel of the gun. A pull of the trigger then releases the hammer, which drives the firing pin into the primer of the cartridge. Recocking the gun moves the cylinder once more, aligning a fresh cartridge with the barrel. This is repeated until all of the chambers have all been fired. Many of the early revolver designs had cylinders with six chambers, and thus they were called "six shooters."

## The Three Types of Revolvers

Revolvers, like semiautomatics, are divided into categories. The three main categories of revolvers are single action, double action, and double action–only. All of these action types are similar in the fact that they function by the mechanical rotation of a cylinder that aligns the cartridge to be fired with the barrel.

The first type of revolver to be developed was the single action revolver. This is the oldest revolver design, and the venerable Colt 1873 revolver, the quintessential "cowboy gun," was a single action. In a single action revolver the trigger performs only a single function: It releases the hammer to fire the gun. Because there are two main steps involved in firing a revolver (cocking and releasing the hammer), the term "single action" refers to the function of the trigger. The only thing that the trigger can do is release the hammer to fire the gun. You will have to manually cock the hammer each time you prepare to fire. Single action revolvers are often abbreviated SA.

Double action revolvers are designed so that the trigger serves two functions. First, the trigger can cock the hammer to initiate the firing process. The trigger also releases the hammer and fires the gun. For this reason it is not necessary to cock the hammer on a double action revolver each time you fire. You can fire a double action revolver by simply pulling the trigger again and again, cocking the hammer and firing the gun with each pull of the trigger. Double actions can thus be fired in two ways. The shooter can also cock the hammer manually and then pull the trigger, which is referred to as "single action firing" because the trigger is performing only one task—releasing the hammer that was manually cocked. Double action revolvers are typically abbreviated DA.

The final type of revolver is the double action–only revolver, the majority of which are instantly recognizable because of the lack of an external hammer. In all other respects, however, the DAO revolver, as it is commonly called, looks like a standard revolver. As the name indicates, the DAO revolver cannot be fired in single action mode by manually cocking the hammer before firing. The trigger *must* perform both operations. The lack of an external hammer offers several advantages for a concealed carry gun, and most DAO revolvers are designed for self-defense. Hammers can hang on clothing and holsters when you try to draw them, especially in a hurry and under tense circumstances. DAO revolvers are simple to operate and simple to maintain; there is no safety and no hammer, so you simply draw the revolver and pull the trigger.

▶ Finding the right holster makes pistol carry much easier. This model from Laser Lyte is designed for a revolver with a laser sight. Photo courtesy of Laser Lyte.

## The Revolver as a Self-Defense Firearm

The design of revolvers makes them extremely durable, and revolvers with heavy frames are capable of handling extremely powerful cartridges like the .480 Ruger, .500 S&W, and the .454 Casull. However, no one needs this level of power for armed self-defense, nor would they welcome the accompanying weight of such revolvers, which can weigh as much as four pounds. These revolvers are designed for hunting large game and defense against big predators like grizzly bears.

There are, however, plenty of revolvers that make excellent concealed carry guns. Revolvers are very reliable and easy to use, as stated earlier. Simply pull out the gun, aim, and pull the trigger. Maintenance typically involves pressing the cylinder release button on DA and DAO revolvers, swinging out the cylinder, wiping down the internal parts, and cleaning the barrel periodically. This combination of unfailing reliability and minimal maintenance requirements makes revolvers an obvious choice for beginning concealed carry.

Revolvers are not without their drawbacks, however. The ergonomics and heft of revolvers make them more difficult to carry concealed than compact semiautos, and while a passerby might see the square shape of a poorly concealed semiauto and mistake it for a cell phone or wallet, revolvers are much more recognizable as firearms when they are improperly concealed (the ability to see a gun is called "printing"). This is one reason that ankle holsters are so popular when concealing revolvers.

The weight of revolvers is sometimes an issue, although companies like Taurus, Ruger, and Smith & Wesson make ultralight versions of their revolvers designed specifically for concealed carry. Standard compact revolvers weigh up to thirty ounces, which is considered heavy for daily concealed carry. However, the new generation of lightweight revolvers are true featherweights. Ruger's LCR revolver, for example, weighs only thirteen and a half ounces when chambered for .38 Special+P. If you are planning to buy a revolver for concealed carry, these ultralight guns are a good choice for all-day carry.

Another consideration when purchasing a revolver for self-defense is limited ammunition capacity. Most ultralight, compact revolvers have a capacity of five rounds in .38 Special, whereas the average 9mm semiauto has an average magazine capacity between ten and (if local law allows) seventeen rounds. Even small caliber revolvers, like those chambered in .22 Magnum, rarely hold more than ten rounds. Some buyers are turned away from revolvers because they want a gun that is capable of shooting more rounds in less time. It's a valid argument; you can certainly put more bullets in the air with a semiauto than you can with a revolver, provided that the semiauto is feeding and firing correctly.

I personally believe, however, that the advantage is largely theoretical and the odds of needing more than five or six rounds in a concealed carry gun are pretty low. Personal experience has taught me that high-capacity semiautos give a false sense of security to inexperienced shooters who believe that the best defense is to just keep shooting in the general direction of the target without taking the time to aim properly. The goal of self-defense shooting, as we will discuss in later chapters, is rapid, *aimed* firing.

In the late 1990s, there was a police dashboard camera that caught footage of a shootout between Ohio State Troopers and a pair of armed felons. On the video there is clear footage of one of the troopers and one of the criminals, both of whom are carrying semiauto pistols, firing at each other at close range. In

the matter of a few seconds something like thirty-two rounds were fired while the shooters squared off at point-blank range, each trying to fire while backpedaling to reach available cover. Nearby houses, trees, and cars were riddled with bullet holes, but despite the volley of shots at very close range, neither the trooper nor the criminal was hit.

What does the above situation teach us? Simply put, it is far more important to shoot well than to shoot a lot. I don't profess to know what it feels like to have a felon standing less than ten feet away, trying in earnest to shoot me again and again, but I will assure you that your conscious mind is of little value under such circumstances. The conscious mind is trying in vain to register the events that are occurring at that moment, and when you speak to people who have been involved in shootings, they will tell you that the conscious mind is usually not doing a very good job getting you out of that situation alive. Muscle memory, the trained, repetitive movement of a practiced shooter, does not rely on the conscious mind for support. Therefore, whether you choose to shoot a revolver or semiauto, it is important to understand that you must practice with either gun until the movements become natural and instinctive. When you reach that point, you aren't relying on the conscious mind and all of its complexity and frailty to keep you out of harm's way. Practice is the key, and to practice a lot you need a gun that works for you. If the gun you choose fits your hand and you are comfortable loading, unloading, and firing that gun, you will spend more time practicing, whether that gun is a revolver or a semiauto.

## Loading the Revolver

Single action revolvers are typically loaded by swinging open a gate (called a "loading gate") on the rear of the frame to expose one of the cylinders. The hammer is then half-cocked to release the cylinder (hence the term "going off half-cocked") so that the cylinder can be rotated and the gun can be loaded or unloaded. In front of the cylinder where the gate is located there is a "plunger" that you can press to slide empty cartridge cases from the cylinder. It is important to note that although the term "half-cocked" indicates that the hammer is cocked halfway, this is usually not true. In reality, most single actions only require about a quarter to a

▲ Some revolvers like this Ruger have adjustable sights. Note the arrows cut into the cylinder of this revolver that indicate which way the cylinder turns. Photo courtesy of Benjamin Gettinger.

third cock to release the cylinder. For routine shooting, the cylinder is not removed from the frame.

I'm not going to spend equal amounts of time discussing single action and double action/double action–only guns, because the vast majority of revolvers used for self-defense are either DA or DAO guns. Single action guns require much more time to load and unload, and you must cock the hammer before every shot. Single actions, therefore, must have an exposed hammer, which is prone to hanging on clothing, belts, and skin when the gun is drawn. Single actions are interesting to shoot, and the popularity of "cowboy action" shooting matches is on the rise. However, for the beginning concealed carry student, I believe that single action revolvers are a poor choice.

Double action and double action–only revolvers, however, are easy to load, unload, and shoot, which accounts for their current popularity. Loading and unloading DA and DAO revolvers requires releasing the cylinder from the frame. For most current production revolvers the cylinder release button will be located on the left rear portion of the frame. Some companies like Taurus, Charter Arms, and Smith & Wesson have buttons that slide forward to release the cylinder. Simply press the button forward and push on the right side of the cylinder to swing the cylinder out of the frame. Other companies, like Ruger, have a cylinder release button that must be pressed down instead of slid forward. Pressing on the right side of the Ruger cylinder will cause the cylinder to swing out into a safe position for loading. Though gun companies may differ slightly in the size or shape of the cylinder release button, the basic concept is the same across different brands.

After pressing the cylinder release button and swinging out the cylinder, it will be possible to spin the cylinder freely with your hand. It is always a good idea to check each cylinder before loading, taking the time to examine them for obstructions or wear. It's also worth noting that when the cylinder is released from the frame the revolver is safe because the gun cannot be fired. After spinning the cylinder and checking each chamber to be sure that it is empty and free of debris, you can begin loading the revolver.

▲ Pressing the cylinder release button (shown here on a Ruger revolver, just behind the cylinder) allows the shooter to swing the cylinder out of the frame for loading, unloading, and safety. Photo courtesy of Gettinger Photography.

Each chamber in the cylinder will hold one cartridge. Load each cartridge so that the bullet enters the chamber first. When all of the chambers are loaded, swing the cylinder back into the frame until you hear a clicking sound. This metallic click is the sound of the cylinder locking into place. If the cylinder does not lock in place, it is a good idea to try and twist the cylinder in the frame with your fingers, being certain to keep the gun pointed in a safe direction at all times. When the cylinder is locked in place and all of the chambers are loaded, you can begin firing the revolver.

## First Shots with a Revolver

As always, safety is paramount when shooting any firearm. Before you begin shooting your revolver, be sure that you are shooting at a safe target and that you know what lies beyond it. Bullets can travel for miles, so be sure that you have a proper backstop before firing. Always keep the revolver pointed in a safe direction, which is usually toward the target. Hearing

and eye protection should be worn at all times when shooting.

Techniques for proper grip and stance are located later in this book and should be reviewed before taking your first shots, particularly because it is easier to learn proper grip and stance when you begin shooting than it is to try and fix bad technique once it has become ingrained in your muscle memory.

Shooting revolvers is simple and straightforward, which is one of the main reasons that they are so popular for concealed carry, particularly with beginning shooters. Since most concealed carry revolvers are either double action or double action–only guns, the majority of this lesson will be dedicated to explaining how to fire DA and DAO guns. As previously stated, single action revolvers are rarely used for concealed carry.

When firing a double action revolver with an exposed hammer, the shooter has two options with every shot. They can either cock the hammer and then pull the trigger to fire, which is referred to as "single action firing" because you are manually cocking the hammer and the trigger is only serving a single purpose, or you can simply pull the trigger to fire each round, which is known as "double action firing" because the trigger is performing the action of cocking *and* firing the gun. For beginners, I recommend single action firing, because it breaks the process down into two simple steps. First, with the revolver pointed at the target, pull back (or "cock") the hammer with the thumb on your strong hand. As you bring the trigger back toward the grip of the gun you will hear a single, metallic click and the hammer will be cocked.

The next step in the process of firing the revolver involves pulling the trigger. By cocking the hammer on your revolver manually, you have reduced the amount of work that the trigger is required to do, which greatly lessens the amount of trigger force necessary to fire the shot. This reduced trigger travel and weight is the reason I recommend that beginning shooters learn to fire DA revolvers by single action firing. When the hammer is cocked, a light trigger press will fire the gun. Repeat this process as you fire each cylinder. Remember the steps in the process as you fire the remaining cartridges. Cock the hammer, align the sights, and press the trigger.

Double action firing does not require cocking the hammer. Get back into proper stance and hold the gun with a solid, two-handed grip. Align the sights on the target and squeeze the trigger. The trigger pull will be much harder and heavier, requiring additional force. However, you will not have to cock the hammer between each subsequent shot. Double action firing is difficult for some beginners, because heavier trigger pull causes them to lose their sight pictures and the gun begins to move as they are trying to fire. Practice staying focused throughout the duration of the shot and learning to pull the trigger smoothly (called "trigger control"). Only the last joint of your index finger should be contacting the surface of the trigger; placing more of your finger on the trigger, also known as "choking" the trigger, makes it difficult to shoot smoothly and accurately.

With DA revolvers, it is fine to shoot one round in single action mode, cocking the hammer before firing, and then to follow that shot with a shot in double

action mode and vice versa. DAO revolvers must be fired as double actions since there is no external hammer to cock.

For the beginning shooter I recommend practicing both single action and double action fire if you have a DA revolver. Learn to shoot both ways, practicing both methods as you begin to familiarize yourself with your firearm. Don't worry about accuracy on your first shots; you are simply familiarizing yourself with the way in which your firearm works and becoming comfortable shooting. The goals of these first few trips to the range are *safety* and *familiarity* with the firearm. Accuracy can be improved upon later, and it is easy to get discouraged when you purchase a gun for self-defense and you feel like you aren't a good shot. Remember, the process of becoming a good shooter occurs in stages. Are you a safe shooter? Are you becoming more familiar and comfortable with your gun? If so, you have accomplished something very important, and that's a lot for one day on the range.

## After Firing

When you are finished firing the revolver, use the thumb on your strong hand to press the cylinder release while keeping the muzzle pointed in a safe direction and keeping your finger off the trigger. The cylinder will swing out once more. If you have fired all of the rounds in the revolver, each primer should be dented from the impact of the firing pin. If you have cartridges that have not been fired, take note of this. Also, look for any problems with the primers. Are the primers struck completely through, leaving behind a hole? Are the primer strikes irregular and varying greatly in depth? If so, you need to contact a qualified gunsmith to examine the revolver for any problems. For the most part, though, revolvers are consistent and reliable.

To remove the empty cartridges from the cylinder, you can press the extractor rod on the front of the cylinder with the palm of your hand. This should elevate the cartridges so that they either fall out or can be removed manually. The ejector rod will remove both fired and unfired cartridges safely. Occasionally, cartridges will swell in the chamber, a phenomenon known as *obturation* that is caused by the pressure of expanding gases inside the cartridge as it is fired and

▲ The author firing a Taurus .357 revolver. Revolvers are simple to use and easy to carry, making guns like the Taurus very popular among new shooters.

the resulting swelling of the cartridge case. This can sometimes make cartridges difficult to remove from the cylinder. Do not pound the ejector rod against hard surfaces because you may bend the rod and cause permanent damage to the gun. If you cannot remove the empty cartridges easily, you may have to pry them out of the cylinder by hand or with a small screwdriver. This is an uncommon occurrence, though, especially in new guns firing quality ammunition.

## Revolver Safety

When shooting a revolver, all of the standard gun safety rules apply, but it is worth repeating basic safety instructions. First and foremost, treat every gun as if it is loaded *at all times*. Not when you think it might be loaded, not in the span of time before you press the cylinder release and swing out the cylinder to check and see if there are any cartridges in the chamber. All of the time.

Treating a gun as though it is loaded means always being aware of the direction the muzzle is being pointed. I'll touch on this multiple times throughout the book, but one of the most dangerous aspects about working with new shooters is that they do not keep track of where the muzzle of their firearms are pointed. It seems simple enough, but on multiple occasions I've seen new shooters turn the muzzle of a loaded gun on their instructors simply because the shooter got caught up in the excitement of the moment and lost track of the location of his or her gun barrel. This is never acceptable.

One of the most important aspects of gun safety is learning to index the trigger finger. When you are not actively firing, your trigger finger should be *outside* the trigger guard. Practice this enough that your finger automatically lands on the same position on the gun each time you pick it up and remains there until you are ready to fire. Immediately after you have finished firing the trigger finger should be removed from the trigger and positioned back along the frame. For more

▲ Ruger's SP 101 .357 Magnum has checkered grips, a stainless steel finish, fiber optic front sight, and a full-length underlug (steel beneath the barrel) for added stability while shooting. This is an excellent revolver for target shooting and hunting but is pushing the upper limit of size for practical daily carry. Photo courtesy of Sturm, Ruger & Co.

on indexing the finger, see Chapter VII, "Firearm Safety."

Eye and ear protection should be worn at all times. Firing a revolver generates enough noise to do permanent damage to your hearing.

Be aware of your target. Remember that a bullet can travel long distances and still carry enough energy to kill or injure others or damage property. You should have a solid backstop behind your target, something capable of stopping the bullet. Most shooting ranges use large piles of dirt. Always be aware of where the bullet is traveling.

When you are at the shooting range, there is no need to load your firearm before you reach the shooting position, and loading your gun before you are in a position to shoot is even more dangerous when there are shooters ahead of you. Until you are ready to shoot, keep your revolver in the SAFE position, which means that you have pressed the cylinder release button and the cylinder is removed from the frame of the gun. When the cylinder is removed from the gun a revolver cannot be fired, which protects you and those around you while simultaneously demonstrating to other shooters that the gun cannot be fired until the cylinder is pushed back in place in the frame.

Revolvers lack a mechanical safety, which causes concern for some shooters. This lack of a safety does not make revolvers inherently unsafe; however, it is important that you learn to index your finger and keep the gun pointed in a safe direction. My favorite carry gun is a double action revolver, which I carry in a holster that fits inside the waistband of my pants, and when properly carried, stored, and handled I don't worry about the lack of a manual safety. In addition, if I need to draw my revolver to protect my life or the lives of others, I don't have to worry about a manual safety; I can simply draw the gun and press the trigger, so don't let the lack of a manual safety discourage you from purchasing a revolver for concealed carry. Safeties are mechanical devices, and all mechanical devices are prone to failure. Carry your gun safely (see Chapter XII, "Carrying a Concealed Firearm" for more details) and keep your gun safely secured while you are at home (see Chapter XIII, "Firearm Maintenance").

Slow-motion video of a revolver being fired shows that gases from the burning powder are vented from the front and sides of the cylinder each time the gun is fired. This cloud of residue covers our hands each time we fire a handgun, though we rarely notice. However, improperly holding a revolver, such as placing your hands around the front of the cylinder while firing, can cause this residue to burn your hands. Residue burns are not a problem if the revolver is held correctly, which means that one hand (the strong hand) holds the grip firmly and the other hand wraps around it, creating a stable shooting platform and keeping the hands out of the way of escaping gases. Though residue burns are rare and almost exclusively the result of an inexperienced shooter holding the gun improperly, wearing a pair of shooting gloves helps reduce the risk of burns from escaping gases.

When firing a revolver with an exposed hammer, it is important to place the hands so that when the hammer falls it will not pinch the skin of the hands and fingers. With a proper grip, there is virtually no chance that the hammer will pinch the fingers, so take the time to learn to properly grip the revolver when you are shooting. Remember that the strong hand wraps around the pistol grip, the weak hand wraps around the strong hand. Be sure to keep the hands away from the moving parts of the gun. DAO revolvers that lack an exposed hammer eliminate any chance of pinching the hands.

### Decocking a Revolver

One important skill to learn when shooting a revolver with an exposed hammer is how to decock the revolver. Let's say that you are at the range and preparing to fire your revolver at the target. You raise the revolver, cock the hammer with your strong-hand thumb, and prepare to shoot. Suddenly, someone next to you yells, "Ceasefire!" and you see a dog running across the range. You want to make your gun safe, but the hammer is cocked and all that is required to fire the revolver is a light press on the trigger. What do you do?

Lowering the hammer on a revolver is a skill that every shooter needs to learn. On most revolvers, once you cock the hammer you can't simply swing the cylinder out to make the gun safe. You must lower the hammer first. However, when the hammer falls it strikes the pin and fires the gun.

Relax. It is possible to safely and easily lower the hammer and then open the cylinder to make your gun safe. First, most modern DA and DAO revolvers have a *transfer bar*, a piece of steel that lies between the

▲ Sliding the cylinder release button forward allows the shooter to press the cylinder on the right side and swing it out of the frame.

▼ Loading the revolver means placing cartridges into each cylinder. In revolvers, the cylinder acts as the chamber (where the cartridge is fired), and with each pull of the trigger the cylinder rotates to align a new cartridge with the barrel.

firing pin and the hammer. The transfer bar system was designed to prevent accidental firing when shooters attempted to lower the hammer or when the hammer was struck by an object like a rock or tree branch. Older revolvers have firing pins that are located on the hammer. Rather than the smooth, flat front surfaces found on most modern revolvers, these older revolvers have an exposed hammer that is plainly visible when the revolver is cocked. Pulling the trigger releases the hammer, which drives the firing pin into the primer of the cartridge, firing the cartridge. Exposed hammer guns are rare today because they lack the transfer bar, which means that the firing pin is already aligned with the exposed primer, which is more likely to result in accidental discharges.

The problem with these older revolvers with firing pins mounted on the surface of the hammer is that sometimes a hard blow to the back of even an uncocked hammer would cause the gun to fire unexpectedly, which was indeed a very serious and dangerous problem. Modern guns, however, rely on the transfer bar system to separate the hammer and the firing pin. For this reason, striking a lowered hammer will not cause the gun to go off.

Returning to our scenario, when you have a revolver with a cocked hammer and you want to lower it, there are several important steps you must take to make the revolver safe once more. First, keep the revolver pointed in a safe direction, so that if the gun happens to go off it will not be a danger to you or others. Keeping your hands away from the front of the cylinder and the barrels, pull the hammer back *farther* than the cocked position and, with a solid hold on the grip of the gun, slowly pull the trigger and lower the hammer. Some experts suggest placing the "meat" of the thumb in front of the hammer as you lower it. The only problem with placing your thumb in front of the hammer is that if the hammer slips it will pinch the thumb. Uncocking a revolver takes practice, so as you familiarize yourself with your revolver it is important to practice cocking and uncocking your revolver when you are sure that you have an empty cylinder and that the gun is unloaded.

As with any gun, use only appropriate ammunition for that gun. I recommend that all new shooters purchase factory ammo and not shoot reloaded ammunition, even if they know the person who reloaded it.

Yes, there are very good handloaders that produce excellent ammo, but there are also plenty of reloaders who do a poor job, and you don't want to be shooting improperly loaded ammo in your gun! In the beginning, the best option for novice shooters is to purchase manufactured ammunition that has been subjected to quality assurance tests in the factory.

### Misfires

If your revolver fails to fire when you pull the trigger, *do not* lower the firearm or immediately begin to examine it. Misfires (when the gun fails to fire) do occur, but hangfires (when the gun fires after an appreciable delay) can be dangerous. When a hangfire occurs the hammer may fall, the gun may click, and after a period of time the gun may go off. For this reason, if you fire on a loaded cylinder and the gun does not go off, keep the revolver pointed in the direction of the target for at least thirty seconds. Hangfires are extremely rare, but they can be very dangerous. For more information on hangfires, see Chapter VII on "Firearm Safety."

## Revolver Advantages

We've briefly discussed some of the advantages of shooting revolvers, but here's a brief recap. First, revolvers are simple to operate. You simply swing the cylinder out of the frame, load rounds into the chambers, close the cylinder, and fire. And while revolvers don't hold as many rounds as semiautos, they are quite reliable and malfunction is very, very rare. Revolvers are easy to clean, maintain, and shoot, and that's why many new gun owners opt to carry a revolver.

## Common Cartridge Choices for the Revolver

**Note:** Most revolvers will have a stamp on the left side of the barrel that indicates which cartridge they are chambered for. Check to be sure that the ammunition you are using matches the information on the barrel. If you have any questions, consult a firearms professional.

### .22s

There are two main cartridges referred to as ".22s" when speaking about revolvers. The first and most common is the .22 Long Rifle (never mind the moniker, it fires just fine in revolvers). The .22 LR is cheap to shoot, producing virtually no recoil, or "kick." As you'll read later in the chapter of this book that examines practice methods, I believe that shooting a .22 is some of the best practice available, and for those of us who grew up shooting .22 pistols and revolvers, learning to handle larger calibers was not difficult because we had practiced on the smaller, lighter, cheaper, quieter .22 LR.

There are other .22 rimfire variants, too (see Chapter III, "Basic Firearms Terminology," to learn the difference between rimfire and centerfire cartridges). There are cartridges labeled ".22 Short" and ".22 Long." These other variations are rarer than the ubiquitous .22 LR. Some revolvers will fire .22 Short, .22 Long, and .22 Long Rifle cartridges, but many will not. Very few semiautomatic pistols will fire all three.

The .22 LR is far and away the most common of the .22 rimfires, and when instructors or gun enthusiasts refer to a ".22" they are, in all likelihood, referring to the .22 LR. Generally not regarded as a self-defense gun, the .22 LR produces roughly 100 ft-lbs of energy. The more common .38 Special revolver produces about twice that much, and the .40 S&W semiautomatic produces almost *five* times that much energy! There are, however, plenty of people who carry .22 LRs for self-defense, and it is certainly better to carry a .22 LR revolver than nothing, as many instructors will tell you. There are now .22 LR revolvers designed for carry, such as Ruger's DAO .22 LCR, and there are rumors that ammunition companies may begin developing .22 ammo for self-defense. The .22 is certainly fun and easy to shoot, and it lends itself well to lots of practice, which is paramount to surviving a dangerous shootout. Ultimately, the .22 LR is at the extreme low end of the power spectrum for concealed carry, but it will certainly provide a level of protection against an attacker. In the end, the choice belongs to the individual shooter. If you hate shooting anything larger and feel

▼ Revolvers like the Ruger SP101 .22 shown here are simple and reliable. With the cylinder swung out of the frame like it is here, the gun is ready to load. The SP101 .22 is a double action revolver. Photo courtesy of Gettinger Photography.

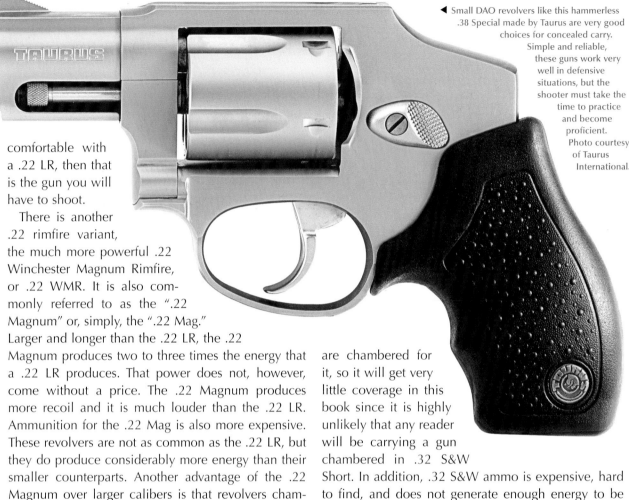

◀ Small DAO revolvers like this hammerless .38 Special made by Taurus are very good choices for concealed carry. Simple and reliable, these guns work very well in defensive situations, but the shooter must take the time to practice and become proficient. Photo courtesy of Taurus International.

comfortable with a .22 LR, then that is the gun you will have to shoot.

There is another .22 rimfire variant, the much more powerful .22 Winchester Magnum Rimfire, or .22 WMR. It is also commonly referred to as the ".22 Magnum" or, simply, the ".22 Mag." Larger and longer than the .22 LR, the .22 Magnum produces two to three times the energy that a .22 LR produces. That power does not, however, come without a price. The .22 Magnum produces more recoil and it is much louder than the .22 LR. Ammunition for the .22 Mag is also more expensive. These revolvers are not as common as the .22 LR, but they do produce considerably more energy than their smaller counterparts. Another advantage of the .22 Magnum over larger calibers is that revolvers chambered for this round typically hold about ten rounds in the cylinder, which is four or five more rounds than the standard .38 carry revolver. Though not nearly as common as .38 revolvers for defense, there is a loyal group of .22 Mag shooters who believe it to be the best carry revolver cartridge on the market.

### .32s

.32-caliber revolvers come in a wide and oftentimes confusing variety. Currently there are no fewer than seven varieties of .32-caliber handgun ammunition produced commercially, of which four are typically found in revolvers. The rarest, oldest, and least likely to be the cartridge your revolver is chambered for (unless it is a very old gun) is the **.32 Smith & Wesson Short**, a cartridge that was developed in 1878 and is fading into obscurity. No new commercial concealed carry guns are chambered for it, so it will get very little coverage in this book since it is highly unlikely that any reader will be carrying a gun chambered in .32 S&W Short. In addition, .32 S&W ammo is expensive, hard to find, and does not generate enough energy to be considered a top choice for self-defense.

The next step up in power and popularity for .32 revolvers is the **.32 Smith & Wesson Long**, a cartridge that is itself no youngster (it first appeared in 1896) and that produces only slightly more power than the .32 Smith & Wesson Short. Like the .32 S&W Short and all other .32 cartridges listed here, the .32 S&W Long actually fires a bullet that is .312 inches in diameter. Like the smaller .32 S&W Short, the .32 S&W Long is not a popular choice for concealed carry, and most of the ammunition designed for the .32 S&W Long is engineered for target shooting, not self-defense.

The next step up in power and cartridge length is the **.32 Harrington & Richardson Magnum**, which came on the scene in 1984. Commonly called the .32 H&R, this revolver packs considerably more punch than the other two .32s listed previously, and there are still revolvers for sale that are currently chambered for the .32 H&R with bullets that are designed specifically for self-defense. The .32 H&R produces manageable recoil and enough energy to be relied upon to effectively stop an intruder. I think that revolvers chambered in .32 H&R should be on your short list of the best concealed carry revolvers.

Lastly, we have the latest addition to the .32 family, the **.327 Federal Magnum**, which was introduced to the shooting public in 2008 as an "improved" version of the .32 H&R. Here, finally, was a .32 revolver that provided substantial punch and plenty of power to work as a self-defense .32 revolver, and the .327 Federal Magnum is growing in popularity. As a concealed carry gun it makes sense for a variety of reasons. First, the .327 Federal Magnum produces more energy than standard .38 Special loads, and because the .327 is smaller in diameter than the .38 Special, most concealed carry revolvers hold six .327 rounds as opposed to five for most .38 revolvers. Several major handgun makers are currently building revolvers in .327 Federal Magnum, and ammo companies have engineered .327 Federal Magnum ammunition designed specifically for self-defense. If you are considering a revolver for concealed carry you should consider a revolver chambered in .327 Federal Magnum.

Two important things to note about the various .32s: First, all of the .32 revolver cartridges listed here actually fire bullets that are .312 inches in diameter. The name given to a cartridge does not always designate the true diameter of the bullet it fires. Even the mighty .44 Magnum actually fires a bullet that is .429 inches in diameter, though the ".429 Magnum" perhaps doesn't sound as magnificent! For this reason, all of the "longer" versions of the .32 revolvers will fire cartridges from shorter rounds. For example, guns that are chambered for the .327 Federal Magnum will fire .32 H&R ammo, but not vice versa. A .32 H&R will fire .32 S&W Long ammo, but a gun chambered in .32 S&W Long will *not* fire .32 H&R ammo. If you have any questions, consult a gun shop professional.

### .38s

The **.38 Special** cartridge has been around for over a hundred years, and it is one of the successful revolver cartridges ever designed. Originally introduced in 1898, the .38 Special has been used by military and police as well as civilians, and today it is the most popular cartridge for self-defense revolvers. Revolvers chambered for .38 Special are available from a variety of companies in DA and DAO variants that are designed specifically for concealed carry. In addition, .38 Special ammunition is readily available. And although I wouldn't say that any loaded ammunition is currently "cheap," .38 Special ammo can be bought in bulk for a relatively reasonable price for use in practice, and premium self-defense ammo for carrying in your revolver is available as well. The .38 Special provides enough power for self-defense and moderate recoil that even the newest shooter can, over time, learn to master it. For these reasons it has become the most popular self-defense revolver cartridge.

The .38 is not perfect, though. The larger cartridge diameter means that most compact .38 revolvers only hold five rounds in the cylinder. In addition, though the .38 produces ample energy to be considered a legitimate concealed carry cartridge, it does not generate near the power of cartridges like the .40 Smith & Wesson. However, the .38 Special is a good choice for someone considering a revolver for concealed carry. Even a lightweight, compact revolver chambered for the .38 Special cartridge does not generate extreme recoil.

In the 1970s, ammunition companies began loading .38 Special ammunition for higher pressure levels. This increase in energy meant more power, and the ammunition became known as **.38 Special+P** or simply, ".38+P." This ammo *cannot* be fired in standard .38 Special revolvers. However, if you purchase a revolver that is stamped with .38+P on the barrel, then it is capable of firing .38+P loads. When you purchase ammo, be sure to check the box to be sure whether you are purchasing .38 Special or .38 Special+P ammunition. Such .38+P revolvers like Ruger's LCR and Smith & Wesson's 38 Bodyguard are .38 +P rated but will still shoot standard .38 Special ammo, which is cheaper and produces less muzzle blast and recoil. For this reason many shooters who own a .38+P revolver purchase .38 Special ammunition to practice with at the range but load more powerful .38+P ammunition in their revolvers when they are carrying concealed.

You cannot fire .38+P ammo in a standard .38 Special handgun, though, because pressures are too high. If you have questions, consult your owner's manual.

Very rarely you can find ammunition that is rated +P+, which is an even higher pressure .38 load originally developed for law enforcement. This ammunition is infrequent today, and guns chambered **.38+P+** are a rarity. The odds of even finding +P+ ammo are low, but it *cannot* be fired in .38+P revolvers since the pressure levels are too high.

The most powerful of the .38 revolvers commonly carried for self-defense is the **.357 Smith & Wesson Magnum**, more commonly called the .357 Magnum.

Despite the name, the .357 Magnum, .38 Special, and .38 Special+P all fire the same bullets, which are .357 inches in diameter. The .357 Magnum has a longer case than the .38 Special or .38+P, and it generates considerably more power. The .357 Magnum also generates more recoil and muzzle blast than either of the .38s, and for most novice shooters, the .357 Magnum represents the upper power limit for concealed carry. The long cartridges require long chambers, so the cylinder of .357 Magnum revolvers is typically larger, resulting in a heavier gun. One advantage of revolvers chambered for the .357 Magnum is that you can also fire .38 Special and .38+P ammo in them. You cannot,

▼ The two revolvers are both chambered for the powerful .357 Magnum cartridge. The smaller gun is a Taurus Model 605 designed for concealed carry. The larger gun is a Ruger GP-100 designed for target shooting and hunting. Today there are a wide variety of revolvers in different calibers and finishes.

▲ A .357 Magnum revolver can fire all three of these cartridges (from left): .38 Special, .38 special +P, and the .357 Magnum. Despite the numeric differences, all of these cartridges fire .357-inch bullets.

however, safely fire .357 Magnum ammo in either a .38 Special or .38+P revolver. The .357 Magnum will certainly work very well for concealed carry, and it generates plenty of stopping power. Ammo is readily available, and there are a number of good .357 Magnum defense loads.

### Larger Revolvers

There are larger revolvers that generate more power, more recoil, and more muzzle blast. For the most part, these larger revolvers are designed for hunting and protection from large bears. Will they work for self-defense? Absolutely. But for most beginners these guns represent a level of power and energy that can be overwhelming. In addition, most of the guns chambered for these rounds are typically much heavier than revolvers chambered for smaller cartridges like the .38 Special and .327 Federal Magnum. Large revolvers are typically anything above .40 inches and include the **.41 Remington Magnum**, **.44 Special**, **.44 Remington Magnum**, **.45 Colt**, and the real brutes like

the **.480 Ruger**, **.454 Casull**, **.460 Smith & Wesson Magnum**, and the **.500 Smith & Wesson Magnum**. All of these revolvers have their place and purpose, and some, especially the .44 Special and .45 Colt, are sometimes carried for self-defense. For the beginning shooter, however, these revolvers represent energy levels beyond what is required for most concealed carry.

### .410 Revolvers

One of the latest trends in defensive handguns is revolvers chambered to fire **.410 shotshells**. The introduction of the Taurus Judge revolver, which is capable of firing both .410 shotgun shells and .45 Colt ammunition, represented a new subclass of self-defense revolvers. Shotguns typically fire a swarm of pellets rather than a single projectile like most handguns. This cluster of pellets, or shot, carries a great deal of energy at close range and strikes a much larger area than a single bullet. Shotguns have long been used for home defense, and tactical home defense shotguns are popu-

▲ Taurus's Judge revolver fires both .45 Colt cartridges and .410 shotshells. Though the Judge is at the upper size limit for a carry revolver, it is a very effective and popular defensive handgun. Photo courtesy of Taurus International.

◄ The anatomy of a defensive .410 shotshell. Winchester's PDX-1 Defensive line of .410 ammo fires twelve pellets and three "Defensive Discs" instead of a bullet. At close range, this is a deadly combination in .410 revolvers. Photo courtesy of Winchester Ammunition.

lar today. However, the Judge (and other .410 shotshell revolvers like Smith & Wesson's Governor) made shotgun power more portable and more compact. Since the .410 shotgun was traditionally used for hunting small game like rabbits and quail, most shotshell loads were designed for that purpose. Ammunition companies like Winchester have now designed .410 shells specifically for defense. Rather than firing a swarm of pellets, each 2 ½-inch Winchester PDX-1 .410 shell fires three "Defense Discs" and twelve plated BBs with each shot. The result is an effective short-range weapon with the power and penetration to stop intruders cold.

All of the various .410 revolvers are large and heavy for concealed carry, though there are some who choose to carry these large revolvers, and companies are currently making carry holsters specifically for these large-frame revolvers. These .410 revolvers are more typically used for home defense. If you purchase one of the .410 revolvers, it is important to note the chamber length. All .410 shotshells are available in both 2 ½-inch and 3-inch lengths, and every .410 revolver should be stamped with the chamber length. Use the correct length shells for the revolver that you have.

# VI. The Semiautomatic Handgun

Semiautomatic handguns are the most popular sidearm for military and police around the world, and semiautomatics are also the most popular choice in handguns for concealed carry. Rather than a revolver, which has multiple chambers that rotate inside of a cylinder, a semiautomatic handgun has a single chamber that remains aligned with the barrel of the gun. This is why loading a cartridge from the magazine (often, but incorrectly, referred to as a "clip") is referred to as "chambering" a round. Semiautomatic handguns differ from fully automatic handguns in that semiautomatics feed a new cartridge into the chamber after each successive shot but require the release and pull of the trigger to fire again.

The immediate and obvious advantage of the semiautomatic handgun is that you can fire more shots (typically seven to seventeen) in rapid succession without reloading. Understand that there is quite a difference between firing ten shots and firing ten *aimed* shots, and increasing the number of shots that can be fired without reloading does nothing to increase the number of effective shots. Learning to shoot a semiautomatic handgun correctly involves learning to fire, aim, fire, aim, and so forth.

Semiautomatics make excellent concealed carry guns, and there are many good semiautomatic carry guns available today. Semiautos are, however, more complex than revolvers, and they do contain more moving parts. Routine cleaning and maintenance of semiautos requires some level of disassembly, which can, depending upon the model, range from a simple task to a frustrating ordeal that takes quite a bit of time. The slightly more complex nature of semiautos means that they require more time to learn to shoot and maintain than the average revolver. Semiautos are, however, an excellent choice for concealed carry if you spend time familiarizing yourself with the gun.

Today's crop of concealed carry semiautos is expansive, and there are many excellent choices for the beginning shooter. They are available with frames of varying sizes, and many modern metallurgy techniques have made it possible to build guns that are

▼ There are a variety of choices in semiautos with regard to frame size, action type, caliber, and finish. These three Kimber semiautos may look different, but in the hands of a practiced shooter all three would make excellent concealed carry guns. Photo courtesy of Kimber America.

▲ These guns represent all three action types for semiautos (from left): a single action .45 Auto, a double action .45 Auto, and a double action–only 9mm Luger.

light enough to carry all day without discomfort. Many modern .45 ACP semiautos are smaller, lighter, and easier to carry than .38 revolvers! Today's semiautos are available in a wide variety of chamberings, from .22 LR up to the powerful .45 ACP and even larger. Several ammo manufacturers have specifically engineered bullets for defense, and there are multiple options for carrying a concealed semiauto. In addition, there are a host of aftermarket options like grips, sights, and magazines that allow you to customize your semiauto to fit your needs.

## Semiauto Basics

Like revolvers, semiautomatic handguns come in three main operating types; single action, double action, and double action–only. And, like revolvers, these names give an indication of what function the trigger performs. However, there are a few ways in which the actions of semiautos and revolvers vary. The most obvious and significant difference is that a revolver holds ammunition in a round cylinder that turns as the gun is cocked and fired. Semiautos house their extra ammunition in a magazine that is almost always housed in the handle (grip) of the gun. As the semiauto pistol fires, the slide (moving part) of the action moves backward, picks up another round from the magazine, and slides forward, chambering the round. This action is repeated over and over as the gun is fired. If there are no jams in the process, the action continues to

slide backward, picks up another round, and slide it forward to the chamber with each trigger pull until the magazine is empty. Usually, but not always, the action remains open and the slide remains locked rearward after the last round is fired. The energy required to push the slide back after each shot is generated by the energy of the previous shot being fired. Some guns use the force of the recoil to push the slide back (these are called recoil-operated semiautos) and others use the pressure from escaping gases created by the shot to generate the movement of the slide (referred to as "gas-operated semiautos"). It's not vital as a beginner to know which type of operation your gun uses for regular firing, and many experienced shooters can't tell you whether the gun is gas or recoil operated. Guns of both types shoot in much the same way.

It is, however, important to understand if your gun is a single, double, or double action–only. Knowing the differences between these different types of semiautos will help you better understand how your semiauto works and will help keep you safe.

With all semiauto handguns a round must be *chambered* to fire, which is important to understand as we begin examining the basic operation of the semiauto. To chamber a round from the magazine on most semiautos, the slide *must* be moved to a rearward position, so placing a loaded magazine into a semiauto with an empty chamber generally means that you will have to pull the slide rearward to chamber a round and prepare to fire. I say generally because there a few exceptions to this rule, most notably the Beretta semiauto carry guns that offer tip-up barrels; in that gun, the first round can be chambered by popping the barrel up, which is done by pressing a button, allowing the shooter to load the chamber without pulling the slide back. By and large, most semiautos require pulling the slide back and releasing it to load the first cartridge into the chamber.

It is important to note that if the slide is already locked in the back position and a loaded magazine is inserted into the gun, a cartridge will be chambered when the slide is released and moves forward. For safety reasons, it is important to know when a cartridge is in the chamber, and some guns have an accessory known as a *loaded cartridge indicator* that gives a visual signal to the shooter anytime a cartridge is in the chamber. Once a cartridge is loaded into the chamber, firing the gun will automatically load another cartridge from the magazine into the chamber. With each shot that is fired, the slide will move backward, pick up another cartridge, and load it into the chamber until the magazine is empty.

### Single Action Semiautos

Single action semiautos have exposed hammers. One of the most popular handgun designs of all time is John Browning's Colt 1911 semiauto, the .45 semiauto that served as the US military sidearm for more than seventy years after it was introduced. The "1911," as the gun is often called now, has served as a popular platform, and many single action semiautos today are clones of the original Browning concept, including a crop of smaller single actions that are designed for concealed carry.

The single action semiauto functions differently than the single action revolver. With a single action revolver, the

shooter cocks the hammer, fires, and cocks the hammer again to fire each successive shot. When shooting a single action semiauto, the shooter can manually cock the hammer or pull the slide back to cock the hammer. The most common method of loading an SA semiauto is to place a loaded magazine into the gun and pull back the slide. By pulling the slide rearward, you are chambering a round *and* cocking the hammer, so the gun is ready to fire. When a shot is fired, the movement of the slide chambers another round from the magazine and automatically cocks the hammer, meaning the trigger can be pulled again and again without recocking. If the hammer is cocked and the chamber is loaded, the hammer can be released by pulling the hammer back, pulling the trigger, and slowly lowering the hammer. For more detail about safely lowering the hammer on a loaded chamber on a single action semiauto see Chapter VII, "Firearm Safety." Once the hammer is lowered on a single action semiauto, you must manually recock the hammer using your thumb before the gun will fire.

▲ The Taurus PT 730 is slim, compact, and simple to operate. In addition, the stainless slide is resistant to wear and corrosion. Small semiautos are easy to conceal and provide the firepower needed to protect you in dangerous situations. Photo courtesy of Taurus Manufacturing.

▲ Colt's compact Mustang is one of the most popular carry guns from the past, and the gun was recently reintroduced by Colt. It is a single action semiauto that is easy to conceal. Photo courtesy of Colt Manufacturing.

Most decockers are built into the safety. Guns with safety decockers generally have three positions. There is a SAFE position where the gun cannot be fired, and moving the safety lever one direction from SAFE mode will put the gun in the FIRE position, while moving the safety in the opposite direction will activate the decocker and safely lower the hammer. Such is the case on the Beretta M9, the FNH line of double actions. In the case of both the Beretta and the FNH pistols, the safety lever is located just ahead of the hammer. In the SAFE position the lever lies roughly parallel to the barrel. By pressing the safety lever upward it goes into the FIRE position, while pushing it down from safe activates the decocker and safely lowers the hammer. While you activate the decocker be sure that the firearm is pointed in a safe direction and that you have a firm grip on the gun. The hammer will drop, which can be alarming to the novice shooter, but guns with decockers are designed to safely drop the hammer. It is important to familiarize yourself with all of the mechanical functions on your firearm, including the decocker.

## Double Action Semiautos

Like double action revolvers, double action semiautos have a trigger that serves two purposes: Pulling the trigger will both cock the hammer and fire the gun. Double action semiautos can be fired in single action mode by cocking the hammer manually and then firing the gun, but unlike single action semiautos you can pull the trigger when the hammer is lowered and fire without manually cocking the hammer. In many regards the double action and single action semiauto work in much the same way. The standard shooting protocol requires you to place a loaded magazine into the gun and pull back the slide to chamber a round from the magazine. At that point you can fire the gun with each successive pull of the trigger.

Many double action semiautos have a decocker, which will automatically lower the hammer for you so that you do not have to do so manually. If, for instance, you load a magazine and pull back the slide, you will have a gun with a loaded chamber and a cocked hammer. By pressing the decocker button you can automatically lower the hammer. The gun can still be fired without cocking the hammer by pulling the trigger, but the trigger pull will be heavier and the trigger will have to travel farther as you pull it because you are performing both the cocking procedure and the firing procedure.

## Double Action–Only Semiautos

Double action–only semiautos are the simplest type of semiautos for most beginning shooters. There is no exposed hammer, so you don't have to worry about manually cocking and decocking the gun with the hammer. The trigger always serves two purposes. When a cartridge is in the chamber pulling the trigger serves two functions: cocking and firing. The lack of an exposed hammer and the simplicity of DAO guns make them very popular for concealed carry, and shooters who are considering purchasing their first gun should consider purchasing a DAO gun. Many compact and ultracompact carry handguns are DAO. The operation of DAO guns is similar to the operation of other semiautos. The magazine is placed in the grip of the gun, and pulling the slide back and releasing it chambers a cartridge. Some DAO guns have manual safeties while others do not.

There is a subgroup of semiauto pistols known as "striker fire" guns. Striker fires guns lack a hammer (both internally and externally). Instead, the firing sequence begins when a "striker" (a piece of metal or plastic that is cocked with a spring) is released by pulling the trigger. Backward movement of the slide recocks the gun, so if you dryfire a striker fire gun like the Ruger SR9 or a Glock the trigger will be "dead," and you must pull the slide back slightly to recock the gun. While shooting the gun, the rearward movement of the slide automatically sets the striker for the next shot, so it is only necessary to pull the slide back slightly to recock the gun when you are doing nonfiring drills.

▶ The CZ 75 compact 9mm is a double action semiauto with fixed sights and a blued finish. This gun is an excellent choice for defensive carry because it is lightweight, compact, and reliable. Photo courtesy of CZ-USA.

Because striker fire guns operate in much the same way as DAO guns (no hammer), some shooters classify these guns as DAO guns. In reality, striker fire guns are not DAO. By definition the trigger on a DAO *always* serves two purposes: cocking the hammer and firing the gun. Striker fire guns like Glocks have a trigger that only fires the gun, thus the trigger only serves one purpose. Technically, striker fire guns would be classified as having single action triggers.

Compact DAO guns are available in several calibers, but the two most common chamberings for concealed carry are the .380 ACP (.380 Auto) and the 9mm Luger. Both of these cartridges are acceptable for concealed carry and today's crop of self-defense bullets make these two cartridges suitable for concealed carry. Compact DAO pistols are also chambered in .25 and .32 Autos, which are at the low end of the power spectrum for concealed carry, and there are some small DAO .40s and .45s as well, though these larger calibers can prove to be quite a handful when chambered in small, light handguns.

DAO guns are available with or without manual safeties. Safe gun handling techniques and a long, heavy trigger pull make it possible to carry loaded DAO guns that do not have a manual safety. However, many models do have an exposed safety, which provides some shooters with extra peace of mind. Understand that the lack of a manual safety doesn't make a gun unsafe (nor does a gun with a manual safety mean that the gun is safe in the hands of an inexperienced or irresponsible shooter), and guns without manual safeties work just fine for concealed carry. In addition, the lack of a safety means that the gun can be pulled from the holster and fired immediately. If having a manual safety on your gun makes you feel more secure, then you should select a model with an exposed safety, but it is also important to practice taking the safety off every time you fire so that you develop muscle memory and so that moving the safety into the OFF position becomes a natural step in the firing process.

## The Semiauto as a Self-Defense Firearm

Semiautos are extremely popular for police and military use as well as self-defense. There are hundreds of compact and subcompact semiautos available from a variety of different firearms companies, and the choices can be overwhelming. Should you purchase a single action, a double action, a double action–only, or a striker fire gun? How large is too large to carry? Which caliber?

The rise in concealed carry permits across the United States has resulted in a new wave of guns that are lighter, smaller, and easier to carry. There are several guns currently on the market that work well for concealed carry, and ammunition companies have developed loads that are specifically engineered for defensive shooting. There are a few guns that are bad choices for the new shooter, but there are also plenty of options that will fit your needs and your budget.

Semiautos range in price from about a $300 to several thousand dollars for a new gun, and used guns can be purchased for less than that. When purchasing a used gun, however, it is important to have someone who is familiar with semiautos (preferably with that particular model) examine the gun. If possible, take the gun apart and see how well it has been maintained; guns that haven't received proper cleaning will bear the signs on their internal working parts, namely dark fouling that accumulates from shooting the gun. Also look for obvious signs of wear like thinning finish, which will expose the metal underneath, corrosion, and other signs of heavy or hard use.

▶ This is Springfield Armory's XDM .40 S&W with a 5 ¼ inch barrel. The XD line is popular for concealed carry. The large cutout in the slide reduces the weight of the gun. Photo courtesy of Springfield Armory.

Semiautos make excellent carry guns since they are compact, easy to carry, and hold several rounds of ammunition. However, semiautos are not without their faults. First, semiautos require more time for maintenance than revolvers. A simple wipe down of the metal parts and cleaning the bore is sufficient to maintain most revolvers. With a semiautomatic handgun, you need to be able to disassemble the gun, which can be a chore in itself. Some guns, like the Beretta M9, Glocks, the various SIG models, and others like them, are easy to disassemble and reassemble. In a few moments you can have the gun apart and back together, so cleaning is a relatively simple task. Other guns require more time and are more difficult to disassemble. If possible have someone knowledgeable show you the process for disassembly and reassembly. Some guns require special tools to disassemble, and

those are usually included with the firearm. Since disassembly procedures vary from one brand of semiauto to the next, it doesn't make sense to cover each individual model here.

However, the takedown process for most any semiauto requires the disassembly of four main parts. When the gun is broken down, these four distinct parts include the slide, barrel, spring, and frame. Typically the slide must be removed first, and it will contain the barrel and the spring. The barrel and spring can then be removed from the slide and each part can be cleaned and inspected to be sure that there are no mechanical problems. If your semiauto is easy to take apart, the cleaning process is relatively simple and takes only a bit more time than cleaning the revolver.

▼ The author shooting Ruger's new 1911-style .45 Auto. The Colt 1911 and similar models like this Ruger are single action semiautos, which means that the hammer must be cocked before the gun can be fired.

▲ This shows a Kimber Solo with the chamber open to reveal the cartridges in the magazine. Releasing the slide will push one of the cartridges from the magazine into the chamber and the Solo will be ready to fire. Photo courtesy of Kimber America.

## Clearing Jams

One of the disadvantages to carrying a semiauto as a concealed carry gun is that the number of operations performed with each shot—extraction, ejection, chambering, locking—means that semiautos will, on occasion, jam. Oftentimes this is not the fault of the gun directly. The reason that the gun is not functioning properly may have to do with choice of ammo, and low pressure cartridges can sometimes cause a jam. In addition, defective magazines, dirty or improperly cleaned guns, and even poor shooter form can cause jams. Some guns rarely jam, and I've had a few over the years that *never* jammed.

Magazines, gun cleaning, and shooting form will all be covered elsewhere in this book. It is very important, however, that when a jam occurs you know how to clear it and keep firing. With properly broken-in guns (it takes several hundred rounds sometimes before a semiautomatic is properly broken in and ready to be carried) that are well maintained and when firing quality ammo, jams are, thankfully, rare. Understanding how to clear a jam is one of the most important components of learning to shoot a semiauto properly. First, a shooter must examine the different types of jams that can occur in a semiauto handgun so that we can understand how to clear each one.

### The "Tap and Rack" Method

Sometimes jammed semiautos can be fixed by a simple "tap and rack." Tapping on the bottom of the magazine to be sure that it is in place and pulling back the slide (aka "racking" the gun, hence the name) will oftentimes clear the jam. For most new shooters, this is the simplest method to clear a jam and it will oftentimes be all that is required to bring the gun back into battery and be ready for the next shot. Many instructors advise students to twist the pistol 90 degrees as they rack the

◄ It is important to familiarize yourself with the mechanical function of your firearm. On the side of this Kimber Solo we see the magazine release button located just behind the trigger. The safety is located just under the rear of the slide, and directly in front of the safety is the slide lock, which holds the slide on for cleaning, loading, and safety. The Solo is a compact 9mm designed especially for concealed carry. Photo courtesy of Kimber America.

slide. This is so the empty cartridge case that failed to eject will fall free from the chamber due to gravity and won't remain in the firearm and cause another jam.

### Double Feed Jam

The "double feed" occurs when a loaded cartridge is pushed into the chamber by the slide and then a second cartridge from the magazine feeds in behind the first, creating a condition that prevents either cartridge from firing. Double feeds can occur for a variety of reasons, but one of the most common is that new shooters often pull the slide back and ease it forward rather than pulling it back completely and releasing it as intended. Sometimes "overhandling" the slide by controlling how fast it goes back into the forward position and then pulling the slide back again before it slides completely forward can cause a double feed to occur. Learn to pull the slide back fully and release it.

When a double feed occurs, it is usually recognizable because the action will remain open and a cartridge will be partially fed from the magazine into the chamber. Sometimes the first cartridge that was fed into the chamber will be immediately visible, and sometimes it will not be. When you suspect a double feed has caused the problem, you can rotate the gun on the axis of the barrel so that the gun is parallel to the ground and pull the slide back fully. Sometimes this will clear the double-feed jam. Other times it is necessary to press the magazine release button (located behind the trigger) and drop the magazine out of the firearm. Afterwards, racking the gun should extract any chambered cartridges.

Double feeds are usually a result of shooter error, and one of the best ways to prevent double feeds is to avoid softly pressing the magazine into place or closing the action slowly. Semiautos are designed to function correctly when the magazine is pushed firmly into place and the slide is drawn back and released without pause. "Babying" the gun can actually cause jams. Rack the slide with authority, and if the slide is locked backward when you loaded the magazine, press the slide release button and let the action close on its own (keeping your hands clear of the sliding action). Many new shooters are intimidated by the loud metallic clap of the action closing, but that is how the gun was designed to function.

### Stovepipe Jam

So called "stovepipe jams" occur when a spent cartridge case fails to fully eject from the gun before the slide moves forward. In this case the action closes on the empty cartridge, holding it in place. Oftentimes the jammed cartridge case sticks straight up from the partially closed action, which holds the cartridge case in place (hence the name "stovepipe"). Stovepipe jams often occur for a variety of reasons. Weak loads, dirt, poor shooter grip and stance, and mechanical or design problems with the gun can all be responsible for stovepipe jams.

When a stovepipe jam occurs, the cartridge case is typically not being held by the extractor on the gun, which means that the cartridge case is loose in the action and simply pulling back the slide will not eject the cartridge. Turn the gun so that it is parallel to the ground and then pull back on the slide, allowing the empty case to fall out with the force of gravity. Sometimes pulling the slide back, allowing the empty to fall out onto the ground, and releasing the slide will solve the problem. Other times a stovepipe jam can be more difficult to clear and may affect the feeding of subsequent cartridges. In that case you'll have to drop the magazine, rack the slide a few times, and hope that solves the problem. Remember to keep the gun pointed in a safe direction at all times while clearing your jam, since frustration can lead to ignoring basic safety rules and causing a dangerous situation.

◀ Ruger's LCP (Lightweight Compact Pistol) is chambered in .380 Auto and is one of the most popular carry guns on the market because it is light, easy to conceal, and chambered in a popular defensive cartridge. This particular LCP is equipped with a laser sight under the barrel that projects a beam onto the target. Photo courtesy of Sturm, Ruger & Co.

As previously stated, there are a number of things that can cause a stovepipe jam, and the cause of the jam is not always immediately apparent. Semiautos require the shooter to provide a platform against which the gun can "push" to allow the action to work correctly. Holding the gun limply or loosely can cause the action not to cycle correctly, because the shooter is not keeping the arms locked, a mistake that is often referred to as "limp wristing" by shooters. Dirty and weak ammo can also cause this problem, as many actions do not cycle correctly with ammunition that is underpowered or causes residue buildup.

### Failure of the Slide to Close

For a semiautomatic gun to fire, the action must be closed. On some occasions the action will not return to battery and will not allow the gun to be fired. There are a variety of reasons for this, ranging from an ill-fitting magazine to excessive fouling in the chamber to foreign objects inside the gun and manufacturing problems with the firearm itself. Thankfully, these jams are rare. A thorough cleaning of the firearms will sometimes eliminate this problem, as dirty chambers, feed ramps, and slides will sometimes cause this malfunction. Sometimes the ammunition doesn't fit, either because of an error that occurred when the ammo was loaded or possibly because you are using the wrong caliber ammunition.

The first step in clearing this type of jam is ensuring that the magazine is all the way into position inside the grip by giving it a firm tap on the bottom of the magazine. If that fails, drop the magazine and pull the slide back, ensuring that the action is empty. Begin by looking at the action and the cartridge. Are there excessive scuff marks on the cartridge case? Does it appear that the cartridge case was jammed into the action, that the cartridge was too big for the chamber? Sometimes changing ammunition helps alleviate the problem. If that doesn't work, try running your finger over the feed ramp that leads the cartridge from the magazine up into the chamber. In most disassembled semiautos the feed ramp is attached to the barrel and is a short, usually slightly concave metal piece that guides the cartridge into the chamber. Feel the feed ramp with your finger and pay special attention to the lip where the cartridge from the magazine first contacts

the ramp. Is it dirty or rough? If so, a good cleaning may be in order, or perhaps a gunsmith could smooth the ramp with a fine file.

Also be sure to check the magazine to be sure that cartridges load easily and feed correctly. Magazines sometimes become worn or dented, making it more difficult for cartridges to feed and occasionally causing jams. Sometimes simply purchasing a new magazine will solve the feeding problem. Before purchasing a new magazine, look for obvious signs of damage to the existing magazine.

If the ammunition, magazine, and a dirty gun aren't to blame, it may be that a mistake was made during manufacturing and you have a firearm that simply doesn't work as it should. In that case it is best to contact the company or a qualified gunsmith to determine what is causing the feeding problems.

## Loading the Magazine

Loading the gun may sound relatively simple, but magazine loading is one of the most difficult steps in the firing process for many new shooters. First, let's examine the component parts of the magazine, the device that stores ammunition that will be fed into the action and fired. Often mistakenly referred to as a "clip," magazines for semiautomatic handguns are comprised of a plastic or metal container that is formed to match the inside of the grip and lock in place during shooting. Inside the container is a spring that pushes the cartridges up toward the top of the magazine. Unless the spring is old and extremely worn, it places constant upward pressure on the cartridges above it, which are prevented from falling out of the top of the magazine by a lip. As the slide moves back and forth during firing, it catches the back of the top cartridge in the magazine with its return (forward) stroke and pushes the cartridges out of the magazine and into the chamber.

Between the top of the spring and the cartridges is a piece of metal or plastic referred to as a "magazine follower." This is what the bottom cartridge in the magazine rests upon, with all the cartridges above resting atop one another in a stack. Some magazines are referred to as "single stack" magazines, where each cartridge sits directly above the cartridge below it. The other common type of magazine, known as a "double stack" magazine, is designed so that cartridges rest above and to the side of each other inside the magazine, creating a zigzag appearance of the stacked cartridges. Double stack magazines have a higher capacity (which means they hold more cartridges) than single stack magazines; however, double stack magazines are wider and usually require a fatter grip to accommodate them.

The first step toward loading the magazine is determining which direction the cartridges should be loaded. This is covered in the owner's manual. Since the magazine should only fit into the grip of the gun in one direction, the cartridges should be positioned so that the bullet is pointed toward the front of the magazine. This way when the magazine is inserted into the grip of the pistol, the forward action of the slide will push the cartridge into the chamber.

Begin practicing magazine loading by examining an empty magazine. Many magazines have numbered ports that allow you to see inside the magazine and determine how many cartridges you have loaded into the magazine. Holding the magazine firmly in your weak hand, put pressure on the follower (top of the portion where cartridges will be loaded) with your index finger on your strong hand. When you place pressure on the follower at the top of the magazine you should feel pressure as the spring inside the

▼ This is a conversion kit for a Kimber semiautomatic handgun that allows the gun to be converted from a .45 Auto to a .22 LR. This allows the shooter to practice with the .22, firing cheap, low-recoiling ammunition, then switch back to .45 for defensive carry. Photo courtesy Kimber America.

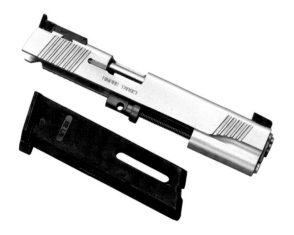

magazine begins to compress. Repeat this a couple of times, familiarizing yourself with the level of pressure required to compress the spring. Different magazines from different gun companies have different spring strength, and new magazine springs are usually pretty heavy to account for the spring weakening over time. As the spring weakens it will become easier to load the magazine.

Loading semiauto magazines can be difficult, and it takes some time to learn the proper technique. If you plan to shoot a lot, you will have to load several magazines, and the stress on the hands and fingers can be heavy for even experienced shooters. As you prepare to load the magazine, familiarize yourself with which direction the cartridges should be loaded. I like to press the spring down slightly a couple times before loading, placing my finger on the top of the magazine follower and pressing down to see how much force will be required to push the magazine far enough down so that the cartridges will slide into place under the lip.

There are several methods for loading, but the one that works best for me when loading magazines without the help of tools is to grip the magazine in my left (weak) hand, holding it so that the front of the magazine is in the center of my torso and pointed to the right. Taking one cartridge between the thumb and index finger of my right hand, I push the follower down into the magazine until I can slide the cartridge into place under the lip, ensuring that the cartridge is held firmly and properly in place. Continue this until the magazine is full, but remember that as more cartridges are loaded and more pressure is applied to the spring it will become harder and harder to compress the magazine spring enough to fully load the magazine. When you have a magazine fully loaded, gently tap the side of the magazine, which ensures that the spring is seated correctly and that the cartridges will feed properly.

Many shooters prefer to use magazine loaders, which are simple and inexpensive. Magazine holders are usually plastic and help hold the spring in the magazine compressed so that it is easier to load cartridges into the magazine. Such tools are available from a variety of companies like Uncle Mike's, and some gun companies provide magazine loading tools with the purchase of a

▲ Step 1 in the loading and firing process for a semiauto: Shove the magazine into the grip.

▼ Step 2: The magazine is inserted and is locked in place.

▲ Step 3: The slide is pulled back firmly.

▼ Step 4: Release the slide. When the slide moves forward it will pick up a cartridge from the magazine and push that cartridge into the chamber. The semiauto is now ready to fire.

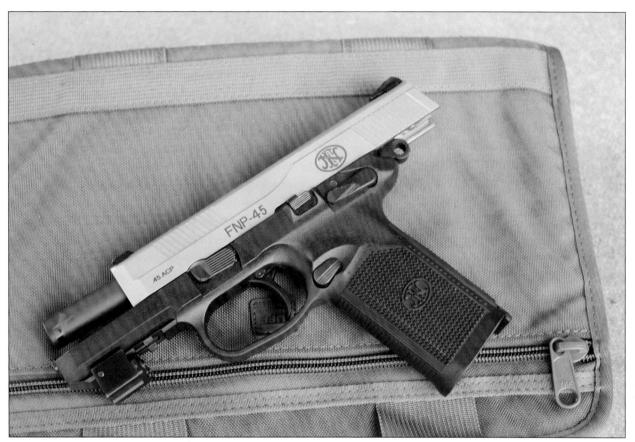

▲ This FNH .45 Auto has the slide locked back. When the slide is in this position on a semiauto, the gun cannot be fired, but you should always keep your finger away from the trigger and keep the muzzle pointed in a safe direction.

semiautomatic firearm. The majority of these tools slip over the top of the magazine, and pressing down on the top of the tool compresses the spring for easy loading. Loading tools are not essential to owning and loading semiautomatic handguns, but they certainly make the job of loading magazines much more pleasant.

Leaving magazines loaded when not shooting will soften the spring and make the magazines easier and faster to load. Provided you can safely store the magazines, this is an effective method of spring softening and it prevents having to load the magazines prior to your next round of practice at the range. In addition, having loaded magazines on hand means you won't have to load before the next time that you shoot, so you will be more inclined to head to the range and practice if you know that all you have to do is slide a magazine into place and pull the slide to be able to fire the gun. When I finish shooting my semiautos, I immediately load two additional magazines and place them in the gun safe with my pistols in anticipation of the next time I shoot. Most new semiautos come with two magazines when you purchase the gun, but I usually purchase additional magazines and prefer to have about five magazines per pistol.

## Maintaining a Semiautomatic Handgun

Semiautomatic handguns are more likely to jam than revolvers because of the complexity of their design. However, well-maintained semiautomatics firing quality ammunition should rarely have problems with feeding, extraction, and ejection. After all, this is a firearm that you are counting on to save your life, so you need it to perform!

I've been very fortunate and have had good luck with most of the semiautos that I have purchased. They haven't all been perfect, but if I maintained them properly and used good ammunition when practicing, all have been at least reasonably reliable. I wouldn't count on all of them to save my life, but I do have a couple semiautos that have never had a feeding problem even after thousands of rounds, which is the kind of reliability that I expect when carrying a gun to protect myself and my family.

There are a lot of reasons that semiautos consistently fail to fire. Some are mechanical, but some are a result of improper or irregular maintenance. If you plan to carry a semiauto, you should regularly inspect and maintain the firearm, the same way that you would with a revolver.

Understanding how to disassemble your semiauto is essential for proper cleaning. Though they are more complex than revolvers, most semiautos break down and reassemble with very little hassle, which makes it less of a chore to clean them. One of my favorite semiautos is my Glock 17, which has been totally reliable for me through thousands of shots. Glocks are well-made guns, but I also clean and lubricate that gun every time I'm at the range because it is so simple to take apart, clean, and put back together. In a matter of a few seconds I can have it apart without any special tools. It takes the same amount of time to reassemble.

It would be impossible to describe the process for disassembling every semiautomatic on the market. However, the basic breakdown procedure is similar in principle. To properly maintain most semiautos you need to be able to remove the slide, barrel, magazine, and spring from the frame. The good news, however, is that most firearms companies have made this process simple. They too understand that proper maintenance is important to reliability, so they have an impetus to make it as easy to clean their firearms as possible. We all have a task at home that is a nuisance, requiring a great deal of time and effort to accomplish. Oftentimes these are the tasks that we put off until they are absolutely necessary. The same is true of gun maintenance: If cleaning your gun is a nuisance and a chore, you are less likely to take the time to properly maintain the gun. If the gun comes apart and goes back together quickly and easily, then cleaning is not as time consuming as with guns that require more assembly/disassembly time.

▼ This Kimber has a skeletonized trigger, which helps reduce weight to an absolute minimum. Pressing the button located behind the trigger releases the magazine. Photo courtesy of Kimber America.

Most semiautos require regular minimal maintenance to function reliably. The main things to remember when cleaning a semiauto handgun are to remove fouling (debris left from the firing process), check basic mechanical function, clean the exterior of the firearm, and lubricate the high-friction portions of the gun. Lubrication is important, and your firearm's manual should tell you key points that require lubrication, but it is important not to apply too much lubricant to the gun since that can lead to "gumming" and failures to properly cycle. A thin layer of lubricant is all that is required, so more is not always better. With minimal basic maintenance, most semiautos can be counted on to consistently fire.

## Selecting the Right Semiauto for You

As with so many other things, the perfect semiauto for you depends on a variety of factors, including your own personal tastes and preferences. It is impossible to tell how a gun feels by looking at a photo in this or any other book or magazine. The best way is to spend time at gun shops handling different firearms and deciding which one fits your hand the best. As I explain in Chapter XII, "Carrying a Concealed Firearm," large national conventions like the annual NRA convention are a good place to shop for a gun that fits you because you can look at and handle such a wide variety of firearms from dozens of different companies. In addition, each company will have experts on hand who can be relied upon to provide you with factual and practical information about their products. This is one of the reasons I suggest that new shooters attend the annual conference. It may cost a bit of money, but it will pay off when you find a gun that you really like that suits you and you have an expert on that firearm available to answer questions about function, disassembly, maintenance, and other topics related to that particular firearm. Gun shop owners can certainly provide much of the same information, and many of these owners have an incredible knowledge of firearms and are great resources.

Chain store employees vary greatly in their level of knowledge of firearms. Some gun shop employees are real gun experts, but many have limited experience with firearms. If you are inexperienced with firearms, it's hard to tell the difference between good advice and

▲ Kimber's Solo has gained a reputation as an excellent concealed carry gun because of its compact size and shooting qualities. The Solo is available in 9mm Luger, a favorite defensive cartridge. Photo courtesy of Kimber America.

bad advice, so it's always good to have an expert available to help you determine whether or not the advice you are getting is accurate and reliable.

There are many things to consider when purchasing a semiauto pistol. The most basic question is what you plan to use it for. Is it going to be a gun you use primarily for on-body carry? If so, it will have to be of appropriate size and dimensions, since it's very difficult to comfortably conceal and carry a large-frame semiauto. For on-body carry, I'd look at compact and subcompact semiautos. The good news is that the nationwide increase in states issuing CCW permits has caused a major increase in the number of semiautos on the market designed for concealed carry. The prob-

lem is that there are so many choices it can sometimes be difficult to select a firearm that is best for you.

Any semiauto you purchase for self-defense should, however, be compact enough to carry and should fit in your hand comfortably. A semiauto that fits your hand properly should have a grip that your hand can comfortably wrap around and you should be able to easily and rapidly find the trigger. Guns that are too large and too small aren't fun to shoot, and if you don't practice with your carry gun, you aren't totally prepared to protect yourself and your family. There are several ways to judge for appropriate frame size, but my favorite method is to index my finger above the trigger, holding it in the same position I would if I were

▼ The Beretta Tomcat is a unique design that incorporates a tip-up barrel. Instead of loading the magazine and pulling back the slide to chamber a cartridge, the .32 Auto Tomcat allows the shooter to load a magazine, tip the barrel up, and place a cartridge directly in the chamber without having to pull back the slide, which can be difficult on some semiautos. The innovative Tomcat is a favorite carry gun.

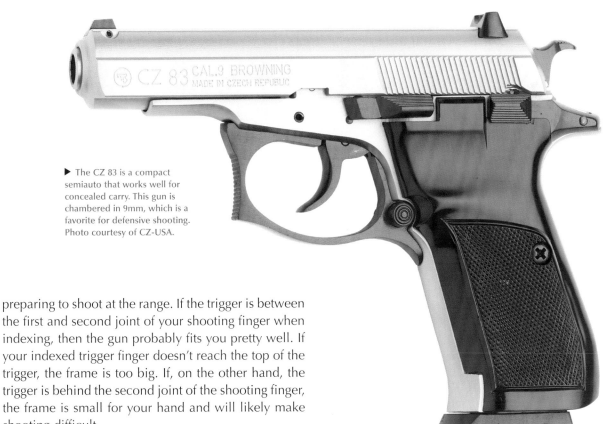

▶ The CZ 83 is a compact semiauto that works well for concealed carry. This gun is chambered in 9mm, which is a favorite for defensive shooting. Photo courtesy of CZ-USA.

preparing to shoot at the range. If the trigger is between the first and second joint of your shooting finger when indexing, then the gun probably fits you pretty well. If your indexed trigger finger doesn't reach the top of the trigger, the frame is too big. If, on the other hand, the trigger is behind the second joint of the shooting finger, the frame is small for your hand and will likely make shooting difficult.

Deciding between single, double, and double action–only variants is largely a matter of personal choice. Unlike single action revolvers, which are rarely used for concealed carry, single action semiautos are popular choices. The SA Colt 1911 and its clones, which are mentioned throughout this book, are a favorite choice for experienced shooters and law enforcement professionals. There are a variety of 1911s designed specifically for concealed carry, and companies like Colt also produce smaller .380 SA semiautos that are perfect for carrying concealed. Most of these SAs have external safeties, and 1911s have grip safeties, which means that the shooter must be gripping the gun to fire. SA semiautos are often carried in the "cocked and locked" position, which means that there is a cartridge in the chamber, the hammer is cocked, and the safety is on.

Double action semiautos can be fired in SA or DA mode. Many of these guns also have a decocker, which, when pressed, safely lowers the hammer. Most DA semiautos are carried with a loaded chamber and with the safety on, provided the gun has a safety. Some DA guns do not. However, because the DA does not require you to manually cock the hammer or pull back the slide before firing like an SA semiauto does, most DA semiautos are not carried in the cocked position because the trigger can be pulled to fire the gun even when the hammer is down.

The simplest semiautos are double action–only guns, which means there is no hammer. Once a cartridge is chambered, the gun is cocked and firing requires turning off a manual safety (provided the gun has one) and pulling the trigger. Striker-fire guns are similar in function to DAO guns in that they do not have a hammer. These guns are typically carried with a round in the chamber and the safety in the ON position.

Choosing a caliber is difficult, and most of the arguments that arise regarding the "best" cartridge for semiauto handguns are largely theoretical and are not based on fact. There are, however, many popular choices that are considered "effective" for self-defense, though the data used to classify a caliber as effective or not doesn't take into account bullet construction and shot placement. Images of bullets knocking victims over tables and out windows is the work of Hollywood; the reality of how effective a cartridge is has to do with the transfer of kinetic energy and what happens to the bullet when it enters the body. Therefore, being able to shoot accurately and choosing a bullet that is designed to perform in defense situations is critically important.

The most popular semiauto defensive cartridges are the .32 ACP (aka .32 Auto), .380 ACP (aka .380 Auto), 9mm Luger, .40 Smith & Wesson, and .45 ACP (aka .45 Auto). This is a good list from which to begin selecting your personal defense firearm. Energy levels and recoil are in direct proportion, so guns chambered in .32 ACP won't produce as much energy as the .45 ACP, but the .32 also produces considerably less recoil in guns of comparable weight. Additionally, .32 ACP ammo may be more difficult to find. But good .380 ACP, 9mm Luger, .40 S&W, and .45 ACP defensive loads abound and their popularity keeps store shelves stocked and prices reasonable. The 9mm is the most popular choice, and it's a fantastic option that combines effective stopping power and high capacities with manageable recoil and an enormous range of ammunition. Additionally, I like having a few spare magazines with my gun. This allows you to practice magazine changes and speeds things up at the range—so long as you've loaded your extra mags at home.

.22 LR semiautos are popular for "plinking" and competitive target shooting. They are fantastic practice guns and are a great caliber to train new shooters and sharpen the skills of experienced ones. Ammunition for .22s is very cheap and the recoil level is very low. Every year there are thousands of new CCW permit holders that elect to carry .22s, but the .22s do not produce high levels of energy, and finding a true defensive bullet for the .22 is difficult. These semiautos are great for

training and casual shooting, but they are typically considered "underpowered" for most defensive situations.

Select a semiautomatic firearm that fits your needs, learn how the gun works, and practice with it frequently until you become comfortable with your gun.

▲ Loading the magazine can be difficult for beginning shooters. The spring inside the magazine must be depressed, and cartridges are loaded. This magazine loader from Glock helps depress the spring, making it easier to load cartridges.

# VII. Firearm Safety

Safety is paramount when handling firearms. Proper gun handling greatly reduces the chances that you will injure someone while shooting, and it is critically important to learn gun safety *before you have a loaded firearm in your hands.* As previously addressed, the vast majority of accidental firearms injuries are related to improper handling. In this chapter, we will examine the essential elements of gun safety that will keep you and others around you safe while at the range.

## Getting on Target

The first step toward safe gun handling is finding a place where you can shoot without running the risk of damage, injury, or death. The key element to remember when shooting a firearm is that once the bullet leaves the gun, there's no chance of correcting errors. Consider where you will shoot and be sure that the area is suitable for firing a gun. In many cases, it is illegal to fire a gun within village, town, or city limits, so be certain that there is no law or ordinance preventing the discharge of firearms in the area where you plan to shoot. It is well worth calling ahead to local law enforcement to be sure you are not in violation, and it could save you from legal trouble down the line.

When you've established that you can shoot, the next question is whether or not you *should* shoot. It is vital that you shoot into a backstop, something that will stop the bullet. The most common backstop is dirt, and dirt usually works just fine as a backstop, provided you have plenty of dirt to stop the bullet and prevent it from passing through the backstop and there are no rocks or metal objects. Shooting ranges oftentimes have specially designed, high-density walls that are specifically engineered to stop bullets. These foam walls are expensive, though. It is essential to always be certain of what you are shooting into and what is beyond it. Do not shoot into any objects that a bullet can pass through, such as wooden planks

◀ Is this target set up safely? No, because the hill slopes away behind the target and the bullet will travel over the ridge to parts unknown. It is essential when you are shooting that you have a backstop so that you can be certain the bullet will be stopped.

▲ The author indexes his finger on a Ruger .45. It is essential to train yourself to always index the finger and not place it on the trigger until you are ready to fire.

or particle board, unless there is a suitable backstop behind the target. Never shoot anything with a hard surface or water, because the bullet could potentially ricochet. Do not fire guns inside unless you are on a range specifically designed for indoor shooting, since the gases produced by discharging firearms are hazardous.

There are many quality indoor and outdoor ranges across the country. For assistance finding a shooting range, visit www.nssf.org.

## The Keys to Firearms Safety

**Muzzle:** The muzzle is the point where the bullet exits the barrel. It is essential that the muzzle is always pointed in a safe direction so that if a bullet were fired accidentally, it would not cause harm to people or property. As simple as this seems, keeping the muzzle pointed in a safe direction is something that many new shooters forget. Making sure that the muzzle is aimed in a safe direction is critical, and it should be something that is learned early and practiced often. As Lieutenant Colonel Jeff Cooper of Gunsite Academy

says, "never point your muzzle at anything you aren't willing to destroy." Sound advice.

**Trigger:** Inexperienced shooters have a natural inclination to place their shooting fingers (index finger on the hand they shoot with) on the trigger as soon as they pick up a gun. This is a bad habit and an extremely dangerous one. At the range, a shooter that is inclined to carry their gun with their finger on the trigger is a hazard, and I've seen one perpetual trigger-toucher asked to leave the range and not return! Resting your finger on the trigger is one of the worst and most dangerous habits for shooters. Safety dictates that you only place your shooting finger inside the trigger guard when you are ready to fire. This means that the range is "hot" (this command is the all-clear from the rangemaster to shoot), the muzzle of the firearm is pointed downrange, and you are ready to deliver the shot. Until that moment, you should index your finger.

Indexing the finger is an important habit that new shooters should learn as they begin to handle guns. Indexing means that you place the shooting finger outside the trigger guard on the side of the frame above the trigger. With your finger indexed, there is very little chance that the finger will contact the trigger unintentionally and result in an accidental discharge. Finger awareness is important. Make a habit of indexing your shooting finger anytime you pick up a firearm. It is one of the easiest ways to prevent injury.

**Action:** Action refers to the moving parts in a firearm. In the case of the semiauto the term "action" refers to the slide, and in revolvers the action is the cylinder. Firearms only shoot when the action is closed; therefore, if you keep the action of your firearm open, you eliminate the chances of accidental discharge. An "open action" cannot be fired, and therefore guns with open actions are considered to be safe. For revolvers this requires that the cylinder button is pressed and the cylinder is swung out of the frame. An open action on a semiautomatic firearm means that the slide is locked in a rearward position; the gun cannot be fired until the slide stop is pressed to allow the slide to move forward. When you are shooting, always keep the action open as you are loading and moving toward the line to shoot. It is only when you are at the line that the action of your gun should be closed as you prepare to fire. The action of a revolver is closed by pushing the cylinder into the frame, and the action of a semiauto is closed by pressing down on the slide stop. When the action is closed, be prepared to fire.

**Ear/Eye Protection:** It is critical to wear ear and eye protection while shooting. Every shot from a modern concealed carry handgun produces enough noise to damage hearing, and every shot expels residue into the air. The use of safety glasses and hearing protection is mandatory on most ranges, and even if the range you are shooting on doesn't have specific guidelines mandating eye and ear protection, it is essential to always protect your hearing and sight at the range. In addition, shooters who do not wear hearing protection are more likely to develop a flinch, an involuntary reaction to the loud blast generated by each shot. Repeatedly shooting without hearing protection can cause permanent hearing loss and other conditions like tinnitus, or ringing of the ears.

## Checking the Firearm

One of the most critical skills involving firearms is the ability to safely check a firearm to be sure that it is unloaded. In addition, you should always check to be sure that a firearm is unloaded when you receive it. As an outdoor writer, people oftentimes want to show me their new guns and simply hand me a firearm without any indication of whether the gun is loaded or unloaded.

◄ Familiarize yourself with the mechanical function of your firearm. This FNH .45 DA pistol has a safety with a built-in decocker. In this photo the hammer is cocked and the safety is ON.

▶ In this photo
the safety has
been moved to
the OFF position
on the FNH .45.
The red dot
indicates that
the gun is ready
to fire.

◀ When the safety/
decocker lever is
pushed down beyond
the safe position
as shown here, the
hammer is safely
lowered. Decockers
allow DA semiautos to
have their hammers
lowered safely. This is
just one example of
understanding how
your firearm works.

If someone hands you a firearm that is not already safe (action open and visible), then your first responsibility is to ensure that that gun doesn't pose a threat to you or anyone else. This is accomplished by making sure that the gun cannot fire. For the purposes of this text, I'm simply going to refer to making the gun "safe."

Revolvers are very simple to make safe. Begin by holding the revolver in a safe direction where even an accidental discharge would not cause damage, injury, or death. Keeping your hand well clear of the trigger and always outside of the trigger guard, locate the cylinder release button, which is usually located on the left side of the frame behind the cylinder, and press the button to open the cylinder. On revolvers made by Smith & Wesson, Taurus, Rossi, and others, the cylinder release button must be pushed forward to release the cylinder. Ruger guns require you to press down on the button and apply pressure to the right side of the cylinder as you do so. With the cylinder release button pressed you can swing the magazine out of the frame. You will immediately be able to determine if there are any cartridges in the cylinder. Likewise, a revolver with a cylinder that is open (out of the frame) cannot be fired. Still, keep your finger off the trigger and keep the muzzle pointed in a safe direction. One of the signs of an inexperienced shooter (and one of the quickest ways to get invited to leave a shooting club or range) is to treat safe guns as though they weren't loaded. When questioned about this, many new shooters claim that the gun is safe and that the cylinder is out of the frame. Remember that it is essential to treat all guns as if they were loaded and to keep your finger away from the trigger. Even when the cylinder is opened (which means that the gun can't fire), keep the muzzle pointed in a safe direction.

Semiautomatic handguns are simple to make safe as well. As with revolvers, semiautos should always be handled so that the finger remains off the trigger and the muzzle is pointed in a safe direction at all times. The first step in the unloading process is to press the magazine release button, which is usually located on the left side of the gun near the grip (handle). Pressing this button allows the magazine to slide out of the gun. Once the magazine is out of the gun, pull the slide back vigorously two or three times to be sure that the chamber is empty. Also do a visual check of the chamber. Can you see that it is clear? If so lock the slide back by pulling it into the rearward position and pressing up on the slide stop, which is usually, located on the frame of the gun. Always be careful when manipulating the slide of a semiauto because having a finger or skin pinched by a closing slide is extremely painful (I can personally attest to this), so always keep your hands and fingers away from the moving slide. When the semiauto has had the magazine removed and the slide is locked back and the chamber is empty (you can see this with the slide pulled back), a semiauto gun is considered "safe."

## Hangfires, Misfires, and Squib Loads

These three terms represent malfunctions of either the firearm or the ammunition to fire correctly. Thankfully, hangfires, misfires, and squib loads are rare, but it is important to recognize these three malfunctions and understand how to handle each one if they should occur while you are shooting.

**Hangfires** are delays between the striking pin contacting the primer and the ignition of the shot. Hangfires are particularly dangerous because when the firing pin strikes and there is no ignition, many shooters (including experienced shooters) immediately lower the gun and begin assessing the problem. It is essential to understand that the delay resulting from a hangfire can take *several* seconds to ignite the powder. In cases of hangfires, shooters and bystanders have been injured because the shooter does not keep the muzzle pointed downrange or opens the action of the gun as the powder ignites. To prevent injury, remember that if you pull the trigger and the shot does not go off, *always keep the muzzle pointed downrange for at least thirty seconds.* As I said previously, I've seen seasoned shooters immediately open the action when the shot didn't ignite. This is a dangerous habit, so don't develop it as a beginning shooter. When you pull the trigger and nothing happens, be sure that you keep the gun pointed downrange for the recommended thirty seconds. To practice safely holding the gun downrange to prevent injury from a hangfire, see the drills in Chapter XI, "Range Etiquette and Proper Practice."

**Misfires** result when ammunition fails to fire after the firing pin contacts the primer. There are multiple

▲ Having a qualified instructor helps the shooter remember safety procedures. New shooters need to remember to *always* keep the muzzle of the firearm pointed in a safe direction and keep the finger off the trigger until the gun is ready to be fired. Photo courtesy of the National Shooting Sports Foundation.

reasons why ammunition doesn't fire. Sometimes there is a malfunction with the cartridge itself, such as inoperative primers or the failure of the ammunition company to drill the hole in the cartridge case that connects the primer and the powder. In addition, some misfires are caused by the gun, usually as a result of a shallow or weak firing pin strike. Treat every misfire as though it were a hangfire. Keep the gun pointed downrange and be prepared for the cartridge to fire for at least thirty seconds. Afterwards you can examine the cartridge to determine what happened. If the firing pin is dented normally, then the problem probably lies with the ammunition. If there is a shallow dent, then the problem is usually a result of a malfunction with your firearm and you need to take the gun to an experienced gunsmith to resolve the issue.

**Squib loads** result when loads do not achieve normal pressure, usually as a result of too little gunpowder in the cartridge case. Squib loads result in weak shots, which usually generate less recoil and noise than normal loads. When shooting a semiautomatic gun, a squib load oftentimes does not generate enough recoil or gas to properly cycle the action. If you suspect a squib load, it is very important to clear the barrel before firing another shot. Sometimes a squib load is so weak that it doesn't generate enough energy to push the bullet down the barrel. If you fire another shot, the bullet that is in the barrel will likely cause a barrel eruption, which can cause serious injury or death. Always stop firing and examine the barrel after each squib load.

As previously stated, hangfires, misfires, and squib loads are rare. Many shooters never encounter any of these problems in their shooting careers. However, it is vital to understand what they are and what you should do if you ever encounter these situations.

## Special Safety Considerations for the Revolver

Revolvers are easy to maintain, simple to operate, and a cinch to clean. They are also very safe. Modern revolvers have transfer bars that prevent a cartridge from being fired by accidentally dropping the hammer, recoil shrouds that protect the shooter from debris, and hand grips that help minimize the painful effects of recoil. However, it is still possible to injure yourself through carelessness when shooting a revolver. First, extended shooting sessions make guns hot, so grabbing the barrel of a revolver that has just been shot dozens of times at the range can result in a burn. Although most of these burns aren't serious enough to warrant medical attention, avoid touching the metal parts of revolvers that have recently been fired multiple times.

A slow-motion video of a revolver shot indicates just how much gas and debris escapes around the front edge of the cylinder during a shot. Therefore, it is important to keep your hands and fingers away from the cylinder at all times while shooting the revolver. Learning the proper grip technique (see Chapter XI, "Range

Etiquette and Proper Practice") is essential when firing any handgun, revolvers included. As a general rule, keep your hands and fingers away from the cylinder, the hammer, and the muzzle when shooting. When closing the cylinder, be sure to keep your hands clear. Obturation can cause cartridge cases to swell, so when you are finished firing and swing the cylinder out of the frame to unload the empty cartridge cases, jamming the palm of your hand down onto the end of the ejector rod can cause injury. To prevent this, place the heel of the hand or the fingers on the ejector rod and push with steadily increasing pressure. Most injury from unloading revolvers occurs when a novice jams the palm of his or her hand onto the ejector rod.

## Special Safety Considerations for Semiauto Handguns

Semiauto handguns are considered "safe" when the action is locked open and the magazine is removed, and the gun should remain this way when approaching the bench and preparing to shoot. In addition, the muzzle should always remain pointed in a safe direction and the finger should always remain indexed on the frame and away from the trigger until you are ready to fire.

Semiauto handguns have a reputation of being "dangerous." In reality, improperly handling any firearm is dangerous, no mat-

▲ Hearing and eye protection should be worn at all times when shooting. Notice that the author has his trigger (right) finger indexed along the frame of the gun because he is not prepared to fire.

ter what type of gun it is. One of the most important elements to remaining safe while handling semiautos is to familiarize oneself with the various mechanical functions of the gun and to understand the basic mode of operation for that firearm. The best way to familiarize yourself with the mechanical function of the firearm is to consult the owner's manual that is provided with the gun. If no owner's manual was present when you purchased the gun, you should contact the manufacturer, as they frequently supply owner's manuals for their products at little or no cost.

Sometimes an owner's manual is not available. An example of this occurred when a friend of mine was cleaning out her grandfather's house. A younger sibling was helping empty drawers in a bedroom and walked into the kitchen carrying a pistol. The adults in the room were rightfully stunned, but no one knew what to do with the gun. Luckily for everyone involved, the firearm was unloaded, but if it *hadn't* been, what could have happened?

This example illustrates why everyone, even children, should be taught the basic rules of firearms safety and what to do if they encounter a loaded firearm. Guns should always be respected for the damage they are capable of causing, and this is why it is important for everyone in the home to understand that firearms

▼ The hammer is cocked on this .45 Auto and the safety is in the ON (upward, in the case of this particular firearm) position. In addition, the gun has a grip safety that requires the shooter to be holding the gun to fire. Safeties are mechanical devices and they can fail, so the shooter must always remember to handle the gun as if it were ready to fire at all times.

▲ Practice at the range can be fun and challenging, but the shooter must first learn the basic rules of gun safety. Knowledgeable shooters can enjoy a lifetime of enjoyment with firearms without risk of injury. Statistically, target shooting is one of the safest of all sports. Photo courtesy of Kimber America.

can be dangerous if mishandled. The notion that some parents have of never exposing their children to anything related to firearms is neglectful, and this is a perfect example of why that is true. Consider that everyone in your home understands that you have a car, and that a set of keys will set that car in motion. However, it must be made clear that only those who are experienced drivers should operate that vehicle. The same is true with guns. Kids that understand that guns are potentially dangerous if handled incorrectly and that are taught basic gun safety rules are far less likely to cause injury in a situation like the one mentioned above. Somehow we have come to the conclusion that keeping our children away from firearms is safer than teaching them to respect guns. This idea is misguided and, ultimately, dangerous. Gun safety shouldn't be a topic discussed only among parents; teach everyone in

the home to respect guns and to stay away from them if they aren't old enough and experienced enough to handle them.

## Holstering Safety

Most negligent discharges occur during holstering. It bears mentioning, then, that you should never reholster your firearm in a hurry. The practice is known as speed holstering, and I can't find any instructor who encourages the practice, especially for civilian CCW permit holders. When you place your firearm back in the holster, do so slowly, and after you have finished firing take your finger out of the trigger guard. If the gun has a manual safety, engage the safety before holstering, and be absolutely certain that your trigger finger is indexed before placing the gun back in the holster. It's critical to your safety and the safety of those around you.

# VIII. Choosing a Firearm for Concealed Carry

## Selecting a Revolver

eciding which revolver to purchase can be difficult. After all, you are relying on this gun to protect your life and the lives of your loved ones. Fortunately, there are a number of good revolvers for sale that are designed for defensive carry.

There are several important points to consider when selecting the right revolver for you. First, it has to fit your hand and be comfortable. If you have very small hands, then you'll want to find a revolver with small grips, and if you have big hands, you'll need a gun that has a large enough grip to allow you a firm and proper hold. Most concealed carry guns are built to an average, so they will fit the shooter with an average-sized hand. If you purchase a gun and decide that the grip doesn't fit you or isn't comfortable, you can purchase aftermarket grips from companies like Hogue.

Beginning shooters should avoid single action revolvers in most instances. Single actions are fun to shoot, but they require cocking between each shot, and loading and unloading require a lot of time. Instead,

▼ Selecting the right firearm can be tough, but the good news is that there are several companies that make quality handguns for concealed carry like these from Kimber. Photo courtesy of Kimber America.

▲ Select a firearm that you are comfortable with and practice often. Most new shooters need to stick with guns chambered for mild recoiling cartridges like the .380 Auto, .38 Special, and 9mm Luger. Photo courtesy of the National Shooting Sports Foundation.

choose one of the double action or double action–only revolvers designed specifically for concealed carry from companies like Ruger, Smith & Wesson, Taurus, Rossi, Charter Arms, or another revolver maker.

The key to being successful with any concealed carry gun is practicing a lot (certainly a lot more than the criminals you'll potentially have to defend yourself against), and the key to practicing often is to buy a gun with which you are comfortable and familiar. Therefore, when you select a concealed carry revolver, it has to be chambered for a caliber that you can shoot without pain or fear and that also generates sufficient power to stop an attacker. Many experts say that it is important to choose a powerful cartridge that has "knockdown power," which is a relative and objective term for the power generated by a handgun cartridge. Instead, you should be balancing effective power with controllability, which is vital in selecting a revolver that will work for you.

The most popular concealed carry handgun cartridges are the .38, .38+P, and .357 Magnum. All of these will work, and there is quality self-defense ammo available for each of these cartridges, which is another key element when selecting a gun. The .38+P is perhaps the most popular chambering for concealed carry guns today, because it fires everything from .38 Special light loads (which have reduced recoil and muzzle blast and are comfortable to shoot for long periods on the range) all the way up to full-power defensive loads. For this reason the .38+P is probably the most common chambering in new carry revolvers and one of the absolute best choices for a new shooter thanks to its versatility. The .357 Magnum is another viable choice, but .357s require larger chambers and increased weight. In addition, the .357 Magnum loads produce hefty recoil and muzzle blast, particularly in lightweight, compact revolvers, and there are very, very few circumstances where a .357 Magnum is truly needed instead of a .38 Special+P.

The .38+P certainly isn't the only appropriate option for concealed carry. The introduction of the .32 H&R Magnum in the 1980s created a powerful and versatile .32-caliber revolver cartridge that would work for defense purposes, and the .32 H&R remains a viable choice for anyone planning to purchase a concealed carry revolver. In addition, the .32 H&R Magnum will also fire .32 Smith & Wesson Long cartridges, which generate very little recoil. In the late 2000s, Ruger and Federal teamed up to develop the .327 Federal Magnum, which will fire .32 S&W cartridges, .32 H&R Magnum, and .327 Federal Magnum ammunition. The selection of quality ammunition for the .32s is growing each year, and .327 Federal handguns are very versatile. Some of these new additions to ammo families are cartridges designed for defensive carry, and the .327 Federal should be on the short list for anyone looking for a defense revolver.

The effectiveness of .22-caliber handguns for self-defense is frequently debated, and while one side says that the .22 LR isn't powerful enough for defensive situations, a logical argument can also be made that a .22 LR revolver is better than having no gun at all, and the low price of ammunition and minimal recoil

and muzzle blast mean that owners of .22s can (and, in my experience, typically do) shoot more often. The minimal mass and diameter of .22 LR bullets mean that this cartridge won't generate as much kinetic energy as larger bullets, which have more mass and a wider diameter. Nevertheless, .22s have been effectively used in defensive situations, and there are several compact DA and DAO revolvers chambered for the .22 LR that are light and small.

Another option for the revolver shooter is the .22 Magnum. .22 Mags deliver considerably more energy than the smaller .22 LR and have a cylinder capacity that exceeds larger calibers like the .38 Special. The .22 Mag is on the low end of the defensive spectrum regarding power, but ammunition companies are now loading defensive .22 Mag ammo. Ruger offers a .22 Magnum (also known as .22 WMR) double-action revolver in their LCR line, and the North American

▼ This shooter's hand is too small for the grip on this gun, a Ruger .44 Magnum revolver. Because this shooter's hand does not fit this gun well and it is chambered for a powerful magnum cartridge, this shooter is unlikely to be successful shooting this gun. The trigger should be between the first and second joint of the shooting finger.

Arms line of micro revolvers include one of the only single-action revolvers that are commonly carried for personal defense. The North American Arms Pug is a five-shot .22 Magnum SA revolver that weighs just 6.4 ounces and measures 4.56 inches long, making it one of the lightest and easiest revolvers to conceal. It's slow to reload, but this miniscule .22 Magnum can be carried concealed under the lightest clothing.

There are a handful of revolvers from companies like Charter Arms and Taurus that are chambered in cartridges normally reserved for semiautomatic handguns, namely 9mm Luger and .40 Smith & Wesson. These revolvers are typically designed for concealed carry, with low-profile hammers on DA revolvers or hammerless DAO models. They make excellent defensive guns, though the .40 S&W produces a fair amount of recoil in small, light revolvers.

Just like with a car, it is also better to actually test a gun first before purchasing, as it is impossible to determine the balance, feel, and grip size relative to your hand until you actually pick up the firearm. Many gun stores will allow you to see the gun before you purchase it. The gun should fit your hand well and be comfortable. Remember, one of the keys to successful armed defense is a lot of practice, and if the firearm you carry isn't comfortable, then you won't want to shoot it any more than necessary.

When choosing a concealed carry revolver, choose a model that has sights, hammers, and cylinders that won't hang up on clothes or holsters as you draw the gun and that is light enough to carry all day without fatigue. I personally prefer DAO revolvers, which have no external hammer to get hung up as I draw. In addition, the lack of a hammer doesn't "print" as a firearm, meaning that people are less likely to recognize that you are carrying a gun. You have to make some compromises when purchasing a gun with low-profile, nonadjustable sights. Although they carry well and don't print, these guns aren't as accurate as models with large, adjustable sights. Then again, most violent encounters happen at a few feet, and the risk of hanging large, adjustable sights in clothing as you draw the gun make them a poor choice for most concealed carry situations. All of my concealed carry revolvers have simple, fixed sights, and I feel confident shooting them out to twenty feet, which is plenty. There are, however, new low-profile adjustable carry sights that are small and designed not to hang up and are also adjustable for windage and elevation.

Concealed carry revolvers shouldn't be excessively large or heavy; guns weighing more than thirty ounces are heavy for daily carry, and many new revolvers weigh less than twenty ounces. Keeping weight to a minimum is important to prevent the gun from being uncomfortably heavy. A concealed revolver that is a burden to carry and wear is likely to be left at home, which defeats its purpose. Before selecting a firearm, you must have an idea of how you plan to carry. The best way to carry a concealed revolver is on the body, so these guns should be lightweight and compact. However, off-body carry, such as in a purse, allows for carrying larger, heavier guns. The disadvantage is that you are only protected when that purse is with you, which may not be the case in a sudden violent attack. If possible, it is advisable to keep your firearm on your person.

There are a variety of lightweight metals and alloys that have reduced the weight of revolvers. Examples include guns with aluminum, scadmium, or titanium parts that reduce the weight of the gun. Remember that recoil energy is partly determined by the weight of the gun, and lighter guns produce more felt recoil. Many concealed carry revolvers have ported barrels, which means that there are holes drilled into the barrel to allow trapped gases to escape, reducing the jarring effects of recoil and reducing muzzle flip. However, these recoil-reducing ports also increase muzzle blast.

In choosing a concealed carry gun that works for you it is important to understand that there is a balance between recoil, muzzle blast, gun weight, and caliber. Heavier guns are harder to conceal but they produce less recoil. Powerful revolvers like those chambered in .357 Remington Magnum produce a large amount of energy, but that energy is coupled by increased muzzle blast and sometimes unpleasant recoil. Shooters who choose handguns that produce hefty recoil and cost a great deal of energy to shoot typically practice less and are therefore less proficient with their guns. Choosing the right revolver for you is a matter of compromise, and the more revolvers you have the opportunity to shoot, the better equipped you will be to make selections about the right gun for you.

Finish is an important consideration when purchasing a firearm. Concealed carry guns, particularly those used for on-body carry, are exposed to human sweat and moisture on a daily basis. Traditionally, guns were "blued," a chemical treatment that gives the barrel a blue-black sheen. However, this type of finish doesn't usually stand up well to constant concealed carry and requires frequent cleaning to prevent corrosion. Stainless steel is a popular alternative, as the metal parts of the firearm are protected against corrosion from sweat and moisture. Another alternative to traditional bluing is proprietary finishes like Cerakote, which is a ceramic coating that protects the metal parts of a firearm.

## Choosing a Semiautomatic Handgun for Concealed Carry

Compact semiautomatic handguns are a popular choice for concealed carry, and as more states have adopted right-to-carry laws, manufacturers have produced more small semiautos perfect for defensive shooting. Today there are many good choices when selecting a semiauto to carry concealed, but it is important to find a gun that you feel comfortable with and are willing to shoot regularly.

As with revolvers, less weight makes a semiauto easier to carry, and today's crop of new concealed carry guns are lighter than ever. Many companies have examined the needs of CCW permit holders and have designed guns just for carry. These guns are typically very lightweight, simple, and reliable, and while they aren't designed for accurate target shooting at long distances (most have simple gutter sights and heavy trigger pulls), these guns serve exceptionally well for daily carry and might save your life.

When choosing a semiauto the first step is choosing which type of trigger action you need. Many of today's carry semiautos are double action–only, or DAO. This is a good place for a beginning shooter to start because DAO guns are very simple to operate. Most of these guns do not have exposed hammers to hang up in clothing as the gun is drawn, and once a round

▼ It is a good idea to speak to a qualified professional when selecting a firearm. Since not all firearms will fit every shooter the same, it helps if you have a chance to hold the firearm to be sure it fits your hand comfortably. Photo courtesy of the National Shooting Sports Foundation.

is chambered, the gun can simply be drawn and fired without worrying about manipulating the hammer.

DAO guns certainly aren't the only option, though. The rising number of concealed carry permit holders has compelled dozens of companies to offer up their own versions of the ideal carry gun, and many of these are single and double action semiautos. Double action semiautos designed for carry typically have low-profile sights and small hammers, and they have the added benefit of being capable of firing in DA or SA mode.

Single action semiautos are most often carried in the "cocked and locked" position, which is to say that the hammer is cocked and the safety is placed in the ON position while the gun is carried. In addition, these guns oftentimes have a grip safety, which requires pressure from the shooter's hand on the rear of the grip before the gun can be fired. Some shooters aren't comfortable carrying a gun that is cocked and fear that the odds of an accidental discharge are higher. However, many shooters carry their single action semiautos in this fashion (virtually everyone that carries a Colt 1911-style semiauto), and I do not know of a single accident involving a single action sidearm.

There are a number of suitable calibers for concealed carry guns, but the most popular choices today are the .380 Auto, 9mm Luger, .40 Smith & Wesson, and the .45 ACP. Gun enthusiasts spend a great deal of time debating which of these is best, but the reality is that all of these calibers are suitable for concealed carry. In terms of numbers, the 9mm Luger is probably the most popular, and there are dozens of compact and subcompact semiautos chambered in 9mm. In addition, there is a wide selection of premium defensive ammunition for the 9mm—ammo that is designed and tested to perform in dangerous situations—so the 9mm Luger is a good choice for concealed carry. The same could be said of all three of the other cartridges listed, though. Some shooters feel that the .380 Auto is too light for concealed carry, and there are others that believe the .45 ACP is overkill and generates too much recoil for the beginning shooter. And while you aren't likely to reach a consensus on which of these cartridges is the best, in a dangerous encounter the

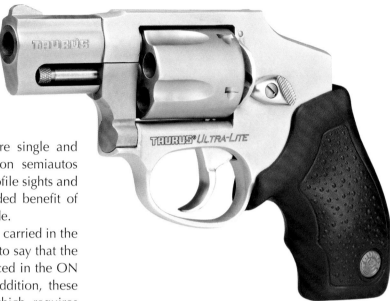

▲ This Taurus Ultra-Lite double action .38 revolver combines many favorable features. It's lightweight and has a stainless finish that is resistant to corrosion. Double action revolvers are simple to use and are extremely reliable. Pressing forward on the magazine release button (visible on the left side of the frame) and pushing on the right side if the cylinder allows for loading and unloading of the gun. Photo courtesy of Taurus Manufacturing.

gun you are carrying is *always* the best! These four cartridges do represent the major choices in semiautomatic carry guns. Which one you select is largely a matter of personal taste. The .45 does generate stout recoil, but I know of at least one petite woman who shoots a .45 regularly and is quite proficient. Fans of the .380 Auto will doubtlessly hear that the cartridge is underpowered (likely from someone who has never seen a .380 used in a defensive situation), but the reality is that .380s can stop an attacker and a number of defensive guns are chambered in .380.

There are a host of other suitable cartridges for concealed carry, though they are not as popular as the cartridges listed above. As with revolvers, there are several .22 LR semiautos that are small enough to carry concealed, and there are a number of permit holders who carry .22 LR guns. The .22 LR certainly can kill an attacker, and there are plenty of cases that support this presumption. However, the .22 LR certainly remains at the bottom of the power spectrum for concealed carry.

▲ It is important to choose a gun that fits your lifestyle and your carry needs. Also, it should be a gun you are willing to shoot often so that you become comfortable with it. Photo courtesy of Kimber America.

The .25 Auto and .32 Auto are also questionable for defense as well. Both certainly *can* stop an intruder, but experts tend to agree that both of these cartridges are somewhat underpowered for dedicated carry duty.

In 1994, SIG Sauer announced a new pistol cartridge, the .357 SIG. The cartridge was designed in cooperation with Federal Ammunition, who provided cartridges for SIG's new lineup of semiautos. The .357 SIG is recognizable because it is a bottleneck cartridge, which means that the bullet is smaller in diameter than the widest part of the cartridge body, and thus the cartridge has a "shoulder" and a "neck" like a rifle cartridge. In the case of the SIG the cartridge was developed by taking a .40 S&W cartridge and "necking it down" (shrinking the diameter of the neck of the cartridge) to accept smaller .357-caliber bullets. When a smaller bullet is used in a larger cartridge case, the bullet typically travels at a higher velocity. In the case

of the .357 SIG, the cartridge was designed to come close to mimicking .357 Magnum revolver energy levels. This means that the .357 SIG packs plenty of punch, and it is a very powerful gun for new shooters. In addition, choice of carry firearms and ammunition is limited. That's a shame, because the .357 SIG has all the qualities that make for a good carry gun cartridge.

There are several other cartridges that will work just fine for defense, including the .38 Super, the 10mm Auto, and the .45 GAP. These cartridges are undoubtedly effective, but ammo can be difficult to find and there aren't a lot of carry guns chambered for these cartridges. They all pack plenty of power, but none of these are probably as good a choice for new shooters as more popular cartridges like the 9mm Luger and the .380 Auto.

No matter which cartridge you choose, it is essential that you purchase quality ammunition designed for defensive carry. Good ammunition is absolutely critical to surviving in a defensive situation, so selecting a bullet that will perform well under the worst circumstances is a top priority when purchasing a concealed carry firearm.

Proper maintenance of a semiauto handgun requires disassembling the firearm so that the barrel, slide, and mainspring can be removed for cleaning. The procedure for disassembly varies from gun to gun, and some are much easier than others. Since these procedures are so varied, it wouldn't be effective to try and list the procedure for each semiauto firearm, but the general method of disassembly involves pulling the slide backward. Sometimes this requires locking the slide, but this is not always the case. Some guns like Glocks and Beretta M9s have release buttons that allow the slide to be removed from the gun when the slide lock is released, while others require the removal of a pin. Understanding how to disassemble a semiauto is important, though it is only in rare cases that you need to do more than remove the slide, barrel and mainspring. Cleaning and repair work that goes beyond that level is generally best left to a gunsmith.

### Other Firearms

Semiautos and revolvers certainly aren't the only options for concealed carry guns, though these are the two most popular styles. For over a hundred years, com-

pact single- or double-barreled "pocket" guns have been popular for defense. In the 1700s, Henry Deringer designed small muzzle-loading pistols that could be carried in the pocket of an overcoat, and these compact guns became known as "pocket pistols" or "Derringers," giving credit to Deringer's original design despite misspelling his name.

Today a "Derringer" typically refers to a small hammer-fired pistol capable of firing one or two shots. These guns do not offer nearly the ammo capacity of a semiauto or even a revolver. However, they are simple to use, easy to conceal, lightweight, and affordable. These small Derringer-type pistols are easy to operate, and maintenance is generally quite simple. Some of these small pocket pistols do not have a manual safety, and many do not even have a trigger guard. However, when simplicity and compact size are more important than magazine capacity, these small handguns are a viable option.

Most traditional Derringers have two barrels that are stacked atop one another. Loading the gun requires releasing the barrels and letting them tip forward on a hinge, loading the cartridges into the chambers. When the barrels are tipped back up and the action closes, the shooter must cock the hammer, fire, and cock the hammer again to fire the

◀ Taurus's line of compact .25 Auto pistols are extremely small and easy to carry. The .25 Auto is considered very light for defensive work, so selecting ammunition loaded with premium bullets is critical. Photo courtesy of Taurus Manufacturing.

▶ The DoubleTap is a unique firearm with two barrels. Simply push the side button forward and the barrels tip up, allowing the shooter to place a cartridge in the top and bottom barrel. Although it only offers two shots, the DoubleTap is lightweight and easy to carry. Note that the barrels are ported, which means they have holes to allow gas to escape to reduce recoil. Photo courtesy of DoubleTap Defense.

second barrel. These single action Derringers are available from a variety of companies such as Bond Arms and are available in a variety of different styles and calibers. There are also hammerless pocket pistols with tip-up barrels, such as the DoubleTap Defense line of compact carry pistols. In fact, pocket pistols like the DoubleTap are among the simplest of all defensive firearms. These guns simply have a button to release the barrels, which tip up to be loaded. The barrels are then closed and the firearm is ready to fire. The DoubleTap, like most other pocket pistols, has simple gutter-type sights. Such rudimentary sights make sense on this type of gun, though; since pocket pistols are designed for close-range defense, shots are expected to be at not more than a few paces, and at that range even the simplest sights will generally work well. Plus, as previously stated, gutter sights reduce the odds of the gun becoming hung up in clothing as it is drawn.

These small pocket pistols are not without their disadvantages, though. They only offer one or two shots at a time, and the recoil can be stout. However, they are extremely simple, lightweight, compact, and they generally do not print as much as larger semiautos or revolvers, which makes them easier to conceal.

## Manual Safeties

Many people tend to equate the presence of a manual safety with a "safe" firearm. There are many defensive carry guns that do not have a manual safety, and there are also those who would not buy a carry gun that *does* have a manual safety. So, why the controversy?

We are often trained to rely on the safety of a firearm, and from a young age many shooters are taught that the last thing you do before firing is to move the safety to the FIRE position. Manual safeties are designed to prevent accidental discharges, but relying on a manual safety to protect against shooter error and negligence is dangerous. Manual safeties are actually viewed as a hazard by some shooters who believe that during a confrontation forgetting to move the safety to the FIRE position can cost you your life.

It must be made clear here that a manual safety does not make a gun "safe," and guns that lack manual safeties are not "unsafe." The safety of a gun is a mechanical device, one of several moving parts that can potentially fail. The safety should serve as a last assurance of preventing accidental discharges. It should not, however, become an excuse for poor gun handling.

I have carry guns with and without manual safeties. None of the double action–only revolvers that I shoot have manual safeties, yet I wouldn't hesitate to carry them concealed. Some people are overwhelmed by the fear that pressure on the trigger of a loaded, concealed gun can cause an accidental discharge. In that case, I contest that it was the carry method that was at fault and not the firearm. Properly carrying a concealed firearm greatly reduces the odds of unintentional firing. I personally keep my revolver (again, a gun that lacks a manual safety) inside a stretchable nylon belt holster that protects and secures the gun, and I don't worry about accidental discharges.

Some carry guns, like the venerable 1911, Springfield's XD pistols, and Smith & Wesson's new Shield EZ .380 ACP, come with grip safeties. These firearms will not fire unless the grip safety is depressed, which happens naturally when the gun is drawn.

The choice of carrying a gun with or without a manual safety is up to the individual shooter. Proper handling, concealment, and storage are all essential to gun safety. A manual safety, however, is not. Learn how your firearm operates and be sure to carefully read the owner's manual before firing.

## Grips and Sighting Systems

When selecting a handgun for concealed carry, consider the grips and the sighting system before purchasing. One of the goals of this text is to encourage the reader to shoot often in preparation for a deadly encounter, and it is very difficult to shoot a lot if you aren't comfortable or able to hit your target. Grips and sights play a major role in how successful you are as a shooter. Some grips and sights can be easily changed,

▼ The author fires a Glock Model 19, a compact 9mm semiauto. The 9mm is a very popular caliber for new shooters because it provides sufficient energy without painful recoil. Most lines of defensive ammunition are available in 9mm Luger.

◀ Really small pistols are easy to conceal, and they're great to carry under light clothing or in a pocket. But their small size makes them difficult for shooters with large hands to comfortably grasp.

and a wide selection of aftermarket handgun accessories means that there is a nearly endless variety of products available for shooters. However, most shooters never change their grips or sights.

It can be difficult to find a grip that fits your hand well, particularly if you have very large or very small hands. Many firearms have aftermarket grips available that will fit smaller or larger hands. Other guns, however, come with a single grip or frame size that only fits some shooters. It is important that your self-defense gun fits your hand well, so take the time to shop around for a firearm that fits you properly.

Auxiliary sights are available for most firearms. The two most common types are laser sights and holographic sights. Each of these sighting systems is covered in detail later in the book, but when selecting a concealed carry firearm, it is important to understand the options available to shooters. Holographic sights are mounted on top of the gun and the shooter uses a red holographic dot to center the firearm on the target. This beam does not extend to the target and is visible only when looking through the sight itself. This type of sight is mostly reserved for military, law enforcement, and competitive shooters, but

there are shooters that choose holographic sights for their defense firearms. For the most part, though, concealed carry guns have either iron sights or laser sights. Iron sights are found on virtually every handgun. Iron sights rely on the shooter to align the rear sight, front sight, and the target, with the bulk of the shooter's focus dedicated to the front sight. Iron sights are accurate and easy to use one you have practiced with them regularly, and even shooters who use lasers or some other form of auxiliary sight should learn to properly use iron sights as well, since most firearms do not have auxiliary sights.

Laser sights emit a beam from the firearm to the target. This type of sight usually fits in the grip or the underside of the gun, and they are popular for concealed carry. Laser sights are effective, but they must be sighted in correctly, so follow the manufacturer's guidelines and, most importantly, practice until you are proficient when using a laser sight. Remember that the keys to successful carry are the same no matter what type of sight or gun you choose. The gun should be easy to carry and you should be comfortable with the firearm that you have chosen.

# IX. Shooting Accessories

## Essential Equipment

Before you begin shooting you'll need to be sure that you have all of the necessary equipment. This starts with safety equipment. Eye and ear protection is essential and should always be taken to the range. All handguns produce residue that travels through the air in the form of gas and debris each time a gun is fired, so safety glasses are mandatory equipment when shooting. It's best to choose safety glasses that are designed for protection, since they offer more durable lenses and greater protection against flying debris than standard sunglasses. Firearms produce damaging levels of noise, so always wear hearing protection and do not shoot unless your ears are protected from the damaging levels of noise produced by a firearm.

Besides your firearm, take plenty of ammunition. Target ammunition doesn't always have to be the same ammo you plan to use for defense; in fact, you'd have very high ammunition bills if you only shot premium self-defense ammo. Less expensive "ball" or lead bullets will allow you to shoot more and spend less, though I always like to shoot at least half a dozen rounds of the type of ammo I carry in my gun. Typically when I travel to the range I have at least fifty rounds of ammunition. I also try to carry ammunition that doesn't generate heavy recoil or muzzle blast. I want to be comfortable while I'm practicing, so when I'm shooting my short-barreled .357 Magnum at the range, I load it with .38 Special ammo that costs less and is more pleasant to shoot for long periods of time.

I always bring an extra magazine if I'm bringing my semiauto along as well.

▲ This is a "range kit" that comes with this Smith & Wesson semiauto. Having a hard plastic holster, magazines, magazine belt holders, and a magazine along with your gun in one convenient plastic box makes it easier to keep track of your accessories. Photo courtesy of Smith & Wesson.

▲ Having a good flashlight with your gun is important. In the home, keep a high-intensity flashlight close beside your gun and practice shooting at the range with the flashlight in hand.

It's also a good idea to bring along a portable gun cleaning kit. These kits are typically small and easy to transport, and it is a good idea to have such a kit with you while you are at the shooting range. It is much easier to clean the fouling from a firearm immediately after shooting, so when I am finished on the range I give my gun at least a brief cleaning and wipe down with a soft cloth. In addition, you should also have targets in your range bag. Many ranges will have targets set up, but oftentimes these targets are tattered and have been shot so many times it's difficult to tell which shots you fired and which were already on the target. Several companies make paper targets that are very inexpensive. You can also make your own targets from old shoeboxes, grocery bags, and posters if you prefer. It's also a good idea to take a staple gun and some staples along with you to the range, just in case you need to affix your target to the frame.

I believe it is very important to bring the holster you plan to use for concealed carry along with you to the range. One of the most important elements of practicing on the range is learning to draw your gun from con-

cealment, so therefore I like to actually wear the gun as I would during concealed carry. I don't try to be too fast when I'm on the range with a concealed gun. In fact, I practice the routine of drawing the gun slowly and deliberately, being careful to keep my finger well away from the trigger guard. I'll describe more about holster drills later, but I believe bringing the holster you plan to use for concealed carry with you to the range is vital.

All of your gear can be carried in a range bag, which means that you'll always be ready to head to the range and won't have to gather your gear each time you head out to shoot. Range bags don't have to be fancy; a child's backpack that is no longer being used, a gym bag, or a cloth grocery bag will work. A number of companies make durable and relatively inexpensive range bags that are designed to carry plenty of gear, and although a range bag is not necessary, it certainly makes transporting equipment to and from the range much easier. It's also important to have a means to safely secure your firearm when you are at home and when you are on the road. Companies like Hornady and Vaultek offer security options for traveling with firearms when those guns aren't concealed on your person.

I believe that a high-power flashlight is also an essential shooting accessory, particularly in the home. Good quality flashlights aren't cheap, but they are bright enough that you can have a clear field of view at night. Imagine you are asleep and you hear a loud crashing in another part of your home. As you get up to investigate, you immediately grab your firearm. If a flashlight is not nearby, you are virtually blind and you will have to stumble from one light switch to the next. Also, the brilliant blast of a powerful flashlight will oftentimes leave an intruder blind, giving the home-owner a major advantage in deadly situations.

Many defensive firearms have an accessory rail on the underside of the barrel for mounting items like auxiliary sights and flashlights. The problem with mounting a flashlight on this rail is that the gun is now controlling the direction of the light. You certainly don't want to find yourself pointing a loaded gun at your teenage daughter or your spouse, so I don't recommend mounting a flashlight on the firearm for beginning shooters. Instead, keep a powerful flashlight with fresh batteries close to your gun at all times. It's also a good idea to carry your flashlight with you to the range. Hold the flashlight in the weak hand while shooting. Some shooters prefer to bend their elbows at a 90-degree angle and rest the firearm on top of the wrist that is holding the flashlight. Another option is to hold the flashlight in the weak hand and position it next to the gun, stabilizing from the side.

### Optional Accessories

There are several additional items that find their way to the range with me, and although none of these items is essential, they are nice to have along when I am shooting.

Auxiliary sights are popular today, particularly laser sights. Laser sights are mounted on the gun and project a beam that strikes the target, producing a small red

▼ Carrying all of your gear in a range bag simplifies practice sessions. The author's range bag includes items such as cleaning kits, holsters, gun oil, ammunition, hearing and eye protection, targets, and a variety of other items that might be useful at the range.

dot where the bullet will strike, provided that the sight is properly aligned and the shooter is within a specific distance from the target. And while these sights aren't necessary, they are a popular option and many concealed carry guns are now offered with some type of auxiliary sights. Laser sights are the most common, and when properly aligned, laser sights make it easy to get on target quickly. Laser sights are sometimes mounted on the accessory rail below the barrel in semiautomatics. Other guns have lasers mounted on the side of the frame or integrated into the grip of the gun. Usually these laser sights are triggered by a pressure pad on the grip, so the laser turns on when the shooter grabs the grip. There are certain instances when lasers are an extremely valuable addition to a defensive pistol, primarily because they allow you to shoot accurately when you are in a compromised position and cannot bring the gun up to align the sights. Lasers are also particularly valuable in low-light conditions.

Laser sights can be effective, but they do have their drawbacks. First, some handguns with laser lights require purchasing a special holster for concealed carry. Lasers rarely fail and fall off or quit working, but under those circumstances the shooter must be able to use the iron sights effectively, and many shooters who have auxiliary laser sights on their guns don't practice with their iron sights regularly. Laser sights require adjustment, and these adjustments are usually simple to perform, oftentimes no more than turning a screw to adjust point of impact.

However, don't make the mistake of losing your shooting form because you've got a laser attached to the gun. Remember, in a life-or-death situation, you need repetition and practice to ensure that you can use your gun properly; shooters who use a laser sighting

▲ These laser sights project a beam from the rear sight. Shown here mounted on a Glock, these sights help improve low-light accuracy and allow for rapid sight acquisition. Photo courtesy of Laser Lyte.

system sometimes lose form, dropping the gun and losing proper position as they focus on finding the laser on the target. Don't forget to maintain proper form, balance, grip position, and stance when preparing to shoot. Lasers are effective, but they do require the shooter to practice as much as a shooter carrying a gun with iron sights. Lasers serve as a reference point when shooting; they don't exempt the shooter from learning and mastering proper technique.

Recently, more and more shooters carry concealed firearms with red dot optics, which are oftentimes mounted just in front of the rear sight on the gun. Today's red dot sights from companies like Vortex, Aimpoint, Trijicon, and others are sturdy, easy-to-adjust, and offer very long battery life. In many cases, elevated iron sights allow you to use either the red dot or the traditional sights simultaneously. Red dot sights are lightweight—many around an ounce—but they do create a larger profile and they can make concealment more difficult.

One optional accessory that many shooters find valuable is a good pair of leather or nylon shooting gloves. Constantly loading magazines, pulling slides, and cocking hammers can be a strain on the hands. In addition, gloves offer some level of protection against moving slides on semiautos and gunshot residue that is expelled as the shot is fired. Gloves also make it easier to practice in colder conditions that oftentimes drive other shooters inside. Choose a pair of gloves that fit you well and don't have loose fabric to get hung up in the moving parts of the gun. It's also important to choose shooting gloves that are thin enough to allow you to feel the trigger as you are preparing to fire. Shooting gloves are available from a variety of sources, and a good pair of gloves, particularly nylon gloves, can be purchased for a reasonable price.

▼ A competition shooter takes aim with a red dot sight made by Aimpoint. These sights are rarely seen on carry guns, but they are a favorite among target shooters. Photo courtesy of Yamil Sued.

◀ Ruger LC9 9mm compact semiauto with a laser mounted under the barrel. Photo courtesy of Sturm, Ruger & Co.

▶ These Meprolight self-illuminated night sights provide a clear sight picture even in the darkest conditions. Photo courtesy of Kimber America.

▼ A quality pair of shooting gloves keeps the hands warm and protected when shooting. They are available in leather or nylon.

▶ Range clothing, like this Tru-Spec shooting shirt, is designed with the shooter in mind. They have generous pockets and allow for plenty of mobility. Photo courtesy of Atlanco.

There are a variety of tactical shirts, pants, and vests that make life on the range simpler. Most of these clothes are designed specifically for shooting, and many of these garments are engineered with plenty of pockets and pouches so that you can store equipment that you aren't using. I like to wear a pair of tactical pants and a vest when shooting, though I certainly don't always have these items along. During extended periods on the range, these garments help keep me organized, and after a few shooting sessions I begin to commit to memory the location of all the gear I'm carrying in my pockets. My favorite pair of range pants

has a magazine-sized pocket located on the right leg just below the traditional pocket. Whenever I'm shooting a semiautomatic I can slip an extra loaded magazine into the magazine pocket, and when I've shot the first magazine I can release it, quickly replace it with the one in the magazine pocket, and return to shooting. In addition, these pockets help keep me organized and prevent me from leaving gear behind at the range, which I'm more than a little apt to do. One item that I recommend all shooters buy is a high-quality shooting belt, one with a "spine" that is strong enough to keep a heavy holster in place without sagging and will hold your pants tight when you draw. Companies like BLACKHAWK! offer stiff, durable shooting (sometimes called instructor) belts.

Speed loaders make reloading your gun fast and simple, and in the case of semiautos they take away a great deal of the strain that comes with depressing the magazine spring and loading one cartridge at a time. There are a variety of loading tools available for both revolvers and semiautos, and these accessories range in price from a few dollars to about $50. For revolvers, I like to use either half-moon clips, which hold three cartridges together at a time, or standard revolver speed loaders. Most speed loaders for revolvers allow you to carry enough cartridges to fill the cylinder; cartridges are held in a circular pattern by a metal or plastic ring. When you swing the cylinder of the revolver out, these cartridges slip into place (the design of the loader should match the revolver you are using) and all of the chambers can be loaded simultaneously. When the cartridges are in position in the chambers a turn of the dial on the rear of the speed loader releases all of the cartridges, filling all the chambers at once. Then you simply close the cylinder and you are ready to shoot.

Speed loaders for semiautos make reloads much simpler and reduce the strain and irritation on the fingers and hands that is associated with manually loading magazines. Semiauto magazines have an internal spring that pushes the cartridges up toward the chamber, and this spring remains under constant

▲ A reinforced instructor's belt is a must-have item since it will support the weight of your firearm and holster as well as magazine pouches.

pressure. For each cartridge that you load, you'll have to press down on the spring (which is located under a follower, or piece of plastic or metal, at the top of the magazine) and load the cartridges by pressing them down into the inside of the magazine until they click into place. This process is repeated over and over again until the magazine is full, and on magazines with heavy springs this process of loading cartridges can be very difficult and time consuming. Speed loaders greatly simplify this process, making it possible to reload magazines much more quickly and with less strain and effort. Most speed loaders for semiautos automatically depress the spring in the magazine, allowing the shooter to simply place another cartridge on the top of the stack in the magazine without having to press down on the magazine while trying to load each cartridge.

I like to carry a black marker or pen with me when I shoot as well. This allows me to write notes on the side of a target, usually notes about the load I was using, the point of hold for a particular gun (for example, "I was aiming at the center of the bull's-eye and held the sights just below the center for this group"), or the weather. I personally keep my targets on file, which helps me determine whether I'm shooting better or worse than I have been in the past and which cartridges shoot the best in my gun. Most shooters believe they'll remember this information without taking notes, but I find these notes on old targets to be very helpful. Recently, Rite-in-the-Rain began offering both notepads and targets that are waterproof, so you never have to worry about precipitation ruining the paper. For the new shooter, keeping track of old targets is a great way to track your improvement as you become more proficient with your gun. Besides, if I shoot a really fantastic group, I want to remember it!

▲ Tru-Spec offers these tactical pants, which have extra pockets designed for magazines and other gear. In addition, these pants are designed to allow the shooter to crawl and kneel to reach all shooting positions. Photo courtesy of Tru-Spec.

Though they're not common on concealed carry guns, some shooters prefer threaded barrels that allow them to shoot with a suppressor in place. Suppressors, or "silencers," don't actually make a gun silent but reduce noise levels by about 25 decibels so the noise produced is loud but not damaging. The Hearing Protection Act seeks to lessen requirements to purchase suppressors, but currently shooters must fill out a form and pay a tax ($200 at the current time) to purchase a suppressor.

## Indoor Practice with Lasers

As stated many times throughout this text, I believe that practice is essential to making you a better shooter, and once upon a time that meant firing hundreds or even thousands of rounds each week to maintain proper practice. In reality, though, most of us can't shoot our handguns 100 times a day. Most people don't have their own shooting range at their home where they can practice daily, so spending time shooting means packing up and heading to the nearest range. For many people this just isn't an option; work and family often leave little time each day for shooting. Also, shooting becomes an expensive pastime when you are firing hundreds of rounds each day.

In the last decade laser shooting practice has become popular with military and police, who use programs that simulate actual occurrences for weapons training. These simulations help officers and military personnel practice drawing and firing their weapons in a tense situation. The situation plays out on a large screen, oftentimes incorporating video from real scenes, and a laser is inserted in the barrel of the gun to indicate where the bullet strikes when the officer fires. This allows officers to train with their weapons in real-life situations in order to become better prepared in the event of a real shooting.

Laser training technology has become an important part of civilian firearms practice as well. Today, shooters can purchase a variety of lasers that fit into their firearms and produce a flash on the target when

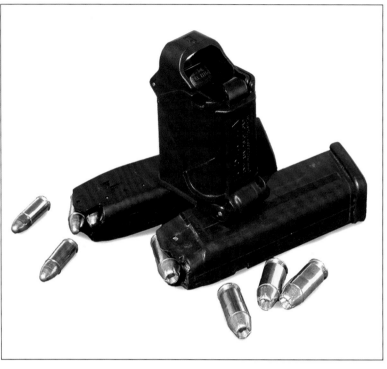

▲ The UpLula is a mechanical device that makes it easier and faster to load magazines. Photo courtesy of Uncle Mike's.

▲ Laser Lyte offers laser training cartridges that are a great way to practice at home. The cartridges are designed to fit in the chamber of a handgun, and each time the firing pin falls, a red dot appears on the target so you know where you would be hitting without actually firing live ammunition. Laser trainers are a fantastic way to improve your shooting skills. Photo courtesy of Laser Lyte.

the guns are fired. These lasers either fit in the barrel (this type of laser typically does not flash when fired but rather emits a beam constantly) or are designed to fit in the chamber of your gun.

Living in Ohio, there are plenty of days when the weather isn't conducive to going out and shooting, so I have to find a way to practice without leaving my home. I use a Laser Lyte practice tool, which looks like a 9mm Luger cartridge with a black rubber pad where the primer would normally be in the back of the cartridge. When I pull the trigger, my pistol's firing pin strikes the pad, firing the laser beam down the barrel. This way I can practice at home anytime I want to, choosing a target on the wall and pulling the trigger. The laser will flash and I will immediately know if I was high or low, left or right.

Laser training tools are a great way to improve your skills as a shooter, because you can fire hundreds of times a day inside the home without spending any money on ammunition. This laser practice does help the new shooter learn to manipulate the gun and align the sights, but perhaps the two most important skills that laser training teaches are trigger control and follow-through. When I have my laser in my gun I always practice trigger pull, trying to keep constant pressure on the trigger until the gun fires. In addition, laser training aids help me practice follow-through by keeping the sights aligned, pulling the trigger, and keeping the gun in place after the shot. Trigger control and follow-through are sometimes difficult to control when you are firing live ammunition because the recoil, muzzle blast, anticipation on the part of the shooter, and flinching combine to distract the shooter from the task at hand.

Laser sight trainers are effective and safe ways to train with your firearm at home. It is important to note that all firearms should be unloaded when practicing with these tools, and the laser training aid must be removed before live ammunition is loaded into the gun. If live ammunition is fired in a gun with a barrel-mounted laser training aid, then the barrel of the gun is likely to explode, causing serious injury. As with any aspect of shooting, laser training requires safe gun handling.

In addition to lasers that fit in the chamber of the gun, companies like Laser Lyte have also developed laser targets that allow the shooter to practice in the home. Available in a variety of styles, these targets record laser hits. This allows the shooter to go through the actions of aiming and firing hundreds of times a day without using a single cartridge. Firing "a laser sight" allows new shooters to practice with trigger control, sight alignment, grip, stance, and follow-through inside the home. If you can afford a laser practice system it will help you to become a better shooter.

▲ This is an "accessory rail" on the frame of a semiauto .45. This is where flashlights, lasers, and other accessories can be mounted. Photo courtesy of Kimber America.

# X. Taking Your First Shots

As a new shooter, it's easy to get overwhelmed at the range. You are still trying to remember a lot of information about safety, grip, stance, eye alignment, trigger control, and a host of other things. It is essential as a new shooter that you understand the process by which you will prepare yourself for those first shots, and some shooting instructors forget just how much information you are trying to absorb, all while being held accountable for safely handling the gun you've just learned to shoot.

Having a solid understanding about the function of firearms is critical. This chapter will walk you through the basics of taking those first shots, and in the next chapter we will take a more in-depth look at practice and drills to make you a better shooter.

## Eye Dominance: Step One to Successful Shooting

Understanding eye dominance is critical to being a successful shooter, yet many people do not know which of their eyes is most dominant. As predatory animals with our eyes set close together in the front of our head, humans have stereoscopic vision. This helps us determine distance and helps us understand dimension. During most of our daily activities we are actually seeing objects in concert between our left and our right eyes, our brain processing what we see as a combination of the image from the right and left eyes. This ability is important to help us understand depth of field. Just as humans are almost exclusively right- or left-handed, there is also a dominant eye. In reality, we observe an object with our dominant eye and our weak eye gives us a sense of dimension, or how far away the object is. This is important, because if both eyes focused on an image and sent the message to our brain simultaneously, we'd have double vision.

Eye dominance is also important when shooting, as we only use one eye (our dominant eye) to align the sights of a gun. Many people share eye/hand dominance, so the side of a person's dominant (strong)

▼ To determine the dominant eye, the shooter can focus on an object at some distance, put the hands up like this so that the object is in the opening between the hands, and slowly bring the hands back to the face while keeping the object in the center of the opening. The hands will come back to one of the eyes, and this is the dominant eye.

hand matches his or her dominant eye. I am right-hand dominant and right-eye dominant, so I hold a gun in my right hand and align the sights with my right eye. My wife Bethany, on the other hand, is right-handed and left-eye dominant, a condition known as *cross-dominance*. Because the shooter naturally holds the gun in his or her strong hand, cross-dominant shooters are often frustrated because they have trouble aligning the sights. Since the right-handed shooter brings the gun up to align with his or her right eye, a left-eye dominant, right-eyed shooter will see two sets of sights, and from a proper stance their dominant eye will actually be focusing on the gun from the side rather than directly behind. Cross-dominant shooters thus may have trouble hitting the target, shooting far from the center of the target as they struggle to align their eyes. But Bethany, like many other shooters, has learned to properly deal with her cross-dominance, and she is now an excellent shot with a handgun.

Determining eye dominance is the first step toward accurate shooting. There are several methods, but two of the most popular involve focusing on an object to determine which of your eyes is strongest.

Method 1: Choose a fixed object at least ten feet away from you. Without thinking, raise your hands, overlapping them and creating a gap between your thumbs and index fingers through which you can see the object. Extend your arms and place the object in the teardrop-shaped gap between your overlapping hands. Slowly bring your hands back toward your face, keeping the object inside the teardrop the entire time as you move your hands closer to your face. Keeping the object visible in the gap between your hands, slowly draw your hands closer to your face. The gap in your hands will automatically travel to your dominant eye.

Method 2: Choose a stationary object across the room. Analog clocks work well, and they are simple to use. Without thinking, point your index finger at the number six on the clock so that the tip of your index finger is located just below the number. Holding your finger in that position, close one eye and then the other. When the dominant eye is open, your finger should remain in the original position, located just below the number six on the clock. When your weak eye is open and the dominant eye is closed, your finger will suddenly move away from the correct position.

If your strong eye and strong hand are the same, then you will simply use that eye and that hand to shoot with. However, if you are cross-dominant, you'll have to find a way to compensate. For many new shooters, the simplest way to overcome this is to learn to shoot using the opposite hand. Because Bethany was a new shooter, she learned to shoot left-handed. It was slightly more difficult, but when the gun (a shotgun in her case) came to her shoulder, her eye automatically focused on the sight and she was ready to fire. Learning to shoot with the same hand as your dominant eye is not too difficult if you are a new shooter. However, many cross-dominant shooters have spent years compensating for the fact that their strong hands and strong eyes are in conflict.

## Grip

How you hold the firearm may seem like a minor detail, but the way in which you grip the gun has a tremendous impact on your success as a shooter. Improper grip can lead to a whole host of issues, from inaccurate shooting to wrist fatigue to recoil and even failure for the gun to function properly with semiautos. Proper grip is one of the keys to good shooting.

First, place the webbing between the thumb and index finger of your shooting hand firmly against the top part of the pistol grip. A low grip can affect accuracy and makes recoil harder to manage. By holding the gun high on the grip you are better able to mitigate the effects of recoil. The shooting hand should be roughly vertical, and the knuckle of the thumb and the index finger of the shooting hand should be about the same height. The fingers should be wrapped tightly around the grip but should not be squeezed so hard that the gun begins to shake. Prior to firing, the shooter should have the index (trigger) finger outside the trigger guard.

Most shooters employ a thumbs-forward grip when firing semiauto handguns. This means that both of the thumbs are on the weak side (the left side of the firearm for right-handed shooters) and both thumbs are pointed forward. This offers a secure hold on the firearm and allows the shooter better muzzle control, but you must be certain to keep your thumbs below the slide to prevent malfunctions or injuries.

Revolver non-shooting hand grip is slightly different. With medium- and large-frame revolvers like the Ruger GP100 and Smith & Wesson 686, there's enough room

▲ Though .22s like this Ruger are perfect for beginning shooters, it is important to learn how to operate the firearm. In the case of this particular handgun, the magazine release button is located just behind the trigger. There are two levers located just below the slide. The rear lever turns the safety on and off. The smaller front lever is the slide catch, which holds the slide back when the gun is not in use. Photo courtesy of Sturm, Ruger, & Co.

on the frame so that you can keep both thumbs on the same side and away from the cylinder. On small revolvers like Kimber's K6S, Ruger's SP101, or Smith & Wesson J-Frames, you'll want to wrap the thumb of the non-shooting hand around the back of the shooting hand so that it is secure and out of the way.

## Extended Stances

There are two main stance types for pistol shooting: the **isosceles stance** and the **Weaver stance**. Both are stable and practical, and as a shooter it is valuable to know both stance types even though you may only ever shoot from the stance with which you are the most comfortable.

We will begin by discussing the **isosceles stance**, which is so named because, when viewed from above, the shooter appears in the shape of an isosceles triangle. The isosceles stance provides a solid platform that allows for accurate shooting. Target shooters tend to stand more upright when shooting from this position, but for self-defense shooting most instructors teach the following method, which is also sometimes referred to as a"defensive isosceles stance."

To position the shooter for the isosceles stance, we begin by positioning the feet shoulder width apart with the toes pointing toward the target. The majority of the shooter's weight should not be on the heels but rather on the balls of the feet, and the shooter should always feel comfortable, not awkward or unbalanced. The knees should be slightly bent, and the upper body should remain slightly forward. One of the problems that most new shooters have with the isosceles stance is finding the proper knee bend. Your knees should never be locked, nor should you be squatting. Weight should remain on the balls of the feet, and the shooter should remain comfortable.

▲ The shooter's knees should be parallel and the knees should be slightly bent when shooting in the isosceles position.

Grip the gun in your shooting hand, allowing the rear portion of the grip to hit against the ball of your thumb the way you would hold the spray nozzle of a garden hose. Wrap the fingers firmly around the grip, and index your shooting finger on the frame above the trigger guard. Wrap your weak hand around your strong hand so that you have a firm hold on the gun. Having a "firm grip" does not mean squeezing the gun as hard as you can, since having stiff muscles will make shooting accurately more difficult. Your grip should be secure and solid without trying to squeeze the gun. When the gun is properly gripped, extend the gun out from the center of the chest. The effect should make it appear that you are being pulled by a rope, with both arms extended out directly in front of the body at about chin height. The arms should remain slightly bent (never locked), and the whole body—shoulders, hips, knees, and feet—should remain square and should be facing the target.

New shooters have a tendency to hold the gun too low and drop their heads to align the sights. This is a mistake. The gun should come to *you*, and you should not have to go to the gun. Keep the chin up and remain focused on the target with the arms still bent. When you are ready to fire, bring the gun up, extend the arms directly forward as though being towed by a rope (always remembering to keep the elbows bent), and make the gun come to your line of sight. Learning to shoot with your eyes focused on your target is essential for defensive shooting, when it is critical that you maintain visual contact with the person who is threatening you. In such cases you don't want to have to look down at your sights and crane your neck to go into shooting position, and if you practice the isosceles stance correctly, the gun should come directly and comfortably into the line of sight. As with any shooting stance, it is important to remain consistent and steady while shooting so that you will improve accuracy.

The other common type of stance is referred to as the **Weaver stance**, which is named for expert pistol shooter Jack Weaver from California. In the 1950s, other shooters began to take note of the way Weaver stood when he shot and began to mimic him. Since that time, the Weaver stance has arguably become the most popular shooting position and the method most often taught in defensive shooting classes.

The Weaver stance looks very different from the isosceles stance. To begin with, the feet are not square with the shoulders. Instead, the foot that is opposite of the shooting hand (for example, I shoot right-handed, so my left foot) is extended forward, usually so that the heel of the forward foot is aligned with the toe of the rear foot. The feet should remain shoulder width apart, and the toes of the lead foot should be pointed at the target while the toes of the rear foot are angled 45 degrees. The shooting arm is relatively straight but the elbow is not locked. The support arm is bent 45 degrees. The majority (about 70 percent) of the weight should be shifted to the forward leg, and the front knee should be bent, which will result in the upper body leaning slightly forward. This is ideal, because you have your weight and balance shifted slightly toward the target and steadied. If you draw a line from the heel of the front foot to the head, the line should be perpendicular to the ground, with your chin located almost directly above the heel of your front foot. Most shooters have a tendency to exaggerate the position, bending their knees too much or leaning too far forward.

### Checklist for the Isosceles Stance:

Feet: Feet should be shoulder width apart and pointed at the target, weight on the balls of the feet.

Knees: Knees should be bent slightly; shooter should feel comfortable and balanced.

Torso: The upper body should lean slightly into the target, though the shooter must be comfortable and balanced.

Shoulders: Shoulders should be squared to the target.

Arms: Arms are extended straight away from the body, elbows slightly bent.

Hands: Shooting hand grips the guns firmly, other hand should be wrapped around the shooting hand to provide support.

Head: The chin should be up, eyes on the target. The shooter should not have to drop the head excessively to get on target.

When viewed from above, the isosceles stance forms a triangle: The shoulders are the base and the arms are the legs.

▲ The isosceles position is so named because the shooter's shoulders and arms form a triangle, as seen here from above. The strong hand grips the gun, the weak hand grips the strong hand, and the hands are kept clear of the front of the cylinder on a revolver or the slide on a semiauto.

▲ The gun has come up and is held well by the strong hand, but the shooter must be aware of the position of the thumb. Getting the thumb too close to the slide can result in injury.

Just like the isosceles stance, the Weaver stance should feel comfortable and balanced.

Unlike the isosceles stance, in which the shooter's shoulders are parallel, in the Weaver stance the strong arm is extended fully and the elbow is only slightly bent. The gun is gripped firmly and lifted into position so that the head does not have to drop to align the sights. The nonshooting arm is bent, and the weak hand is wrapped around the strong hand and grip to provide a stable platform. The strong shoulder will be slightly farther back than the weak shoulder, and the weak elbow will be bent more than the strong arm. The head remains the same as with the isosceles stance and should not be lowered to meet the sights of the gun. Rather, the gun should be brought up into position so that the shooter's head does not have to move down very much. The gun hand presses the gun forward while the weak hand pulls the gun back toward the shooter, and this push and pull (known as isometric pressure) helps keep the gun stable and reduces the effects of recoil. The Weaver stance should be comfortable for the shooter and should provide a steady enough platform for accurate shooting at a wide range of distances. Since the arms are bent, the gun is closer to the body and, as result, the sights appear larger. This allows for rapid target acquisition for close-range

shooting. Additionally, the Weaver stance offers more torso movement than the isosceles does.

## Other Shooting Positions

The isosceles and Weaver stances are the most common methods of shooting a handgun while standing, but they are not the only ways to practice. Oftentimes shooters will tell me that they simply can't get their guns to shoot accurately, and that the guns seem to be low and left on one shot and high and right on the next. If a gun delivers consistent groups (let's say that all of your shots are low and left), then there is a level of consistency and that can be addressed. However, if there seems to be no pattern to the shots, then it is pretty hard to assess the problem. I've heard many new shooters say that their guns "just aren't accurate." In a case like this, I like to test the gun's ability to shoot to a consistent point of impact, but the problem is that many new shooters aren't consistent enough in either the Weaver or isosceles stances to get reliable results about their guns' true points of impact. All they have are papers full of scattered holes.

There are two shooting positions that will help better determine your gun's point of impact, and that is because these two positions are more stable than either the isosceles or Weaver stance. The first stable platform

▲ The fundamentals of the Weaver stance: The shooter places the leg opposite the shooting hand forward and places the majority of the weight on that foot. Feet remain shoulder width apart, the strong hand brings the gun up in front of the face, and the weak hand supports the strong hand.

## Checklist for the Weaver Stance:

Feet: The foot that is the opposite of the strong hand should be placed forward so that the heel of the front foot is in line with the toe of the rear foot. Feet should remain shoulder width apart. Rear (shooting-side) foot should be angled 45 degrees.

Knees: Knees should be slightly bent with the majority of the weight on the front foot.

Posture: There should be a slight forward lean—the chin should be directly above the front knee.

Head: The head should drop very little when aligning the sights; the chin should remain forward and should not be tucked to the chest.

Strong Arm: The gun should be gripped firmly and the strong arm extended directly in front of the face. The elbow should remain slightly bent. The strong arm pushes the gun slightly forward as the weak hand pulls back, creating isometric balance.

Weak Arm: The weak arm supports the gun, so the weak hand should grip the firing hand. The elbow should be bent more than the elbow of the strong arm, at roughly 45 degrees. Traditional Weaver stance has the elbow pointed almost straight down, although some shooters raise the elbow slightly so that the weak arm is more parallel with the ground, though the weak arm should never be completely parallel to the ground.

Shoulders: Unlike the isosceles position, the shoulders are not square. The strong arm shoulder will be slightly farther back than the weak side shoulder.

▲ In this photo we see a shooter who is leaning too far back. A slight lean forward is generally preferred, and the shooter should be comfortable. This shooter is unbalanced.

▲ Here we see a photo of a shooter who is "letting the gun shoot him." In other words, the shooter's head is going to the gun instead of making the gun come up and align with the shooter's eye.

used to determine point of impact is **benchrest shooting**. Shooting from a benchrest requires the shooter to sit down at a stable platform (usually a table) and to rest the gun firmly while shooting. Benchrest shooting is not a position you will use in a defensive situation, but it is valuable to have a very stable platform from which to shoot your gun and determine where the bullets are striking.

Some shooters prefer to use their own rest made from piled towels or old pieces of clothing, but there are a number of very good pistol rests available that are stable, solid, and engineered for benchrest shooting. In addition, you can purchase many of these rests for a reasonable rate.

When shooting from a bench, it is important to be seated comfortably and be able to easily reach the gun and the rest. Some shooters stabilize their arms by resting them on bags, but this is not absolutely necessary. Place the gun on the rest. Pistols should have

their barrels firmly seated on the rest, and semiautos should have the bottom of the slide placed on the rest. The gun should be steady, and the sight picture should remain consistent.

Another option that provides a solid shooting platform is the **seated position**. Though it is not a position regularly taught in concealed carry classes, the seated position is very stable and allows shooters to get more consistent groups. For this position, shooters sit down on the ground, legs drawn up so that the knees are even with the shoulders. The shooter then rests the forearm on the knees and grips the gun as they would for the isosceles stance. Shooting in the seated position is comfortable and stable, but you must be sure that you have a tall enough backstop to ensure that the bullet is stopped. Targets should be placed below the line of sight of the gun so that the bullet does not travel up into the target without hitting a backstop, which is dangerous.

There are a number of various techniques (and even names) for the one-handed extended shooting position, and while it's not as stable as the previously-discussed two-handed positions, it may be necessary in some circumstances. First, the hand extends the firearm straight away from the body and aligns the sights with the target. The arm should be straight but not completely locked. Most commonly, the body is turned at a 45-degree angle and the strong side (shooting-hand) foot is extended one foot or more ahead of the weak side foot. The strong foot points at the target, and the weak side foot is angled at 45 degrees like the body. Leaning forward and placing more weight on the strong side foot will help control muzzle rise and recoil and will allow you to shoot more quickly. The non-shooting hand should be made into a fist and pressed against the center of the chest, both to keep it from interfering with the shooting hand and to aid in close-range defense (i.e., throwing a punch) if needed.

## Ready Positions

There are a number of ready positions, and different instructors and texts use various names for them. Here's a rundown of the four most common—and useful—ready positions. Remember: your finger is indexed and off the trigger in all of these.

In the high ready position, the gun is held a foot or less in front of the body with both elbows bent and the muzzle of the firearm pointed up and away from the shooter. This is a compact position, yet the muzzle remains pointed in a safe direction.

▲ The high ready position shows the gun held a foot or less ahead of the shooter with the muzzle pointed up and away.

Compact ready requires the shooter to bend the elbows and keep the muzzle pointed at the target while the gun is held close to the body. Since the gun is still pointed at the target, this position still allows you to engage attackers, and the "compressed" nature means the gun is easy to retain if an attacker appears at close range. When an innocent person crosses in front of the shooter, they will be in the line of fire when the gun is in this position, so you must be aware of your surroundings. If a bystander crosses your path, you can quickly transition into the Sul position to keep the muzzle pointed away from them.

Low ready is a very basic position in which the gun's muzzle is lowered and points at the ground in front

▲ One-handed shooting is rarely practiced, but it can be valuable in a defensive shooting situation. The arm extends the firearm and the weight of the body shifts forward to manage recoil. The non-shooting hand is pressed against the chest.

of the shooter with the arms still extended. There's a modified low ready position in which the muzzle isn't angled as steeply downward, and this allows the shooter to raise the gun more quickly and get on target.

The Sul position is relatively new and was developed as a means to prevent accidentally pointing the muzzle of a handgun at teammates or innocent people when you are in a crowd of people. In Sul, the non-shooting hand is placed palm against the abdomen with the thumb pointing up. The handgun is held pointed downward and slightly (roughly 20 degrees) away from and in front of the shooter, and the shooting finger is indexed. A practical application of this position for civilian shooters would include a deadly shooting in a crowded area where you wanted to maintain a safe

▲ The Sul position requires the shooter to turn the gun so the muzzle is pointed down and away and the support hand rests behind the firearm. This is a good position to utilize when moving. Notice the shooter's finger is off the trigger.

muzzle direction to prevent pointing the firearm at innocent people, specifically while moving.

## Sight Alignment

Handgun sights vary, but the majority of these sights include a notch or U-shaped rear sight and a post or dot front sight. To correctly and accurately shoot a gun with these sights, the front sight should be aligned so that the front sight is positioned evenly within the rear sights with the top of the rear and front sights at the same height. Use the dominant eye to align the sights. Many cross-dominant shooters (their shooting hands and dominant eyes are opposite) find it difficult to shoot because they naturally want to use their strong hands to shoot, yet they have trouble aligning the sights properly because their dominant eyes aren't aligned with the sights. For cross-dominant shooters there are a few options. First, they can learn to shoot with their weak hands, and after a good deal of practice most cross-dominant shooters become comfortable shooting with their weak hands. The other option is to close their dominant eyes so that they don't interfere with their sight picture. Closing one eye is not ideal because it limits peripheral vision by as much as forty degrees and requires that a shooter does this every time; in a tense self-defense situation, the shooter must remember to close the dominant eye, which is difficult to do in a dangerous situation. This is why the best option is to teach cross-dominant shooters to effectively shoot with their weak hands.

Because humans have a narrow band of focus when looking at an object, it is impossible for us to focus our vision on the rear sight, front sight, and target simultaneously. For this reason, it is best to focus on the front sight, which allows you to align the rear sight and keep your place on the target with your peripheral vision. New shooters sometimes have difficulty because they are trying to focus on the rear sight, then the front sight, then the target, bouncing their points of focus between the three different objects. Practice aligning the rear and front sight while maintaining direct focus on the front sight. When focused on the front sight you will still be able to determine position on the target. At track and field meets hurdlers must do the same thing. If you watch world-class hurdlers, they run the length of the track with their heads up,

▲ Learning to shoot a group is important. By shooting several shots while aiming at the same point, you can assess the issue. In this case the gun is shooting high and left, which can be caused by misaligned sights or "heeling" the gun in anticipation of the shot. Here the responsibility was with the shooter, and after some coaching on trigger control and follow-through, the groups moved closer to center.

▲ These Meprolight sights are properly aligned on target. The rear and front targets are lined up and the center of the front dot is in the center of the target. Focus should remain on the front sight. Photo courtesy of Kimber America.

focused on the finish. It would seem that they should look down at each hurdle, but this would slow them down greatly. Instead, they focus down the track and use their peripheral vision to track the hurdle they are approaching. Shooters have to function in much the same way as a hurdler. Since you can't focus on everything at once, you have to have a focal point and rely on your eyes to help you align what is not entirely in focus (the rear sight and target) with what you have decided to focus your attention on (the front sight).

### First Shot

For many (probably most) first-time shooters, the initial shot they take with a gun is very intimidating. After all, they have to remember range commands, safety rules, grip and stance, sight alignment, and a host of other things. Plus, they have no idea how loud or how much recoil a gun will produce, and they are responsible for the path of the bullet. That's enough to make anyone nervous, and when the stakes are as high as they are when shooting a firearm, there are plenty of reasons to be a bit overwhelmed.

▲ The shooter has a solid grip, the gun is aligned with the target, and the shooter's head is not dropping down to meet the gun. The arms are slightly bent and the wrists are locked, which will help reduce the impact of recoil.

When you take your first shots, remember that safety is the first priority. No matter how accurately you shoot, being safe is your number one job as a shooter. Keep the muzzle pointed in a safe direction, and keep your finger indexed before you are ready to shoot. Take a moment to double check that you have your hearing and vision protection on.

When you are ready to fire and the range is hot, align the sights where you want to hit the target. In most cases, you will be aligning your sights so that the bottom of the front sight is just below what you are trying to hit, which is also referred to as the "pumpkin on a post" position because the target (usually a round circle on a bull's-eye) and front sight resemble a pumpkin sitting atop a fence post. You may have to adjust your sights (if possible) or aim higher or lower. My own concealed carry gun, a 9mm semiauto, requires me to position the top of the front sight so that it just covers the top of the point on the target I'm trying to hit.

### Trigger Control

Once you are in position with a good grip on the gun and the sights aligned, move your finger to the trigger. One of the most important aspects of being a good shooter is trigger control: the ability to apply steady, even trigger control until the shot breaks. This helps greatly improve accuracy.

Triggers vary greatly between different types and brands of guns. For instance, double action–only pistols and revolvers typically have a long, heavy trigger pull, in part because the trigger is cocking and firing the gun and in part as a safety measure to prevent accidental discharges. Single action revolvers and semiautos with cocked hammers, on the other hand, have very light trigger pulls. Double action revolvers and semiautos have a heavier trigger pull in double action mode because, as with DAO guns, the trigger is performing two tasks, but when the hammer is manually cocked on a DA firearm, then the trigger pull is much lighter.

Regardless of whether you have an SA, DA, or DAO gun, the principles of proper trigger control are the same, and learning to properly manage the trigger takes practice. Trigger pull should be as steady and as smooth as possible, with the shooter applying slowly increasing pressure in a consistent rearward direction until the trigger breaks and the gun fires.

When the gun goes off, remain in position, holding the front sight on the center of the target. This is referred to as "follow-through," and it is an important element of other types of shooting sports as well. The best skeet shooters, for instance, swing the barrels of their guns past the clay target as it flies through the air, press the trigger, and continue swinging the barrels

◄ Trigger control is important to accurate shooting. The finger should be contacting the trigger in front of the last joint, and the pull should be steady and straight backward.

even after the target is broken. This may seem odd, but it forces the shooter to learn to maintain a consistent position throughout the duration of the shot. Even though it seems like the trigger breaks and the bullet strikes the target simultaneously, it is possible to move the gun barrel as the trigger breaks and pull the shot away from the center of the target. Shooters who have a tendency to shoot and immediately drop the gun to look at the target sometimes notice that they have trouble shooting accurately. Oftentimes they are actually moving the gun during the process of shooting. Align your sight picture, focus on the front sight, pull the trigger smoothly and consistently, and follow through after the shot by repositioning the front sight in the center of the target.

It sounds like a lot to remember, and for a first time shooter it is. Putting these steps together requires repetition and practice. When you begin shooting, don't fire long strings of cartridges. Instead, shoot once, regroup and refocus, and shoot again.

As a new shooter, one of the best ways to learn to shoot correctly is to have someone read those six steps to you while you are shooting one cartridge at a time. Oftentimes it is best to stop between each shot and go through every step again. I like to give the six verbal commands as shooters learn the process: safety, stance, grip, sights, trigger control, and follow-through. Take your time and repeat the steps again and again. For the first series of shots, a new shooter is typically very nervous, but consistency and repetition help calm nerves. The more often the new shooter hears these commands over and over again, the faster he or she will learn to shoot properly.

## Managing Recoil

Some longtime shooters will tell you that recoil isn't something to worry about, that you must simply learn to deal with the punch that power handguns produce. Some shooters actually say that they enjoy recoil, or they advise new shooters to suck it up. They think you should take your beatings and go about your business, since that's just part of being a shooter.

That's nonsense. The best shooters in the world understand that recoil is the enemy, and the cumulative effects of recoil can affect your shooting, causing physical pain or flinching each time that you pull the

## Checklist for Firing a Gun

1. Safety: Keep the muzzle pointed downrange. Check that eye and ear protection is on, finger is indexed, and you are certain that you have an effective backstop to safely stop bullets. If you are on the range, the range master should have declared the range is hot and that shooters may begin firing.
2. Stance: You should either be in the isosceles or Weaver stance, you should feel balanced and comfortable with your elbows bent, and your head should not drop down too much to align the sights. Lean slightly forward.
3. Grip: Hold the gun firmly and be sure that the gun is secure.
4. Sights: Align sights correctly on the target.
5. Trigger Control: Begin the shooting process by applying pressure with the last joint of the shooting finger, consistently increasing pressure on the trigger until it breaks.
6. Follow-Through: When the gun goes off, the muzzle will jump up with recoil. Try to hold the gun on target so that the front sight is aligned.

trigger. Recoil should be managed so that it doesn't interfere with your shooting sessions. Competitive shooters are always fighting against recoil fatigue, which develops after several hundred (or thousand) shots in a single day.

Recoil is generated by the energy produced when the shot is fired. Recoil for big bore rifles and shotguns places strain on the shoulder and cheek, because the gun is being driven backwards into the shooter's shoulder and then upward into the face. With handguns, recoil energy is transferred back into the shooter's wrists and the muzzle flips upward. This recoil, along with muzzle blast, can lead to flinching. Flinching is the habit of a shooter bracing just before the shot and the result is poor accuracy.

There are several ways to prevent excessive recoil and the resultant flinching. First, don't buy a gun that has heavy recoil if you are a beginning shooter. Guns chambered in .357 Magnum, .45 ACP, and .38 Super produce substantially more recoil than less powerful

▲ This is an incorrect "low ready" position. The arms are locked at the elbows and the shooter will have to swing the gun up to aim. Instead, keep the arms bent and the gun closer to the body with the muzzle pointed down and ahead of the shooter. This way, if you do encounter a threat, you simply extend the arms rather than swinging them up.

▼ This is a better "low ready." Note that the muzzle is pointed in a safe direction but the shooter holds the gun close to himself. In case of danger, the shooter extends the arms straight ahead and fires.

calibers like the .380 Auto, .32 H&R Magnum, and 9mm Luger. That's not to say that relatively new shooters can't get comfortable with larger caliber guns, but they are more likely to cause a flinch.

Proper grip and stance are essential when shooting a handgun. You must have a firm grip on the gun, and the wrists should be roughly parallel to the barrel of the gun (not bent). Your grip on the gun should be as though you were firmly shaking someone's hand, with the top rear portion of the grip striking between the thumb and index finger of the shooting hand. Follow-through becomes critically important to mitigate recoil. When you fire and immediately refocus the sight on the target, your mind becomes accustomed to maintaining a proper sight picture and keeping the gun in position. This causes you to concentrate on keeping the wrist solid and helps control the gun. Do not overcompensate by dropping the front sight every time you shoot, which will result in a consistently low group.

There are a variety of recoil-reducing devices on the market. The most common method for reducing recoil and muzzle flip in pistols is called "porting." Porting involves drilling small holes in the sides of the barrel so that the gases that push the bullet down the barrel can escape through the ports. While muzzle ports are effective at reducing recoil, it should also be known that most ported barrels have increased muzzle blast, which makes the firearm much louder.

The key to managing recoil lies in knowing when to stop shooting, either because your wrists and hands are beginning to suffer from recoil fatigue or because you are in pain. As a shooter, a gun can push you with recoil, but it should never *hurt*. If you are in pain, then stop shooting. In addition, it is important to wear hearing protection anytime you shoot, because the intense muzzle blast of a firearm is registered as pain by your brain. Shooting without hearing protection can cause permanent hearing damage and often leads to flinching to avoid the painful noise generated by the gun. If shooting is unpleasant, then you won't practice, and if you don't practice, this book is of little value to you. Incidentally, so is the gun you carry!

Learning to properly manage recoil makes shooting more fun and allows you to shoot for long periods of time without developing a flinch.

## Targets

As mentioned earlier, you need to be certain that you have a proper backstop before shooting. Paper targets are the most common option and the most economical, and you can easily mount them to a backing board (or, if you don't have a board, a cardboard box in front of the backstop will serve well, too). Birchwood Casey, Champion, and other companies offer a wide selection of targets.

Shooting steel targets is also popular, especially among competition shooters. And while it may seem strange to shoot a bullet at metal, proper steel targets—when used with the right ammunition and when fired at from a safe distance—can be a lot of fun. Plus, you won't need to replace paper targets as you fire. Steel plates are available from companies like Champion, and steel is rated for performance (AR500 or AR550 steel are the most common options). But, as stated, follow the steel target manufacturer's guidelines so that you won't damage the steel. This usually means matching the right steel for the caliber/ammunition you're going to shoot, standing at a safe distance away from the target, and replacing old, broken, or dimpled steel.

# XI. Range Etiquette and Proper Practice

## The Importance of Practice

*I*n the mid-1950s, educational psychologist Benjamin Bloom developed a learning model that included what he referred to as the "three domains of learning." Bloom's theory was that there were three distinct areas of learning and our ability to understand and remember information was related to these three domains, which he referred to as *cognitive, psychomotor,* and *affective.* Simply stated, Bloom believed that our level of comprehension of a subject depended upon how much information we knew about the topic (cognitive), our mindset and attitude about learning (affective), and our coordination and muscle memory (psychomotor).

Bloom's cognitive theory of domains remains one of the cornerstones of educational philosophy. Almost seventy years after the introduction of the three domains of learning, educators and coaches still rely on combining these domains to effectively teach important skills to students and athletes. Basketball players have to have the knowledge to execute a play, the motor skills to make a three-point shot, and the confidence necessary to take that shot. Likewise, educators try to teach basic cognitive skills and encourage their students to apply these skills (such as in a science lab), all while engaging their students and promoting an atmosphere of learning.

Consider what would happen if that basketball player, despite an in-depth understanding of the principles of the game, had never picked up a basketball. Imagine that the student, despite a thorough understanding of the concepts of mathematics, had never picked up a pencil and learned to write. What if you bought a new entertainment center for your home, and after reading the detailed assembly instructions, you realized you didn't know how to use a screwdriver? Motor develop-

▼ A student receives shooting instruction from a coach. Having a patient coach who understands the principles of shooting provides you with the basis you need to become proficient with a firearm. Practice is extremely important. Photo courtesy of the National Shooting Sports Foundation

▲ Students at a "First Shots" seminar learn the basics of handgun shooting. Good coaches help teach new shooters safety, demonstrate range etiquette, and make them far better shooters. Photo courtesy of the National Shooting Sports Foundation.

ment is a critical component of learning, and the same is true when learning to shoot a gun. This is especially true in cases of self-defense shooting, when there is tremendous strain on the shooter.

During my years on a college shooting team we practiced weekly, shooting between 100 and 500 shots per week, because we knew that repetitive practice helped us build the motor skills necessary to succeed in competition. The shots were all the same, but that repetitive motor development allowed shooting to become natural and automatic, so that when we were in a match and our conscious minds were overwhelmed with the stress of competition, our motor skills took over. The repetition of practicing the same shots again and again made it possible for us to succeed.

What was at stake during these collegiate competitions? Not much. At the bigger shoots you might bring home a plaque or trophy if you won, and at small duel meets you might get nothing more than a pat on the back and a blurry photo of yourself in the back of the college newspaper.

One afternoon, I was going through my gun safe and I had all of my firearms laid out on a table as I prepared to clean them. The shotgun I'd competed with in college lay there, the bluing worn and the stock scratched from hundreds of hours on the range. Beside it lay the .38 Special I carried concealed, a gun that looked very much like it had the day I'd picked it up at the local gun dealer. I figured my shotgun, which I used to compete in weekend shoots, had had about a hundred times as many shots fired through it as the revolver, which I relied upon to save my life in critical situations. I realized I wasn't any more prepared to save my own life with that gun than a guy who'd shot a shotgun a couple times was to win the national collegiate trap championship.

Learning to shoot a gun is no different than learning to play basketball, assemble an entertainment center, or solve a calculus problem. You have to have a conceptual understanding of the material. This is Bloom's cognitive domain, the "instruction manual." But you must also have the corresponding psychomotor skills necessary to apply what you have learned.

This text is designed to serve as a reference to help you develop your shooting skills. In the book I explain how to clear a jammed action, clean a firearm, select a holster, safely store your gun, and so forth. In this chapter, I will also provide you with ways in which to practice your shooting skills. However, motor skill development depends on you. To be a good shooter, you have to learn how to shoot correctly and shoot often.

By reading the text and practicing your shooting, you will have covered two of Bloom's three domains. The last domain, the affective domain, examines your mental attitude toward the subject matter. You have to develop confidence in your skill as a shooter, and this requires an understanding of the material in this book and time on the shooting range. It also requires that you have the right gun (one that fits your hand correctly, functions reliably, doesn't generate excessive recoil, and is a gun you feel comfortable shooting) and that you have the time to spend on the range.

▼ Students examine their groups at a "First Shots" seminar. It is important to learn to assess your groups to determine whether or not you are shooting correctly and, if you aren't, how to fix the problem. This is where a professional's help becomes valuable. Photo courtesy of the National Shooting Sports Foundation.

▶ Practice frequently until you are comfortable with your firearm and you have committed the movements associated with shooting to muscle memory. Photo courtesy of the National Shooting Sports Foundation.

The good news is that if you learn the material presented in this book and spend at least three days a week practicing with your firearm on the range, you'll be better prepared for a deadly confrontation than the majority of concealed carry license holders. You'll also stand a much better chance of surviving in a defensive situation. Very few shooters (including the criminals you're defending yourself against) spend adequate time on the range, but those who do have a distinct advantage in times of crisis.

One of the most frequent comments I hear from new shooters after their first day on the range is that they didn't expect shooting to be so much *fun*. Indeed, shooting can be fun. Shooting can be challenging and exciting when you are comfortable on the range, and practicing often makes you a better shot.

## A Perspective on Practice

A few years ago, a nightly news channel presented a program about what might happen if college students were allowed to carry concealed weapons in class, a staged event to challenge the theory that armed students would provide a deterrent to violent crime on college campuses. Students received several hours of basic firearms training under the guise that they were learning about armed self-defense.

Several minutes later, an assailant entered the room and began firing, sending students into a frenzy as he aimed a series of loud shots into the fleeing student body. The professor was "hit" and slouched down, presumably injured or killed, and the students who had professed to be experienced with firearms were struggling to draw their guns from their waistbands. When they did begin firing, there were shots scattered across

the room, hitting innocent bystanders and failing to touch the masked attacker. The scene was a massacre.

The conclusion that the media drew from this staged event was that armed students on college campuses are more of a hazard than a benefit, accidentally shooting fleeing classmates in a moment of panic. However, I challenge that this scenario was flawed in many ways. First, they asked for students who were "proficient with guns." What does that mean? Anyone who has ever fired a single round down the barrel might consider himself or herself to be proficient, and that doesn't mean that these "proficient" shooters have any real knowledge about firearms, particularly defensive shooting. Some of the students claimed to have spent a great deal of time on the range, but that is a vague qualification at best. Second, the student shooters were given guns that were crammed into their waistbands. When the shooting began, these "proficient" shooters spent half of the gunfight trying in vain to draw their firearms from the baggy clothing they wore. And even though these students were given basic training, they didn't have the opportunity to practice long enough after they were initially trained to become proficient.

Despite the fact that I think the media used this as a tactic to thwart efforts to allow students on college campuses to carry firearms, there are some important

▲ Rimfires like this Kimber .22 semiauto make great practice guns, allowing the shooter to practice with light-kicking ammunition. Frequent practice is the best way to become proficient with a firearm. Photo courtesy of Kimber America.

lessons to be learned from this scene. Foremost among these is perhaps the most important lesson presented in this book: *If you want to save your own life, you have got to practice often with your concealed carry firearm, and you must practice correctly.*

The inspiration for this book came, as previously stated, from my years as a collegiate shotgun shooter. I won't say that I was world class or elite, but I held my own for one simple reason—I practiced. I practiced a lot, firing upwards of 300 shells per week, which was actually pretty low for a serious competitive shooter, some of whom go through three times that many shells in the same period of time. The shots were always the same, the stance was the same, and, for the most part, the clay targets were the same. I was the variable. I had to practice bringing my gun to my shoulder the same way, aligning my cheek on the stock the same way, swinging the shotgun smoothly, following through after the clay was broken. The act was repeated again and again, the same simple motions that, over time, helped me build consistency.

The stakes are much higher during an armed confrontation than they are with collegiate shotgun sports, yet how many rounds do most CCW permit holders put downrange each week? The number is certainly lower than 300, which is what even a modest college shooter puts through his or her gun each week *just to stay competitive.*

For some concealed carry permit holders, the idea that they are carrying a gun is enough to convince them that they are safe. They feel that if they simply have a gun—a gun that they can pull out to scare the bad guys away—then they are safe. For those who believe that, I suggest you think about the scenario above, in which shooters who were "proficient" managed to do no more than increase the damage inflicted during the college attack. One of the most important points in this text is that *you cannot rely on the presence of a gun to keep you safe.* You have to know how to use that gun.

To become good with a firearm requires the same practice and repetition required to learn to play the piano or hit a baseball. Being a competent, "proficient" shooter requires practice and the development of muscle memory. You don't have to fire 300 rounds a week, but one of the cornerstones of the lessons in

this book is that first you learn how to shoot and then you must practice.

## Setting Goals

The first goal of this book is to convince you that you can learn to effectively protect yourself with a firearm. The second goal is for you, the reader, to develop a foundational understanding of how firearms work and how to handle them in a safe manner. The final goal of this book is to teach you to practice correctly so that you can effectively build the muscle memory necessary to fire accurately during tense situations. Effective practice is essential to effective concealed carry, and if you are going to carry a firearm, it is your responsibility to learn to use it effectively.

Many new shooters find that once they become accustomed to shooting and are comfortable on the range, they actually *enjoy* shooting. Concealed carry classes have introduced hundreds of thousands of new shooters to the sport, many of whom have realized what an exciting hobby target shooting can be. I know of more than one CCW permit holder who was looking for a single gun to carry and now owns multiple firearms, and I know at least one person who had never shot a gun before taking a CCW class and now shoots competitively.

Your primary goal as a new shooter is safety. Learning to handle a firearm properly is critical. After you have learned the basic safety rules (safety is always a priority regardless of age or experience) and you feel comfortable with the function of your firearm, you can begin setting more advanced goals. Perhaps these goals are lofty: You may want to compete in a sanctioned International Defense Pistol Association (IDPA) match. Maybe your goals are simpler, such as to get all of the shots on the paper target at seven yards. It is also possible that you just want to remain proficient with your concealed carry gun. All of these goals require time on the range, as anyone who claims to be prepared to defend himself or herself in a deadly encounter and does not practice is deceiving himself or herself. Being good with a gun requires time on the range.

## Finding a Range

You have several options when it comes to finding a place to practice. There are many private ranges

▲ The author practices lifting his windbreaker and drawing the gun from his hip.

▲ The gun comes up, the trigger finger is indexed, and the arm goes straight out without the shooter dropping his head.

▲ The shooter has extended the arm and has his support hand in place, ready to shoot. This series of actions seems simple, but it must be repeated over and over again to commit the movements to muscle memory.

and shooting clubs that will allow you to join for a membership fee, and shooting at these ranges typically involves a brief course of range etiquette to be sure that all of the shooters on the range understand the basic rules. Private shooting clubs vary greatly in price. Some are relatively inexpensive (my own club charges $50 a year), while others are far more expensive. Indoor ranges are typically more expensive to offset the cost of the building, utilities, maintenance, and so forth.

Another option is to find a public shooting range. Many state wildlife agencies maintain shooting ranges for the public, and while some of these ranges are heavily used, others rarely have two shooters on the range at the same time. Public shooting ranges are typically well maintained (some are better than private clubs), but this varies from one club to the next. The problem with public ranges is that they are open to anyone, and you cannot be sure how safety-conscious other shooters will be on the range. I've seen very few

people on public ranges who behaved dangerously, but it is always a good idea to be conscientious of others shooters and be cautious when walking downrange. It's not a bad idea to try and lay some ground rules just to be sure that you and the other shooters are on the same rules. If you feel unsafe for any reason, don't shoot at that range.

It's impossible to determine how many ranges there are in the United States, because there are so many private ranges built in backyards where friends shoot from time to time. Backyard ranges make it easy and convenient to shoot, which means you'll likely shoot more, and if they are properly constructed, backyard ranges are a great place to practice. However, be certain that backyard ranges are safe. There should be a solid backstop (usually made of dirt) that will stop any projectiles fired downrange. The problem with many backyard ranges is that the berm (dirt pile) is too low to effectively stop every shot. The berm should be high enough to ensure that no bullets will accidently be

▼ Shooting from the bench is a good way to evaluate how the gun is shooting. Find a secure rest and slowly squeeze each shot off, taking note of where the bullets strike. Photo courtesy of the National Shooting Sports Foundation.

fired over the top of the dirt pile and potentially injure someone. It's also important to be courteous when you are shooting. There are enough people in the world who are against guns already, and firing a 9mm handgun at six in the morning on their day off will certainly not improve your relationship with the neighbors!

The National Shooting Sports Foundation offers a number of resources including a shooting range locator to help you find a range in your area, range safety guidelines, and resources for range owners and managers. Visit www.nssf.org.

## Range Etiquette

Safety on the shooting range is the first priority. Too many new shooters don't know safe range procedures, and I have witnessed some new shooters being shouted at by range officers for safety infractions. Several of these shooters probably won't come back to shoot again; at the very least their confidences will be badly shaken. Many times I've tried to talk with these new shooters after they'd been publicly embarrassed and humiliated, and most of them didn't have any idea what they were doing wrong.

Perhaps these range officers were a bit extreme, and I've seen cases where range officers were totally out of line and self-serving (and, frankly, jerks), but safe gun handling is essential. The range is not the best place to learn basic range procedures, because there is too much happening too quickly. Many new shooters make mistakes because they are overwhelmed and they are trying to learn too much too quickly.

To simplify range etiquette, I've highlighted the basic "rules of the range" below. Remembering these key points will help you have an enjoyable and safe time.

1. **Guns are always unloaded and safe until you are ready to shoot**. This is probably the mistake that gets most new shooters in trouble and presents the greatest level of danger to other shooters. To simplify this rule, understand that you should always keep the action of your gun open until you are on the line and ready to fire. For semiautos this means that the slide should be locked back, and revolvers should have their cylinders swung out.
2. **Do not handle guns while others are shooting.** For the sake of safety and the peace of mind of everyone who is on the line, it is best not to handle firearms when you are behind a line of shooters. If you are going up to join the line and shooting is already in progress, keep the action open and the gun pointed in a safe direction, usually toward the ground. Always keep your finger outside the trigger guard until you are ready to fire.
3. **Protect your eyes and ears at all times**. Whenever you are on a "hot" range (shooters are firing or ready to fire), always wear eye and ear protection.
4. **Always keep the muzzle pointed downrange.** New shooters must understand that the muzzle of the firearm should always be kept in a safe direction, and when you are on the line shooting, the barrel should be pointed downrange while the line is "hot." New shooters have a tendency to turn their entire bodies to their shooting coach or range master for instruction, inadvertently pointing the firearm at others on the range. Bear in mind that the muzzle is your main focus at the shooting range, and therefore that muzzle should always be under control and pointed in a safe direction no matter what. If you cannot focus on keeping the gun pointed in a safe direction and speaking to your coach or range master at the same time, simply make the gun safe, put it down, and engage in the conversation.
5. **Do not distract shooters**. When shooters are on the line, they need to concentrate on shooting, not listening to someone behind them. Be courteous to other shooters by allowing them to shoot while they are on the line, and don't draw their attention away from the task at hand. Distracted shooters tend to lose track of where the barrel of their guns are pointed, and this presents a real hazard to everyone on the range. Save the conversations for when the range has been declared "cold" and the guns are all safe.
6. **Do not walk downrange until a "ceasefire" has been called and the range is "cold."** I was shooting on a "hot" range one afternoon when I heard a shooter to my left shout, "Ceasefire!" A brand-new shooter with her first handgun had fired a group at the target and was walking downrange to collect her target *while the range was still hot and shots were still being fired*. This is one of the most dangerous situations that can occur at most ranges. Ignorant shooters, many of them new to the sport, simply

▲ The author practices on the range. By practicing the same motions over and over the shooter commits these movements to muscle memory. In tense situations, the brain is already hardwired with directions for drawing, aiming, and firing. This training is a result of repeated practice.

◀ This group is high and to the right, a result of "heeling" the gun. The shooter realized this when conducting the "empty chamber drill" with the instructor. The shooter then practiced smooth trigger pull and follow-through with this gun and a Laser Lyte laser. The next group showed marked improvement.

suspect that a shooter is under the influence, don't stay at the range, as you may be placing yourself at great risk.

## First Shots on the Range

Now that you've arrived at the shooting range and you have a gun that you are familiar with and a range bag with all of your essentials, you are ready to shoot. Begin by ensuring that you have your eye and ear protection on as you approach the range, and be sure to walk to the line with an unloaded firearm with the barrel pointed in a safe direction. Most shooting ranges have a bench or a table for you to shoot behind. If this is the case, I place my firearm and my spare magazines or speedloaders (provided they are not in my vest or shooting pants) on the table. Always make sure that the range is "hot" and that it is safe to shoot. Then you can begin loading your firearm.

Taking your first shots with a firearm can be stressful. Many shooters become overwhelmed the first time that they shoot, and for many firearms instructors it has been so many years since they've fired their first shots they can't relate to the experience anymore. The main thing to remember as you prepare to shoot is to relax and remember basic firearms safety. If you don't shoot well, that's perfectly understandable. Shooting takes practice, as previously stated, and if it were just a matter of pointing the gun at the target and pulling the trigger, then there would be no market for a book like this. Most new shooters are so busy trying to remember a dozen or more instructions on sighting, grip, stance, eye alignment, trigger control, and other elements of shooting that they forget the most basic and fundamental rule of shooting, which is being safe.

walk downrange to collect their targets while other shooters are firing on both sides of them, which is, of course, extremely dangerous. Do not walk downrange without calling a ceasefire and ensuring that all of the other shooters on the range understand that the line is "cold" (no more shooting), all shooters have their guns safe, and they are not touching them. Then and *only* then is it safe to travel downrange.

7. **Do not handle firearms when under the influence of drugs or alcohol**. It may seem axiomatic, but firearms do not mix with drugs or alcohol. This also includes prescription medications that affect your mood, balance, cognition, or alertness. If you

One of the major problems on the range is that students feel rushed, and while I listen to instructors complaining about "dangerous new shooters," I try to bear in mind that many times the new shooter felt rushed and overwhelmed and, as a consequence, forgot the basic safety procedures. During your first time on the shooting range, there are two important points that I stress to new shooters. First, *focus on safety*. I don't care if you shoot a nice, tight group. It's not important that you can pull off a perfect double tap to the center of mass. What's important on the range is that you don't endanger anyone else or yourself. If you have a good instructor, he or she understands this concept and wants you to focus on safety. The instructor should control the pace of the shooting and should help with the mechanics.

The second key to a successful first trip to the range is to *take your time*. The rushed novice shooter is a dangerous shooter, and a good instructor will be sure to slow down the pace of shooting rather than speed it up. This is up to the instructor to control, but not all instructors do a good job of keeping control of the tempo of the shooting. In such a case, you as the shooter must either tell the instructor or refuse to shoot. In the long run you'll both be better off for parting ways. When I'm instructing new shooters, I try to slow the pace down to about half speed, which affords most shooters the time they need to handle their guns properly and safely and to shoot well.

So, of all the things you'll be trying to remember on your first day on the range, there are two that are absolutely critical. Every new shooter should remember their two main focal points for the first trip to the range:

# FOCUS ON SAFETY
## TAKE YOUR TIME

Keep these two points in mind as you begin to shoot. Always remember to maintain focus on the range and don't let yourself become distracted, as a distracted shooter is a dangerous shooter.

Once the range is hot, you are at the bench (or the shooting line if there is no bench), and you have your hearing and eye protection in place, you are ready to shoot. Keeping the gun pointed downrange, begin loading by placing cartridges in the cylinder of

a revolver or by inserting a loaded magazine into the semiautomatic handgun and closing the slide.

## Ceasefire

As previously stated, anyone on the range can call ceasefire for any reason. Perhaps you see a dog wandering onto the range, or maybe you see a situation that is unsafe. If you hear anyone call ceasefire, imme-

▼ The shooter was jerking the muzzle down with each trigger pull, which explains why the first three shots were low. After practicing trigger control, the group improved greatly.

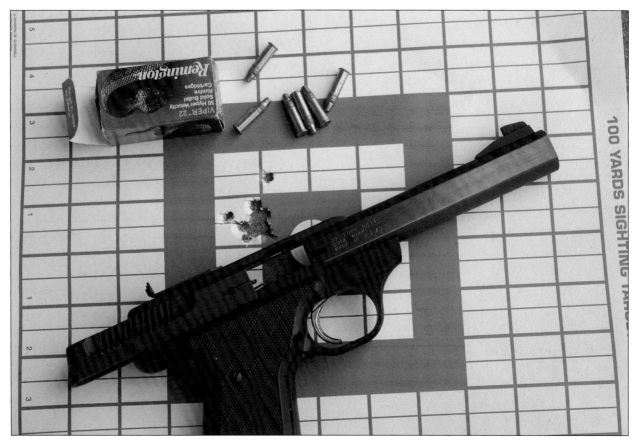

▲ Shooting a .22 LR pistol like this Browning Buckmark is a fantastic way to practice. Ammunition is cheap and recoil is almost nonexistent. Having a good .22 is one of the best ways to improve your shooting.

diately make your gun safe, set it down, and step back from the range.

## Most Common Mistakes on the Range

Most new shooters make similar mistakes on the range. There are very few places where the rules are as strict and the stakes are so high, so it is absolutely essential for the sake of everyone present to be sure that everyone understands the basic rules of range shooting.

First, shooters often forget to wear **ear and eye protection**. This is critical for your safety. I always carry extra ear and eye protection, and there are often people at the range who are willing to share, but if you don't have the right equipment, you shouldn't shoot.

Another common mistake shooters make is **muzzle control**. This creates a very dangerous situation at the range and puts everyone at risk. "The gun isn't loaded" is never an excuse to ignore the direction that the muzzle of a firearm is pointed, and many new shooters simply aren't aware where the gun in their hand is pointed. This is never an excuse, however, since a muzzle that is pointed at someone is always a dangerous mistake that the shooter should avoid.

New shooters sometimes break the rule about **handling firearms behind the firing line** because they don't know any better, but again, this places other shooters at risk and there simply is no reason for doing that. Picking up a firearm and carrying it around with you, especially if the action is closed, causes great concern (and justifiably so) on the part of most experienced shooters and range officers. Leave the gun alone until you are ready to go to the line.

**Leaving the action closed** is another major mistake that rookie shooters make, and this is another dangerous situation. Train yourself to keep the action of your gun open at all times unless you are at the firing line and ready to shoot. An open action indicates that the gun cannot immediately be fired. For revolvers this means that the cylinder must always be open, and for semiautos the slide must always be locked open. A few guns, particularly small semiautos, have actions that will not lock open. Chances are very good that someone at the range will mention to you that you need to keep your action open, which is true, but in the case of these guns there is no way to lock the action open. If you do happen to be shooting such a firearm, be sure to drop the magazine out by pushing the magazine release button and keep the magazine in the opposite hand from the gun. I try to hold the action of these guns open by squeezing the slide back, placing my thumb on the top of the back of the grip, and pressing down while my fingers are wrapped around the slide and pulling up, thus using the leverage of my thumb and fingers pushing in opposite directions to keep the action open when I'm holding the gun. Always index your finger alongside the gun and keep it off the trigger.

**Ignoring range commands** is another problem and one of the most dangerous. Shooters who do not understand or pay attention to range commands place everyone in danger. Pay close attention to the range officer and listen to what he or she is saying to you at all times.

## Practice with Purpose: Drills To Make You a Better Shooter

Now that you have learned range commands and you feel comfortable shooting your gun, here are a few range commands that will help you become a better shooter.

**BlueGuns Drills (No Live Fire):** BlueGuns are replicas of real guns that are made of blue plastic and that do not fire. However, BlueGuns are commonly used by instructors to teach proper grip, stance, and eye alignment when first learning to shoot. Because these guns are unable to fire, the shooter can practice safe gun handling skills without the anxiety of handling a real firearm.

**Laser Sight Training (No Live Fire):** I'm a proponent of laser practice, and I try to practice with the laser in my gun at least three times a week. The latest laser trainers from companies like Laser Lyte fit in the chamber of your unloaded firearm just like a cartridge and fire a laser each time you pull the trigger. You can practice against a wall or other object in the home, or you can purchase one of the laser sensitive targets on the market that record your hits. This allows you to practice for hours without going to the range. Work on improving stance, grip, eye alignment, and trigger control. Even though laser training does not involve live fire, you should always practice handling the firearm in a safe manner.

**Double Tap (Live Fire):** This is one of the most common drills for new and experienced shooters. The term "double tap" means two aimed shots fired in rapid succession. Notice that these are *aimed* shots and it is not a contest to see how fast you can shoot two times.

To practice the double tap drill, aim for the center of mass, or the center of the torso, and fire. Immediately after the first shot is fired, relocate the front sight and deliver a second aimed shot. Once you are proficient at the double tap, the shots should occur less than a second apart, preferably even faster. Again, this drill is ineffective if the second shot is not accurate.

**.22 Training:** As previously stated, the .22 LR is widely considered underpowered for daily concealed

▼ This Laser Lyte target works in conjunction with the Laser Lyte chamber laser. The target records where the laser strikes, so you can practice shooting without actually firing live rounds. This is one of the best ways to improve your shooting skills quickly. Photo courtesy of Laser Lyte.

▲ Adding movement to your drills is important. You may be forced to move in a real confrontation to find cover, and you'll be harder for attackers to hit if you can move.

▲ This competition shooter is "slicing the pie," or shooting at targets as they present themselves from behind cover. The shooter will use the cover as defense and will shoot the outermost target first and work around the edge.

carry. However, .22s make wonderful practice guns; ammunition is cheap, recoil is virtually nonexistent, and the shooter is less likely to develop a flinch that

results from heavier, harder-kicking centerfires with more muzzle blast. You can either buy a .22 firearm or purchase a conversion kit that allows you to turn your carry gun into a .22 by removing the slide, barrel, and spring and replacing them with factory components that help transform your large semiauto into a .22. Use your .22 to train frequently and help work on trigger pull, sight alignment, grip, and stance without the added cost and recoil of larger caliber guns that you will be carrying.

**"Stop" Drill**: When you feel that your life is threatened, the most simple and appropriate verbal response to an attacker is to shout, "STOP!" This makes it clear to the individual approaching you that you don't want him or her to come any closer. Sometimes this command and the sight of your firearm will be enough to stop the attacker. Sometimes it isn't.

Practice giving the "stop" command, pausing, and then firing. You can also practice giving the command with the gun extended and then slowly lowering the firearm, simulating a retreating intruder. This drill teaches the shooter to give a simple verbal command to the attacker if there is any chance of stopping the attack. By shouting, the victim alerts others to the danger.

**Approach Drill (Live Fire):** Many concealed carry permit holders are taught that when the gun is in the low ready position, the arms should be extended with the elbows locked. However, the most common scenarios when the low ready position would be called upon in a real defense situation involve times when the gun is carried in anticipation of having to shoot. Keeping the arms extended and the elbows locked requires the shooter either to swing the gun up like a pendulum or break at the elbow, draw the gun in to the body, and then extend the arms. Instead, keep the elbows bent and close to the body with the gun pointed downward. If you were involved in a real defensive situation, it wouldn't make sense to keep the arms extended. Practice standing back from the target and taking one or two steps forward with your elbows bent and the gun held just above the navel with the barrel pointed at the ground. Extend the gun straight at the target, pushing it up and away until you have proper eye alignment. Practice a double tap, make the gun safe, and step back. Practice this over and over again. If you are in a real-life situation, remember to keep the gun close and the elbows bent in case you have a very sudden, very close defensive situation.

**Near-Middle-Far (Live Fire):** I borrowed and modified this drill from my friend Monty Kalogeras, who teaches sport hunters how to shoot properly. Monty teaches this drill with a rifle, so his "near" target is pretty far away! For defensive handgun, the "Near-Middle-Far" drill means placing three targets on the range side-by-side. The left target should be close, about three steps. The middle target, which is aligned in the middle of the three targets, should be a bit farther back, perhaps four or five steps. The far target on the right should be between five and seven paces, depending on your experience. Begin with the close target and shoot once, then move to the middle target, then on to the right one. Afterwards, practice going the other direction, shooting far-middle-near. As always, be sure to determine what is past your target.

**Empty Chamber Drill (Live Fire):** This one requires a partner, preferably someone who knows firearms and understands how to load and unload guns. Have your partner stand beside you and carefully (muzzle always in a safe direction) hand you the firearm. For revolvers, one of the chambers should be empty. With semiautos he or she will have to hand the gun to you each time you shoot. Go through the steps of proper shooting each time you fire, making sure to have proper grip, stance, and sight alignment. On some occasion you will be pulling the trigger on an empty chamber. When this happens, the firing pin will click but the gun will not fire. It is important to note what happens to the body after the trigger is pulled. Do you flinch or tip the gun forward? Does your sight alignment begin moving just before trigger pull? The best situation is when the firing pin falls and you remain in place, maintaining sight picture. If you flinch, be sure to repeat this drill several times, relaxing and refocusing before each shot. Also, make sure the gun is not causing your flinch. High-powered handguns can cause pain that eventually results in a flinch as you try to brace yourself against the rearward force of the gun.

**Flashlight Drill (Live Fire):** As previously stated, a flashlight should be on your list of "must-haves" when purchasing a gun for home defense, and I believe that it is also valuable to have a flashlight for concealed carry as well. But if you are going to have a flashlight and a firearm, then you will need to practice with both of them at the same time.

As previously stated, I don't have flashlights on my home defense guns. However, a tactical flashlight mounted on the gun makes more sense on a concealed firearm because when a concealed carry gun is drawn you already know that there is imminent danger. However, if your flashlight is not attached to the firearm, you need to learn to shoot without two hands on the gun.

Your flashlight arm should be held across your chest, your elbow bent at a 90-degree angle with the flashlight held so that the beam is pointed ahead of you, and your thumb should be closest to your chest. With your arm in this position, place the wrist of your gun hand on the wrist of the hand that is holding the flashlight. This will help secure the gun, but be sure that the barrel is pointed down in a low ready position. When you decide to shoot, extend both arms straight ahead of you, keeping the flashlight on the target while you shoot. Be sure to keep the hand with the flashlight well behind the barrel of the firearm.

**Failure Drill:** Also known as the Mozambique drill, the failure drill requires shooters to place shots in the center mass and a third shot in the head of a torso target. The idea is that you are shooting an assailant who has not stopped advancing after two shots (the "failure" part of the drill) and you must fire a third shot into the attacker's head to immediately stop the threat. Mechanically, this drill is excellent because it requires you to place two shots on target quickly and then transition to another aiming point to fire the last shot and complete the drill. When you feel comfortable with this drill, you can add movement.

**Interrupted Fire Drill:** This is another one of my favorite drills, because it combines two elements of good defensive shooting—movement and muzzle control while firing. Place two or more targets downrange and place barriers between the targets and the shooter. The idea is that the shooter has to engage the first target (on either the right or left) and must then move laterally down the line, dropping the gun into the Sul position when a barrier is located between the shooter and the target. I prefer to set up four targets (these can be as simple as balloons tied to stakes in front of a backstop) with three barriers between the targets. Barriers can be made of anything, but I like to use torso targets set on one-inch-square posts so I get the feel of shooting around real humans that might cross my path of fire.

**Slice the Pie Drill:** This drill requires the shooter to begin shooting behind cover. Any safe barrier will do, even a tree, but I prefer using target stands. From this position, the shooter must lean around the tree and "slice the pie," or shoot targets as they are presented. The first target you see must receive one or two shots before you can lean further around the barrier and engage the second target. It's critical in this drill to shoot around cover from both the left and right side. You'll probably do better shooting when the targets are on your strong side, but you can't guarantee that will happen in real life, so practice both ways.

These drills certainly aren't the only ones that you can try, but by practicing each of these at least once or twice a week you'll better prepare yourself to deal with a dangerous encounter in the home or in public. Change your practice schedule up as you shoot so that you don't get bored.

### How Far Away from the Target Should I Be When I Practice?

Most new shooters have a tendency to shoot from too far away. This usually results in poor groups, and some novices are immediately discouraged. Defensive situations happen at close range, and if you are shooting at someone from fifteen steps away, it raises the question of whether you are in mortal danger or not. Depending upon which source you use, data suggest that the average self-defense shooting occurs between eight and ten feet away. That's three or four steps, not ten or fifteen. As a general rule I recommend practicing from three steps away from the target to six steps, or roughly nine to eighteen feet away. Practice at this range will cover the vast majority of defensive situations that you will face. Some encounters may be closer, but I believe that three strides is a logical minimum. Be sure to check that your target is not something that will shatter and injure you or others when you shoot.

Remember, one of the keys to successful defensive shooting is practice, so set aside the time needed to remain proficient with a firearm. Notice I didn't write become proficient, because I believe every shooter, no matter his or her skill level, needs regular practice to remain effective.

### Shooting Groups

The most effective way to improve accuracy is to shoot a series of shots (called a group) at a target and analyze the results. Some shooters have a tendency to want to correct for accuracy, an example being someone who decides that his or her first shot was high and right so now he or she will aim low and left, only to find out that the next shot is high and left. This is why we shoot groups. We want a consistent series of shots to indicate our point of impact, eliminating the possible variables like flinch or poor trigger control.

I like to shoot groups of ten to twelve shots before I diagnose where the point of impact of a gun is. Even then you cannot always immediately be sure why the bullets are striking at that point. Perhaps the sights are truly misaligned, but it is also possible that there is another reason why the bullets aren't striking where they are supposed to.

### List of Common Shooting Problems That Result in Poor Groups

#### Anticipating the Shot

Anticipating the shot means that the shooter is moving the gun just prior to firing. This can be a result of flinching, dropping the gun to see the target, or simply losing focus. Oftentimes new shooters are so afraid of the noise and recoil of a gun that they simply "close their eyes and squeeze," as one new shooter told me. This is why follow-through is important, and the "Empty Chamber Drill" listed above can help diagnose this problem. If the shooter moves the gun dramatically when he or she fires the empty chamber, he or she is anticipating the shot. If the gun does not move, then the shooter is not anticipating the shot.

#### Trigger Control Issues

Pulling the trigger seems at first to be one of the simplest steps in the process of firing a gun, but problems with trigger pull are very common. Poor trigger control can cause a variety of accuracy problems, usually resulting in groups that appear low and left or low and right on the target, depending upon the particular trigger problem that you are having. As simple as it sounds, trigger control can be difficult. You need to concentrate on pulling the trigger directly backwards with the last joint of your trigger finger.

### Poor Sight Alignment

The sights should be properly aligned and must stay that way throughout the shot, from the initial trigger squeeze until the shot is fired. Some shooters have poor sight alignment because they are not focused on the front sight, instead paying attention to the target or the rear sight and allowing the sight picture to change while firing.

### Grip Problems

Proper grip is an essential element to accurate shooting, but many shooters don't take the time to examine their grips when accuracy problems start to occur. Grip the gun high, holding the gun firmly without excessive squeezing.

### Stance Problems

Poor alignment of the feet, bad body angle, and improper head positioning can all translate into poor groups on the range. If you suddenly find yourself struggling on the range, begin remedying your poor shooting by evaluating stance. Are your feet shoulder width apart? Feet square? Knees slightly bent? Is the gun coming up in front of your eye or are you craning your neck to see the sights?

### Sight Adjustment

Most concealed carry handguns don't have adjustable sights, but some do, and if the sights are out of alignment they may need to be corrected. However, I advise against changing your sights immediately after you find that your point of impact is not where you need it to be. Examine factors such as trigger control, stance, grip, and follow-through before you change the sight alignment. If you immediately adjust your sights and the real problem is poor stance, you will constantly have to change the sights and will always be "chasing the bull."

## Analyzing Groups

If you find that you are consistently missing in one area of the target, you can use the following chart to help you diagnose the problem. Note that all of these suggestions are for right-handed shooters. Everything will be reversed for the left-handed shooter.

| Group Appearance | Possible Problems | Solution |
| --- | --- | --- |
| Scattered and Inaccurate | No Consistency, Poor Sight Alignment, Poor Mechanics | Hard to diagnose this one. A careful breakdown of your stance, grip, and shooting style is a good first step. Laser training aids are a great help. Also, try shooting from the bench and pay close attention to sight alignment and trigger pull with each shot. |
| Low Right/Low Left | Trigger Control Issues | Practice pulling the trigger straight back. Odds are you are pulling the trigger at an angle. Be sure you are only using the last joint of your index finger to press the trigger. The trigger may be too heavy for you. |
| Consistently Low | Losing Focus, Anticipating the Shot | Practice the "Empty Chamber Drill." Are you dropping the muzzle of the gun? Forcing it down from recoil? Practice with a laser training aid and work on consistent sight picture. Do not drop the gun. Also might be the result of bracing in anticipation of heavy recoil. Sights might need to be adjusted. |

| Group Appearance | Possible Problems | Solution |
|---|---|---|
| Left-Right Vertical Plane | Uneven Pressure on the Grip of the Gun, Losing Sight Alignment | Many shooters have a tendency to turn the wrist when shooting. The wrist should be in a straight line with the hand and should be consistent. You may also be losing focus on the sights, perhaps focusing all your attention on the target. Try shooting from the bench or practicing with a laser or empty chamber. |
| High Left/High Right | Sight Alignment Problem, Poorly Adjusted Sights, Anticipating the Shot | The first instinct in this situation is to begin adjusting sights, if yours are indeed adjustable. Slow down. Begin by examining grip and practicing the "Empty Chamber Drill" to be sure that you aren't anticipating the shot. Many shooters "heel" the gun, applying extra pressure to the bottom of the grip in anticipation of the shot. |

## Ask the Professionals

Sometimes it's very difficult for a new shooter to assess the problem. This is due, in large part, to the fact that you don't know what proper shooting looks like or feels like. Don't get frustrated. Shooting seems like it should be easy, but this book is over a hundred pages and only covers the basics! It's sometimes best to ask for help from an experienced shooter. Although many shooters want to fix their shooting troubles on their own, it is a good idea to consult with an experienced shooter. However, not all shooting instructors are created equal. I think back to my days as a competitive shotgun shooter and all the bad advice I received from well-intended locals at my neighborhood range.

Professional shooting instructors are typically very good shooters with an excellent understanding of shooting mechanics and the skills necessary to help others shoot better. In other words, they understand the problem and can relate the solution to their students. Good professional shooting instructors don't work cheap, but you are leaning on them to help make you a better shooter. Next-level training with qualified instructors can be very beneficial to almost any shooter, regardless of their level of proficiency with a firearm. Continuing your personal defense education is a sound investment.

▲ Continuing your firearm education is a great idea. Schools such as Gunsite Academy in Arizona offer next-level training for shooters of all skill sets.

# XII. Carrying a Concealed Firearm

The options for carrying a concealed firearm have grown tremendously over the last decade in response to the increased numbers of states issuing carry permits and the millions of new CCW holders. In fact, there are so many options that choosing a carry system can be overwhelming. How you choose to carry your firearm is largely a matter of taste, but there are a few key points that you must remember as you select your method of carry.

As discussed previously in the text, there are two main types of concealed carry. The first is on-body carry, where the gun is physically attached to your body. This is the best option in almost all circumstances, as your firearm always travels with you when in public, and if you do need your gun, it's not going to be left behind in a car or ripped out of your hands as a thief steals your purse. On-body carry intimidates some new shooters; they worry about carrying a loaded gun attached to their bodies and fear that the gun will print and become visible to others. There are clothing limitations with regard to what you can wear when carrying on-body, but with some experience you can learn to effectively conceal a gun under most casual or work clothes.

There are times, however, when on-body carry is difficult or impossible. At that point, off-body carry is an option, but again, it's always preferable to have your firearm physically attached to your person in the event of a crisis.

## Key Questions about Carrying

New shooters have a lot on their minds. They have to learn to shoot, handle, store, and maintain a firearm, and they have to overcome the odd feeling of knowing that there is a loaded gun attached to their bodies. Selecting a carry method is difficult, too, because of the seemingly endless options and many varied opin-

▼ The Betty by Flashbang is a simple molded holster that fits easily against the body. The gun is secured and easily accessible. Photo courtesy of Flashbang Holsters.

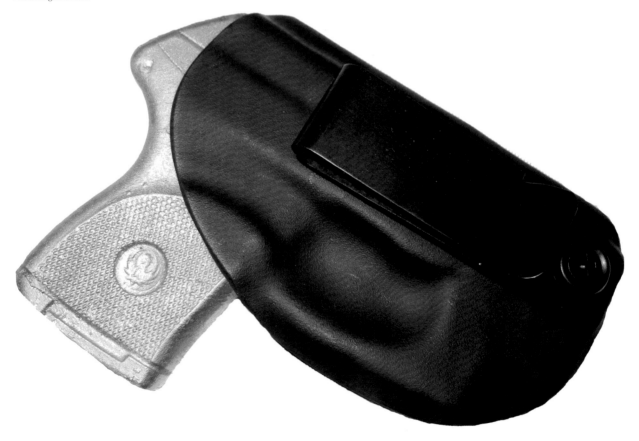

ions regarding the best method. If you ask a dozen CCW permit holders how they carry their firearms, you'll likely receive a different answer from each one.

How you choose to carry your gun is largely a matter of personal taste, and I recommend that you spend some time trying out new holsters to find the one that you are most comfortable with. Ultimately, as long as you are carrying the gun in a safe manner, your opinion is the most important.

As you work your way through this chapter, keep the four following points in mind. These are the critical questions that every new shooter must ask anytime he or she is planning to carry concealed. This will also serve as a guide to selecting a new holster, because if the holster you have chosen doesn't meet these criteria, you'll likely be disappointed and have to purchase more holsters until you are satisfied. Many shooters even stop carrying their guns altogether. Here are the four most important questions you can ask yourself when selecting a holster for concealed carry:

### Is It Safe?

This is always the most important consideration when dealing with firearms. In the case of concealed carry, a holster (or any other carry method) should be safe. Because you are carrying the gun on your body, an accidental discharge could be deadly. However, accidental discharges are thankfully extremely rare, and a good modern holster virtually eliminates any chance that the gun will accidentally fire. Still, be sure that there is nothing in the holster that runs the risk of contacting the trigger.

The gun should also be secure in the holster and should not fall out or move around during standard carry. Having your gun secured prevents it from being lost or dropped.

### Is It Comfortable?

This is an extremely important question, because I've found that if shooters can't find a holster system they are comfortable wearing, then they typically stop carrying their guns altogether, which defeats the purpose of obtaining a concealed carry permit and learning to shoot a firearm. If you can't comfortably wear your holster all day, then you likely *won't*, and a carry per-

mit does very little good if you don't have a gun in a time of crisis.

What is defined as "comfortable carry" is objective. What works for one shooter may not work for another. In addition, many shooters (myself included) have shopped for carry holsters and, after purchasing a holster from a catalog, find that it doesn't fit nearly as

▼ Below is Uncle Mike's Reflex holster, which is made of molded plastic and is designed to fit a specific brand of gun. The gun cannot be pulled straight out, which helps prevent an attacker from getting the gun. The firearm's grip must be twisted toward the body and the gun can then be pulled straight upward. If you practice with the Reflex holster, you can learn to draw very quickly and have the assurance that an assailant won't be able to draw your firearm.

▲ The floor of the annual SHOT Show, which is hosted by the National Shooting Sports Foundation. The SHOT Show is designed for industry professionals, but large national conventions allow new shooters to see the latest firearms and speak with company representatives about their products. Photo courtesy of the National Shooting Sports Foundation.

well as you had suspected it would. I've currently got a collection of holsters that I thought would be perfect but weren't as comfortable as I had hoped. When you purchase your first uncomfortable holster, send it back and buy another one that suits you. Better yet, try the holster on and see if it fits you comfortably. Large sporting goods stores and gun shops sometimes have a selection of holsters, but you are better served to go to larger events, if possible, and try a variety of different holsters. The annual NRA convention, which travels to a different city each spring, is a great place to speak with vendors and try new products. In addition, such events give shooters an opportunity to see the latest concealed carry guns and ammunition.

If you can't travel to a large show, it is important to speak to as many different CCW permit holders as possible, read reviews, and try a variety of holsters. Don't simply purchase the first holster that you find in your local sporting goods store, as it may not fit your needs.

### Is It Accessible?

The ability to access your firearm quickly is critical when carrying concealed. Many new shooters are so focused on keeping their firearms concealed that they forget the whole purpose of carrying a gun is to be able to quickly draw it and defend yourself. This is extremely hard to do when your carry weapon is buried beneath layers of tight-fitting clothes, which render the gun all but useless in critical situations.

▲ This is the Underwraps Belly Band by Galco Gunleather. The wide elastic band wraps around the body and provides a snug, secure fit. Belly bands are one of the easiest and most effective concealment methods. Photos courtesy of Galco Gunleather.

▲ This nylon holster by Uncle Mike's has an extra pocket for an additional magazine. This would be an effective way to carry a gun but might be difficult to conceal.

It is important to understand how you will access the gun when it becomes necessary. This requires practice, and once you have settled on how you will carry, you must decide how you will reach that gun in the event of an emergency. Will the gun be on your hip, or will it be on the ankle? Perhaps you'll use another method of carry, something that requires a completely different method of accessing the gun. No matter how you choose to carry, understand that it is critically important that you can reach your gun quickly and pull it without delay. To have any chance of doing this in an emergency, you'll have to practice frequently until you have the muscle memory necessary to complete a draw, a skill that you learn by repeatedly practicing the steps involved.

You may also have to consider what style of clothes you will wear when you are carrying. There's no need to completely change your wardrobe, but it is impor-tant to wear appropriate clothing. Many CCW permit holders become so fixated on wearing clothes that are loose enough that they forget the same baggy, over-sized clothing that helps conceal your gun may also cause a delay in your draw, resulting in dire conse-quences in a critical situation.

### Does It Print?

Even though you are legally carrying a concealed weapon, you may not want to advertise that to the world. There are plenty of places that I carry where the *idea* that someone was carrying a loaded gun would cause panic, even if I'm perfectly legal to carry. Nobody wants to induce panic or cause a scene, so it's best to be sure that your gun is well concealed.

If a gun prints, or shows through clothing, it will be difficult to conceal. Sometimes the problem of printing is a result of a gun that is too large and clothes that are

▲ This gun is placed behind the hip and the grip is canted forward, making for easy access by a right-handed shooter.

▲ Handbags, such as this one by Galco, provide off-body carry. The good news is that the gun is easily concealed, but the bad news is that the gun is not physically attached to the shooter. In some instances, such as in an office (if it is allowed), off-body carry makes sense. Photo courtesy of Galco Gunleather.

too tight. Other times guns print because of the size or shape of the firearm itself. Certain styles of gun will always print as a firearm, and even someone with very little firearms knowledge will recognize the outline of a concealed gun.

Part of carrying concealed is learning to balance the need to conceal a gun with the need to access it in a hurry. Some instructors advise baggy clothing, but I don't think that baggier is necessarily better. In fact, baggy clothes are a problem for many shooters, who can't draw their firearms because of bunched up fabric that blocks them.

## Do I Have to Carry in a Holster?

Simply put, you don't have to have a holster for concealed carry. Then again, a holster helps secure the gun and makes it easier to practice a consistent draw because the gun is always in the same place. However, the rise in numbers of concealed carry permits has resulted in a new crop of carry options, some of which are holsters and some of which are innovative and effective alternatives to a standard carry holster.

Many shooters carry their concealed firearms in a pocket, which has its own set of advantages and disadvantages. First, it is tough to prevent a gun in the pocket from printing unless you wear thick clothing year round. Second, there are very few shooters who can consistently draw a firearm smoothly and quickly from the pocket of clothing. Lastly, a firearm in the pocket is not secured, which means it can be lost or may fall out during daily activities. Still, pocket carry is simple and the gun is at least held on the body, so there will be people who continue to use this method.

## Off-Body Carry

For reasons discussed earlier in the chapter, off-body carry is not ideal under most circumstances. However, there are situations where off-body carry is the only option. Many professionals, for instance, spend the bulk of their days at their desks. Under these circumstances it isn't logical to keep a firearm tucked behind the crest of the hip or on the ankle, since the hands will likely be on the desk. Laws vary from one state to another, and it would be impossible to condense all of the different requirements for concealment, but in many states a zippered pouch or purse is sufficient.

There are a host of products that are either designed for off-body carry or that will work well in cases where off-body carry is the most sensible method of concealment. Galco Gunleather's Hidden Agenda is one such item, a functional, zippered day planner that doubles as a holster for your concealed firearm. The Hidden Agenda and other products like it look natural in the office yet provide an ideal location for concealing a firearm, and for those who spend the bulk of their days behind the desk, this may be the best carry option. In addition, carrying a day planner looks natural when going to or from the office, so very few people are likely to suspect that you are carrying a gun.

Purses are another option for off-body carry, and although they are one of the simplest ways to conceal a firearm and transport it, purse carry certainly has its disadvantages. Big, bulky purses tend to have contents that shift, and it's very rare that guns carried in these purses are quickly accessible in dangerous situations. However, tactical purses are typically compartmentalized so that a firearm is always separated from the rest of the contents of the purse and is more easily accessible. Like the Hidden Agenda, most of these tactical purses serve a dual role, functioning as a purse as well as a holster. Because most tactical purses are engineered specifically for carrying a firearm, they have internal holsters or pockets that secure the gun much better than traditional purses.

There are a variety of other off-body carry methods, and some CCW holders leave their firearms in their vehicles. However, off-body carry limits the amount of protection that your firearm provides. New products like those listed above provide effective methods of off-body carry, and sometimes such methods are

◄ The Ankle Glove by Galco provides access to the firearm and the support and comfort necessary so that you can wear this holster all day. Photo courtesy of Galco Gunleather.

▲ Pictured above is the Original Flashbang, which is a molded holster that has a leather snap that attaches to the center chest strap of a bra. The gun is drawn by reaching up the shirt and pulling straight downward, a novel and effective carry method. Photo courtesy of Flashbang Holsters.

the only option. Even though off-body carry doesn't offer the same level of protection as on-body carry, it is far better than not carrying a firearm at all. In addition, you don't have to pay as much attention to the clothes that you wear when carrying concealed.

## On-Body Carry

Carrying a concealed firearm on the body is the ideal method, because the gun remains close to you at all times, providing constant protection no matter where you travel throughout the day. Once upon a time a holster on the hip, side, or ankle was the basic method of on-body carry, but creative minds have developed dozens of unique and innovative methods for on-body carry, from body wraps to tactical fanny packs and bras with built-in holsters. The most difficult part is choosing the method of on-body carry that works best for you.

### Holsters

The most traditional method of on-body carry is the holster, which is usually made of nylon fiber, leather, or hard thermoplastic. Some holsters are generic, while others are designed for specific models of firearms. Traditional holsters surround the forward portion of the firearm, leaving the grip exposed so that the shooter can draw when necessary. Some holsters have a retention strap, which holds the gun in the holster from the rear. Other holsters have finger releases on the body of the holster itself, and these holsters are typically made of molded plastic.

There is a seemingly endless variety of holsters and it would be impossible to cover every possible method of carry. Instead, this book will focus on the major types of holsters and most popular positions for concealment. Some shooters prefer ankle holsters, while others prefer a cross-draw or strong-side hip carry. Carry style is very personal, and finding the correct carry position for you may take some time.

There are three basic materials used for holster construction. The first is leather, which is more pliable than the other options and sometimes easier to conceal. Leather holsters tend to grab the gun, making for a very secure fit, and they are often easy to carry comfortably. However, leather holsters are not without their drawbacks. First, leather holds moisture much more than nylon and hard plastic, so perspiration will not dry as quickly on leather holsters as it will on plastic and nylon varieties. It is also important not to store your gun in a leather holster, which can lead to corrosion resulting from leather's tendency to absorb water and oils.

Nylon holsters do not absorb liquids and oils the same way that leather holsters do, and nylon holsters are typically less expensive than leather holsters. However, nylon holsters are not form-fitted like hard plastic and leather holsters, which means that the majority of nylon holsters are sized to fit a generic category of guns. As a result, these holsters do not fit any particular gun perfectly and usually require a retention

▲ Above is the Yaqui Paddle Holster by Galco, which can be removed without unbuckling the belt. The "paddle" holds the gun in place, making paddle holsters very popular. Photo courtesy of Galco Gunleather.

strap to ensure that the firearm stays in place. Nylon is often used in other types of carry devices as well, such as belly bands and fanny packs.

Thermoplastic Kydex holsters are another option, and these holsters are engineered to fit a particular model of firearm. Kydex holsters are impervious to moisture from perspiration, and because they are formed to fit a particular gun, they typically offer a very snug fit, so the gun is likely to be held firmly in place and won't require a retention strap. Some hard molded plastic holsters have a trigger release that must be pressed in order to draw the gun. The primary disadvantage to molded Kydex holsters is that they are very firearm specific.

Most holsters are labeled as either IWB (inside waistband) or OWB (outside waistband). OWB holsters offer easier access to the firearm for rapid and unimpeded drawing of the weapon, but they're hard to conceal. IWB holsters are most common for concealed carry since they offer the best concealment, and today's IWB holsters are lighter, more durable, and more affordable than ever. There are a number of different IWB holster configurations, including "tuckable" models that have a clip that attaches to the belt or top of the pants with space between the holster and the clip so that you can tuck a shirt in over the firearm.

### Other Options for On-Body Carry

Holsters are secure, and if properly positioned, provide easy access to the firearm. They are not, however, the only option that you have for on-body carry. Another popular carry method is a "belly band," which is a wide nylon strap that wraps around the midsection of the body and usually fastens with Velcro. Most belly bands have a built-in nylon holster that is thin and relatively simple, often a stitched pocket within the band that holds the gun in place. Belly bands are effective and simple, and many new CCW permit holders find that belly bands make it easier to conceal the firearm. Some belly bands fit inside the pants, while others ride higher up on the body, holding the gun on the torso. Belly bands are rarely firearm-specific but are designed instead to fit a range of guns. Provided that you can quickly access the firearm, though, belly bands are one of the simplest and cheapest options to carry your gun, and they are usually very comfortable.

Belly bands and traditional holsters are good methods for carry inside the waistband. There are, however, other options as well. Versacarry makes a molded resin clip that holds the gun in place with the use of a piece of plastic that inserts into the barrel, a piece the company refers to as a barrel retention rod. The outside clip hooks on the waistband or belt, and the gun is carried on the inside of the waistband and is held in pace by the barrel retention rod that is inserted in the muzzle. The Versacarry also has an optional trigger guard that prevents anything from accidentally contacting the trigger. The design is simple, lightweight, easy to conceal, and effective.

Flashbang makes a variety of holsters designed to attach to a woman's bra. The company's namesake product attaches to the center strap on the front of the bra and the gun rests just below the bra line, held in place by molded plastic holsters that are engineered to release when the gun is pulled straight down. To access the firearm, the wearer reaches up into the shirt, grabs the grip of the gun, and pulls down hard. The company makes a variety of other holsters for traditional hip carry, both inside and outside the waistband. In addition, the company's Marilyn model is also mounted on the bra, but the thermoplastic holster rides under the arm and the gun is accessed by reaching down the neck of the garment.

There are several manufacturers on the market today who have developed lines of tactical clothing, or garments that are designed specifically for shooting. Many of these shooting garments contain built-in holster pockets that are stitched into the garment to provide a secure and discrete location for concealed firearms. The most common types of tactical clothing with integrated pockets are jackets and vests, and this is a viable carry option provided that the garment provides significant support and concealment. If the garment is comfortable, carries the gun well, and allows for quick access to the firearm, then tactical clothes are a good choice for concealed carry.

Many CCW permit holders carry their guns in their pockets, which is a simple method of carry; however, most clothing pockets do not conceal guns adequately, and retrieving the gun quickly, especially in a tense situation, is very difficult. There are a variety of pocket and wallet holsters designed specifically to conceal firearms in the pocket. Because many people carry

▲ Finding a holster and carry position you like will allow you to be comfortable while wearing your firearm. This IWB holster is compact and holds the gun firmly in place, and the firearm can be concealed with a cover garment like a sport coat.

wallets and cell phones inside clothing pockets, these pocket holsters usually don't raise suspicion, and they provide a convenient method for carry. However, pocket holsters are sometimes difficult to access quickly, which is vitally important in the brief seconds during a fatal attack.

Fanny packs are another option for concealing a firearm, and they are often the only effective method of carry, such as when jogging. Tactical fanny packs oftentimes offer useful pockets for carrying money, cards, and keys as well as a compartment for your firearm. In addition, a quality fanny pack is far more comfortable to wear while running than carrying a concealed gun on your body, and sweat and moisture is less likely to contact the gun while it is in the fanny pack.

Choosing the right carry option for you can be difficult. The good news, however, is that there are a seemingly endless variety of choices available to the CCW permit holder. Body shape, size, clothing options, arm length, and a host of other factors affect the best method of carry, but the ultimate decision must be made by the individual shooter. Remember to choose a method that is safe, secure, discrete, accessible, and comfortable.

## Carry Positions

One of the most common questions that new shooters ask is where they should carry their guns on the body. The answer to that is any place that offers concealment, comfort, security, and the ability to quickly draw the gun when needed. The most common carry position is a strong-side hip carry, meaning the firearm is holstered on the same side of your body as your strong hand. *Where* the gun is positioned is largely a matter of personal taste, provided it meets the criteria listed above. Assuming that the body is a clock face with the navel being twelve o'clock and the small of the back being six o'clock, the most natural position for most right-handed shooters would be to have their guns between the two and three o'clock position on the hip. This is because the strong hand usually hangs near this position, and it is easy to draw the gun in a hurry if your hand is already in position. When clothing does not interfere, this allows a direct elevation of the hand from the side that contacts the grip of the gun and creates a natural draw motion. For left-handed shooters, the gun would be in the nine to ten o'clock position on the left hip.

The problem with direct three o'clock/nine o'clock carry is that the gun rests on the widest part of the hip, making it harder to conceal, and the shooter is more likely to bump the gun against objects like doorjambs. The holster mounted on the lateral point of the hip does not work with the natural contours of the body, meaning the angle of the gun stands in opposition to the line of the body, making the firearm more likely to print. Where open carry is legal and acceptable, carrying a gun on the three o'clock/nine o'clock position makes sense, but for concealed carry this hip position only makes sense if you have a small handgun that you can easily conceal.

Carrying your concealed gun in front of or behind the lateral point of the hip is usually the best option. For a right-handed shooter this means the gun is located in either the one o'clock to two o'clock position or the four o'clock to five o'clock position. Secured in either position, the frame of the gun will lie roughly parallel to the body, which means it will be easier to conceal. Whether you prefer to carry your gun on the front of the hip or the rear of the hip depends on a variety of factors, including arm length; shooters with short arms have a tendency to carry near the two o'clock position. Long-armed shooters often feel more comfortable drawing from the rear portion of the strong-side hip. Again, this is a matter of personal preference.

When carrying on the hip you can choose to carry inside or outside the waistband of your pants. Both methods are acceptable provided they offer effective concealment. Outside the waistband carry is less popular because it makes it more difficult to prevent the gun from showing, and it severely restricts the type of clothing that you can wear. I have found that a belly band holster worn outside and just above the waistband is easier to conceal than most outside the waistband holsters, yet the belly band offers significant support for the firearm and easy access. Inside the

▲ The Versacarry is one of the simplest and most effective carry methods; the barrel of the gun sits on a post and a plastic tab attaches the gun to the top of the pants. The system is lightweight and simple.

waistband carry makes it easier to conceal the firearm, because the natural contours of the clothing help disguise the gun, making it possible to conceal the firearm under a wide variety of clothes.

Hip carry certainly isn't the only option, though. As discussed above, pocket holsters and even bra holsters have become popular choices for carry. Hip carry is still the most popular choice, however, and the majority of holsters are designed for hip carry. One popular type of hip-carry holsters are paddle holsters, so named because they have a wide leather "paddle" that offers support and makes the gun fit comfortably against the shooter's body. Traditional holsters also work for hip carry, though some are canted, or angled, to tip the gun forward for easier access to the handle. Again, this is largely a matter of choice and comfort, so take the time to select a hip holster that fits you well. Like choosing an item of clothing, a holster must be comfortable and practical.

Cross-draw holsters are another option for hip carry. Cross-draw holsters are located on the weak-hand side of the body so that you must reach across midline to pull the gun. For instance, as a right-handed shooter, I would position a cross-draw holster at approximately the eleven o'clock position on my hip with the grip of the gun facing to the right. Cross-draw holsters are occasionally positioned on the back, though this is less common. There are advantages to wearing cross-draw holsters; the gun is usually canted at such an angle that the holster lies almost horizontal to the waistband, which helps aid in concealment because the lateral position of the gun doesn't print as easily and most nonshooters don't immediately recognize a gun in that position. Cross-draw holsters are a favorite for those who wear business suits frequently, because the suit jacket naturally covers the gun.

Ankle holsters are another popular choice, particularly because ankle holsters are easy to conceal with proper clothing, and most casual onlookers won't think to look on the ankle for a firearm. Ankle holsters are popular with permit holders who choose to carry revolvers and small semiautos because both types of firearms fit easily onto the ankle and are small enough to be comfortably worn all day long. Be sure to choose an ankle holster that fits well and is designed specifi-

cally for your firearm. Choosing to wear an ankle holster limits your wardrobe choices; you'll have to wear loose-fitting, full-length pants to conceal the firearm. Be sure to select an ankle holster that remains in place on the leg and is secure, because you won't be able to conceal or draw a gun from a holster that is loose and doesn't stay in place. Choosing an ankle holster means that you will have to reach down on the leg to draw the gun. If you are wearing an ankle holster and find that you must draw the gun in a dangerous encounter, remember not to take your eyes off the threat; if possible, bend down at the knees with your head up, lift the pant leg and draw while you maintain eye contact. Drawing from an ankle holster requires lots of practice and preparation, but ankle holsters are a popular and effective option for concealed carry.

I'll classify carry from the top of the belt line to the armpits as "torso" carry. There are a variety of different options for torso carry, but the two most popular choices are belly bands and shoulder harnesses. Belly bands, as discussed earlier, are stretchable nylon bands that wrap around the belly and fasten together, usually via Velcro straps that allow the band to be fitted to the individual. Belly bands wrap tightly around the body and make it easy to conceal a firearm; however, belly bands positioned high on the torso sometimes make it difficult to draw the gun, because you have to reach so high up the body to remove the gun. Belly bands worn under loose clothing require the shooter to lift the garment and draw the gun, which can be accomplished quickly if practiced often.

Shoulder holsters are generally supported by a harness worn over the shoulders and under the top garment. This setup is popular among detectives, and if you've ever watched police dramas on television, you've seen cops wearing shoulder holsters under sport coats and jackets. Most shoulder harnesses can be adjusted to fit the shooter, and the firearm is usually held just under the arm with the barrel pointed backwards, though some shoulder holsters, particularly those designed for carrying large frame revolvers, are designed so that the barrel of the gun points down to better distribute weight and prevent the gun's long profile from printing under the jacket. Shoulder harnesses work well, but they severely limit your choices when carrying concealed. You'll have to wear a jacket or similar garment that opens in the front to access the gun, yet you'll have to be able to close the cover garment to prevent the gun from being exposed.

### Carrying When Exercising

Carrying a firearm when exercising may seem like a chore, but when you're running, hiking, canoeing, or biking it's worth taking a firearm along just in case. After all, you're isolated, tired, and may be distracted, and that leaves you vulnerable.

I wear different holsters depending upon my activity. For canoeing or biking I prefer a DeSantis Roadrunner, a pouch that fits over the shoulders and rests in the middle of the body. For running, I prefer a lightweight, low-profile carry rig that keeps the gun close to my body and prevents bouncing or rubbing (which can lead to irritation and pain). Any belly band holster from UnderTech, Galco, DeSantis, or others will work so

▲ Runners are vulnerable to attack, so it makes sense to carry a firearm. Some holsters, like Flashbang's Marilyn, are light enough and secure enough to be worn while running. Photo Courtesy Flashbang Holsters.

long as it secures the firearm close to the body. Belly bands are also easy to wash.

### Mindset Training

The late Lieutenant Colonel Jeff Cooper was one of the foremost experts on firearms and defensive shooting, and many of his methods revolutionized modern shooting. The school that he started in Arizona, now known as Gunsite Academy, teaches a wide array of different shooting courses for everyone from civilian shooters to law enforcement and military professionals.

Gunsite teaches a concept that Lt. Col. Cooper formulated called the Combat Triad. The three primary principles of defensive shooting, according to Cooper, were marksmanship, gun handling, and mindset. We've already covered the basics of safe gun handling and marksmanship, so let's take a brief look at the role mindset plays in surviving a deadly situation.

Lt. Col. Cooper was an expert in mindset training, and he referenced color-coded "condition" states to help students identify the various mindsets (and this applies to more than firearms defense; these principles are essential for everyone who wants to play an active role in their personal protection). The first condition is white, which, according to Cooper, is the condition where we are oblivious to attack. We're gardening. We're walking out of the shopping mall with a cart full of groceries and we're trying to locate our car. We're distractedly walking down the street from the office to get a coffee. In short, if we were attacked at these moments, we'd be so shocked and surprised that there's little chance we could defend ourselves. Unfortunately, Cooper says that most people spend their entire lives in condition white, and thus they are perpetually vulnerable.

The next stage is condition yellow, and this is where we need to spend most of our time. This state does not, according to Cooper, make you a "kook"; instead, you are aware. You're conscious of your surroundings. The head is up, eyes scanning. There isn't a specific threat that has been identified, but you are vigilant. One of the underlying principles of condition yellow is that you are in a state of heightened sensitivity to your surroundings. Should an attack occur, you'll be aware and better able to defend yourself.

The next step is condition orange. This stage is when a threat has been identified but not engaged. It

▲ Colonel Jeff Cooper, who founded Gunsite Academy in Arizona, used different color-coded "conditions" when teaching mindset. Mindset training is still part of Gunsite's "Combat Triad."

## Putting It All Together

One of the most difficult parts of concealed carry is choosing the right gun/holster combination for concealed carry. It is vital that you are comfortable and confident with your choice, and you'll have to do some research to determine which setup is best for your stature, your daily dress, and your routine. Choosing a carry method and holster can be also as difficult as choosing a gun. There are several good options available currently, and as more and more Americans take advantage of laws that allow them to carry concealed firearms, more new and existing companies will develop innovative methods of carrying a firearm.

I believe the most important question that you must ask yourself when planning to carry concealed is whether you will buy a holster that fits your clothing choice or clothes that fit your choice of holsters. For instance, if I wore a suit every day, I might consider a shoulder holster or an inside the waistband holster that fit on my right hip. However, my clothing choices are varied, and so I own a number of different holsters that allow me to carry in a variety of ways. When I'm wearing jeans and a jacket, for instance, I usually carry using a clip-on Versacarry or leather holster inside my waistband. Sometimes, however, I'm wearing jeans and a light cotton shirt. In that circumstance I carry a revolver in an ankle holster, a setup that provides quick access, safety, and easy concealment. Many joggers and hikers choose to carry their firearms in a fanny pack, which makes sense while you are on the trails. However, wearing a fanny pack to your job in a law office certainly doesn't make sense. In that case I would consider off-body carry, something like Galco's Hidden Agenda, which I could lay on my desk while I'm at work without raising suspicion. Tactical clothing makes sense for most casual activities, and the Flashbang and other similar holsters have created a whole subclass of holsters designed for female shooters. Having several holsters can be expensive, but it greatly increases the odds that you will be carrying a firearm at that critical moment when you have to defend yourself, which is the point of obtaining a CCW permit. And since that moment typically strikes when we least expect it, it makes sense to spend time choosing a carry method or methods that best suits your lifestyle.

could be someone screaming threats in a parking lot or someone who is lurking in the shadows. The gun remains in the holster, but focus increases. You're ready to act if necessary. If an attack occurs, you're ready to defend yourself. And, when there's a clear threat to life, you transition to condition red—engagement.

Mindset is something that we all need to work on every day. We need to be aware of our surroundings and, equally as important, to we need to have an understanding of what we will do if our life is in danger. But defensive shooting instructors aren't the only ones who are aware of mindset and the effects it can have on the outcome of a confrontation. In a university study that polled violent inmates, it was determined that the potential victim's awareness—or lack thereof—was the primary driving force in target selection by violent offenders. The proper mindset can actually stop an attack before it even begins in some instances.

# XIII. Firearms Maintenance

One of the most important elements of owning a firearm is learning the proper procedures to maintain that firearm and keep it in good working condition. Regular cleaning is one of the best ways to ensure that your firearm will function properly, and since you are relying on your defensive firearm to save your life in a dangerous situation, it is essential to ensure that it is in proper working order.

Improvements in CNC machining, metallurgy, and gun finishes have made the modern concealed carry gun pretty durable, but that doesn't mean that you can neglect regular cleaning sessions. If you are going to practice with your firearm as much as I've recommended in this book, you'll need to have an understanding of how to keep your gun in working order.

Different guns require different amounts of maintenance, and some guns are easier to clean than others.

When you purchase a firearm, it is essential that you understand how to keep that gun cleaned and lubricated. Since all firearms are slightly different, there is no single manual for cleaning all guns, though there are many steps in the cleaning process that are shared by a variety of different firearms.

## Protecting the Finish

Different grips and finishes require different cleaning styles and frequency. Since most concealed carry guns are meant to be utilitarian and aren't designed as show pieces or collectible guns, firearms manufacturers have focused on providing guns that are durable and easy to maintain. In truth, concealed carry guns are subject to far more daily wear than most firearms, except for service weapons and competition guns. We carry our guns with us throughout the day, exposing them to moisture and friction. Some people leave their

▲ Cleaning kits usually contain rods, a T-handle, various brushes, jags and swabs, and a box of patches. This is a universal kit that can be used on virtually any firearm.

Though bluing is still a very common way to treat gun metal, firearms that are blued will still rust if exposed to moisture for extended periods of time. In addition, friction points tend to lose their blued finish, so if you store your revolver in a holster, the perpetual wear associated with taking the gun in and out of the holster will eventually wear the bluing from the cylinder. When the steel beneath is exposed to the elements, the gun rusts more easily.

If you purchase a blued gun, understand that it will require more maintenance than other firearms finishes; however, I own several guns with a blued finish and have never experienced a problem other than thinning (friction causing the blued coating to wear down or "thin," exposing the steel). I am also more careful to clean the exterior metal of my blued guns more frequently than I clean the exterior of my other guns with different finishes like stainless steel. If you inadvertently allow the firearm to become exposed to moisture and it begins to rust, it is important that you catch this early so as to limit the amount of corrosion. Rust typically appears on a gun barrel in small patches that lose their glossy color. Immediately upon finding these initial spots of rust on your firearm, wipe the area down with a rag coated in gun oil. This will help stop the effects of rust. In extreme cases of rust, the gun can be reblued by a gunsmith.

Exposure to moisture and perspiration can damage traditional blued finishes, so firearms companies have developed new methods for protecting their guns from corrosion. Guns made of stainless steel are durable and stand up well to moisture, so that is one option. Many manufacturers also now use a finishing process

concealed carry guns in the holster at all times when they are not actively shooting.

Over time, this daily handling can cause corrosion to the firearm. The good news, though, is that today's gun owner has a wide variety of choices with regard to the finish, and many of these gun finishes are extremely durable, standing up to even the roughest daily handling.

Traditionally, guns are blued. This finish is not really blue at all, but rather black with a blue sheen, and is the result of chemically treating the steel with a protective coating to inhibit rust. Exposure to moisture causes steel to oxidize, which ultimately results in rusting of the metal parts. Bluing slows this process, helping preserve the exterior appearance of the gun. For most of the twentieth century, almost all firearms were blued to help prevent rusting, and today a sizeable portion of firearms are blued at the factory.

to protect exposed metal surfaces. Cerakote developed a ceramic-based finish to help protect a firearm, and there are a variety of color options. Some guns, like the Walther PPS M2, have hardened metal slides that are treated with a Tenifer finish that uses a salt bath to protect the steel. Virtually all concealed carry guns today are designed to withstand the rigors of daily use, but some older models may develop rust or pitting when they are exposed to moisture and perspiration on a daily basis.

In recent years there have been a variety of new finishes released that are designed to withstand even the worst treatment. One of these is Cerakote, which is a baked-on ceramic coating. Cerakote finishes are very tough and highly corrosion resistant, but they can chip. Hard anodizing is another very popular option, and hard anodized guns are among the most durable firearms available. Hard anodizing changes the structure of the steel and makes the firearm impervious to rust.

All the modern firearms finishes are effective, though they require varying amounts of maintenance. Stainless steel, hard anodized, and Cerakote finishes are more corrosion resistant than traditional blued finishes, but a swift wipe down with a light coat of gun oil is typically enough to protect most blued finishes.

## Cleaning Guns

Firearms are mechanical devices, and like other mechanical devices they require a minimum level of maintenance and cleaning to perform correctly. Properly cleaning your gun is the best way to be sure that it will continue to function correctly for years. In addition, cleaning and maintaining your gun adds value to the firearm and helps protect your investment.

Safety is critical when cleaning guns, so the first step in the cleaning process is to be certain that the gun is unloaded before you begin. For revolvers, press the

▼ Wire brushes are used to remove excessive fouling from the rifling of the barrel. Do not overuse these brushes, though. One or two passes down the bore should be sufficient.

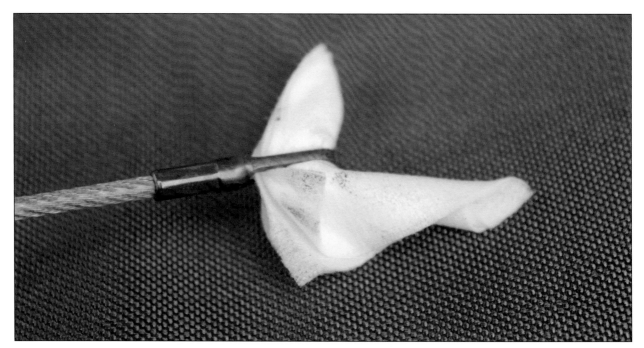

▲ Excess fouling can cause problems in handgun barrels. This barrel shows a bit of fouling after cleaning, but not an excessive amount.

cylinder release button and swing the cylinder out to be sure the gun is unloaded. Release the magazine and open the action of semiautos. Although gun cleaning accidents are a rarity, it is essential to be sure that you are not putting yourself or others at risk.

There are three basic steps involved in cleaning firearms:

### Cleaning the Bore

The bore, or the inside of the barrel, will need to be thoroughly cleaned out periodically, as excessive lead and copper fouling builds up in the rifling and can affect the accuracy of the gun. Rifling is composed of a series of spiral lands machined around the axis of the bore that cause the bullet to spin as it exits the barrel, resulting in far greater accuracy than could be achieved from a smooth barrel that does not cause the bullet to rotate. The spiraling bullet is like a spiraling football thrown by a quarterback; the rotation causes the bullet (or the football) to maintain a steady path through the air, greatly increasing accuracy. The highest points of rifling inside a barrel are referred to as "lands" while the lowest points are referred to as "grooves." These lands and grooves are fouled over time by lead and copper from the outside of bullets

that pass down the bore, and even though a minimal amount of fouling won't affect accuracy, the accumulation of quite a few shots can eventually reduce accuracy. On most semiautos, the barrel can be easily removed to facilitate cleaning, and on most modern semiautos, removing the barrel is a part of the standard disassembly of the firearm required for basic cleaning.

Once you have removed the barrel from the gun of the semiauto (revolver barrels usually will not be removed), begin by looking down the bore. You will see the rifling and any fouling that has accumulated on the lands and grooves. Cleaning the bore will require the use of a cleaning rod (which is available in most retail stores) or a cleaning cable. Depending upon how long the fouling has been in the bore and how badly it has accumulated, a wire brush may be required to remove the heaviest copper and lead. Both cleaning cables and cleaning rods have threaded ends that allow you to attach a variety of tools, which will be included with your cleaning kit. The most common tools are wire brushes (either copper or bronze), cleaning loops, chamber brushes (which are wider than bore brushes), and jags.

Wire brushes can be used for the initial step in cleaning, though if you perform regular routine maintenance, it is not usually necessary to clean the bore with the wire brush attachment. If you elect to clean the fouling from the bore with a wire brush, pull the brush from the chamber to the muzzle, with the brush traveling the same direction that a bullet would. Many shooters who use wire brushes prefer to pull them through the barrel one time and then stop, expecting that the wire bristles have now either removed the fouling or have loosened it enough that liquid solvents should effectively remove any additional fouling.

Once the wire brush has been pulled through, attach the head to your cleaning kit that allows you to slip a cloth patch into the center to be pulled down the length of the barrel. Patches are relatively inexpensive; you can usually purchase several hundred for a few dollars, so don't hesitate to use a sufficient number of patches to effectively clean the bore. The first patch should be sprayed or wetted with a bore cleaning solvent. When using solvents, it is a good idea to wear gloves to limit contact with the skin. After spraying the patch with bore solvent, run the patch through the barrel. Most shooters run patches from the chamber to the muzzle, examining each patch for signs of fouling. Most of the fouling that is removed will be black in color, but copper fouling has a distinct blue-green tint on the white patch. One or two patches saturated in solvent should be sufficient to clean the majority of the fouling from the barrel. Run one or two dry patches (no solvent of any kind) down the barrel. Now when you look into the bore you should be able to see clean, smooth rifling.

Most bore cleaners include lubricants, so the interior of the barrel should look shiny and the rifling should be sharp, or well-defined. When purchasing a used gun, look at the bore to see how well the firearm has been maintained; well-kept guns should have a clean bore with good, sharp rifling. Guns that are fouled, pitted, or that have badly worked rifling should be avoided.

Remember that the longer a barrel is fouled, the harder it is to effectively clean. It's a good idea to carry a range cleaning kit and make an effort to at least clean the interior of the barrel before heading home. This will save additional cleaning work down the line as the fouling is fresh and can be easily removed.

## Cleaning the Interior of the Firearm

This is a relatively easy procedure for most revolvers. On DA and DAO revolvers, simply swing the cylinder out and wipe down the visible metal parts with a lightly oiled rag. It is possible to foul the revolver by putting excess amounts of oil on the moving parts, so a soft cloth with a light application of a quality cleaning oil like Remington Rem Oil will work to keep the exterior of the firearm protected and all moving parts in order. Do not forget to clean less obvious areas like the rear of the trigger, the underside of the hammer, and the channel that the ejection rod rests in when the cylinder is inside the frame. Because revolvers are rugged and reliable, there is very little reason to clean

▼ A bore snake is designed to be pulled down the interior of the barrel to clean away fouling. These products are effective, but they have a limited life.

▲ Uncle Mike's M-PRO7 Tactical Cleaning Kit is great for the field, providing the basics for cleaning your gun after firing. Photo courtesy of Uncle Mike's.

the interior much beyond a thorough wipe down of the metal parts with an oiled rag.

Semiautos are more complex. Some semiautos can be disassembled, cleaned, and reassembled very quickly and easily while others are more difficult. It is important to note that for most semiautos you will only need to remove the slide, barrel, and spring. Anything beyond that is not usually recommended for general maintenance. Consult your owner's manual for breakdown procedures or speak with a qualified gunsmith or other expert who can assist you if you have any questions.

Because the action of a semiautomatic handgun moves with every shot, fouling can build up on the interior portion of the gun that can hinder mechanical function, so it is essential to keep the interior of a semiautomatic gun clean. It is essential to not only keep the interior of the action free from fouling, but the moving parts must also be lubricated so that there will be less metal-to-metal resistance and wear. There are several quality combination solvents/lubricants on the market, items such as Smith & Wesson Dry Lube, which help clean metal surfaces while simultaneously lubricating moving of the firearm.

When you have the gun disassembled, pay special attention to the wear points. Owner's manuals typically indicate where these points in the gun are and will advise you to lubricate them to reduce friction. Signs of wear are usually apparent when the gun is disassembled. Pay attention to places where the finish is being worn down from constant friction and lubricate these points. Wipe down the exterior of the barrel, the spring, and the inside of the slide. Once you have wiped all of the metal surfaces clean, reassemble the gun in accordance with the manufacturer's recommendations.

## Cleaning the Exterior of the Firearm

The simplest step is external cleaning, which oftentimes involves little more than wiping the gun down with a rag to preserve the finish. After shooting, thoroughly wipe down all of the exterior metal with a rag sprayed with quality gun oil. Be certain that the spray or oil is designed for protecting finishes and not some other function, such as eliminating copper fouling in the barrel. Harsh gun solvents should not be used when cleaning the exterior of a gun, as they can damage the finish. Also, do not spray gun oil directly on the firearm itself; instead, spray oil onto a soft cloth and then wipe the gun down. Do not spray or drip oil into openings in the exterior of the firearm unless the owner's manual states that this is necessary, as excessive amounts of oil can foul moving parts and prevent the gun from working properly.

## Degreasing

When firearms are shipped from the manufacturer, the interior and exterior of the gun are oftentimes coated with a heavy oil or grease that is designed to protect the firearm against damage. This layer of grease should be removed before the gun is fired, because this layer of grease can eventually lead to feeding problems as the action becomes gummed. Refer to your owner's manual for more instructions about wiping the grease from a new firearm, although a general wipe down with a soft rag will oftentimes do the trick.

## Storage in the Home

Moisture is very bad for firearms, so it is important to store firearms in a dry place with low humidity. Many gun safes have dehumidifiers that help reduce the amount of moisture in the interior of the safe, thus reducing the risk of corrosion.

When storing firearms in the home, safety is the main priority, but keeping moisture away from firearms is important as well. Many items hold moisture and could promote corrosion, so handguns should not be stored in leather or foam-lined products that could hold moisture. This is particularly true when carrying concealed, as the holster material may have become wet with perspiration while you were carrying the gun.

▼ Wiping down the cylinder of a revolver with gun cleaner after shooting. The stainless finish on this gun is not completely resistant to corrosion, but it does offer more protection than a blued finish.

◀ The author's Glock 19 9mm after a session on the range.

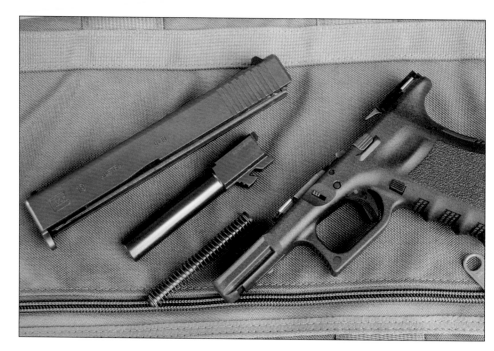

▶ The Glock 19 disassembled and ready for cleaning. From left, the slide, barrel, spring, and frame. The interior of the barrel will be swabbed out and all of the metal parts will have a very light coating of gun oil applied with a rag. Friction points where metal-to-metal wear is visible will receive a light coat of Smith & Wesson Dry Lube.

When you are at home you must be sure to remove the gun from the holster and wipe it down with an oiled rag to prevent the moisture from corroding the finish on the firearm.

## Read the Owner's Manual

Always consult your owner's manual when purchasing a new firearm. The owner's manual usually gives detailed instructions on how to use and maintain that particular firearm, so be sure to consult the manual before you begin shooting. Most owner's manuals contain very specific and detailed instructions with regard to your firearm.

# XIV. Firearms in the Home

Gun owners have a responsibility to ensure that our firearms do not cause injury or harm, and that includes ensuring that our guns are safely stored in the home. The term "safely stored" means different things to different readers, and the definition of safe storage changes depending on the situation.

Many shooters struggle between balancing a gun's quick accessibility in the home and ensuring that the firearm doesn't get into the wrong hands. Guns that are locked in a quarter-ton combination safe aren't going to fall into the wrong hands, but those guns will not be very easy to access in the event someone enters your home with the intent to do harm. Likewise, a gun left lying loaded by the nightstand will be easy to access, but if you have visitors with small children, that gun poses a hazard if it falls into inexperienced hands.

Safe firearm storage in the home can be accomplished in several different ways. The most secure method of home security is a high-quality gun safe. Gun safes vary drastically in weight, capacity, fire resistance, and price, so it is important to understand what is available within the bounds of your budget before making the decision to purchase a safe.

Buying a good gun safe is rarely cheap, but gun safes do offer a level of practicality in the home that extends beyond the storage of firearms. Gun safes are rated against fire, are difficult to steal, and generally have locks that most criminals can't breech, so most people who purchase a gun safe also store other valuables inside. In addition, many safes weigh several hundred pounds and most have the ability to be bolted to the floor, which makes them

virtually impossible to steal without heavy equipment and lots of time. For all but the savviest burglars, a gun safe bolted to the floor is off-limits. These gun safes also have internal dehumidifiers that prevent moisture from damaging valuable firearms and other materials kept in the safe. There are a variety of items that can be kept in gun safes, including external hard drives with data and photos (some new models of safes have ports that allow the owner to keep items plugged in while they are inside the safe), Social Security cards, visas and passports, diplomas, birth certificates, albums, and a host of other items. One

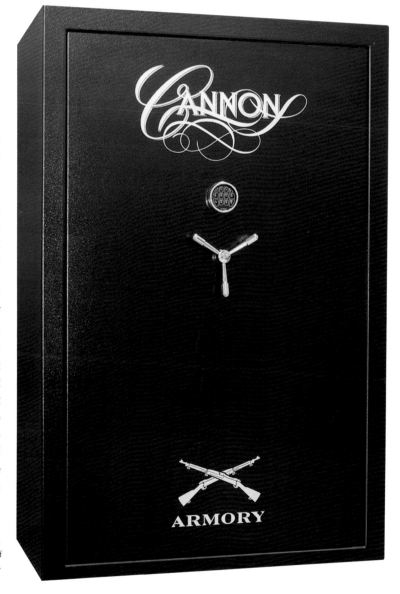

▶ A safe provides the highest level of security for your firearms and other valuables. Most quality safes like this one are rated against fire damage and weigh upwards of a half-ton, ensuring that your guns are going to stay put. Photo courtesy of Cannon Safes.

▲ In home-defense situations rapid access is important, but the need for rapid access must be balanced with the need to keep the gun secure and away from others in the home. Photo courtesy of Kimber America.

dollars upward to several thousand dollars, and moving them is no easy task. Even the average top-end gun safe will weigh between 600 and 800 pounds, and there are several that top the half-ton mark. This creates logistics issues when trying to place one of these safes in the house, and people have been badly injured trying to move heavy gun safes without professional help. The other problem with these safes is that most of them don't allow easy access to firearms, so while the guns are protected in the home, they aren't very effective at protecting the home. Gun safes have drawbacks, but there is almost certainly no more secure way to store your firearms and other valuables in the home.

▼ Gun safes are a place to store other valuables as well. They prevent anyone from finding or stealing your valuables and keep guns out of the hands of those who shouldn't have them. Photo courtesy of Cannon Safes.

individual who lost his home in a fire managed to salvage all the contents of his gun safe, including a baseball signed by Mickey Mantle.

Gun safes are fire rated by independent laboratories to determine how long the contents of the safe will remain undamaged in fires of various temperatures. Fire rating increases as more insulation is added to the safe, and the more airtight a safe is the less heat will be allowed into the safe in the event of a fire. Fire ratings are not standardized, and different safe companies develop their own testing methods. However, most high-quality safes do offer some level of protection in a house fire, and new technology like expandable door seals helps minimize fire damage.

Safes are a wonderful investment, but they are just that—an investment. Good safes aren't cheap, ranging from a thousand

▲ Most handguns come with a lock like this one that ensures the gun cannot be fired until the lock is removed. This is a safe system, and it's a good way to keep a firearm out of the hands of children, but it makes gaining access to the gun very time-consuming in emergency situations.

There are a variety of locker-type gun safes that are lighter and cheaper, but these offer virtually no fire resistance and can be moved by criminals who break into your home. Gun lockers do offer a level of protection against the gun falling into the hands of children and ignorant adults in the home, but they are difficult to access in emergencies. One innovative new option comes from a brand called Tactical Walls, and as the name implies, they supply false walls, mirrors, clocks, and more that hide secured firearms. Tactical Walls don't offer fire protection, but they allow you to securely store your firearms in plain sight and access them quickly if the need arises.

These same statements can generally be extended to small, portable, bedside gun safes. However, there are some companies that have developed ingenious designs that allow you to store a gun safely and access it quickly, which are the two primary factors in effective gun storage in the home. Safes like those

made by the company Gun Vault have recessed slots for the fingers and have pads that can be pressed in sequence by the fingers to release a locked door on the gun safe. After some time practicing with these bedside safes, most gun owners can quickly access their bedside firearm without leaving the gun lying exposed. This allows the home owner to quickly access the gun in an emergency and prevents guests and those unfamiliar with firearms from having access to the gun.

Additionally, some companies offer biometric safes. Vaultek is one of those brands, and their compact safes are among the very best options for homeowners who want quick access to their firearms without sacrificing security. Vaultek safes have a biometric pad that stores fingerprints, so you simply need to touch the finger to the pad to access the firearm. You can also open the safe using a code (the keypad lights up when your hand gets near it for ease of access at night), and there

◄ Tactical Walls offers drop-down shelves that hold firearms as well. Many of these concealment options are RFID coded for fast access.

RFID bracelet, keys, or a code. All three of these safes offer owners the ability to secure their safe to a piece of furniture or other heavy object using heavy-duty hardware, greatly reducing the risk that anyone will steal them.

There are a variety of bed holsters that are available that fit on the bed and allow for easy access to the weapon when needed. Some of these gun holsters are visible and others are not, and although they offer very rapid access to the gun during a home invasion, they do very little to prevent thieves and others in the home from accessing the gun. If you live in a home where you need to limit access to firearms, then this system is not right for you.

Gun locks come with most handguns sold today and prevent those who do not have the key from using the firearm. Many of these locks will not allow the action to close until they are removed, eliminating any chance that the gun can be fired. Most gun locks look somewhat like standard key locks with oversized locking cables or bars. These locks do an excellent job preventing others from accessing the gun and eliminate any

is a key and an RFID fob that allows access as well. There's even a Vaultek app for your phone that allows you to unlock the safe remotely, as well as a "drop alarm" that sounds when someone tampers with the safe and that message is sent directly to your phone. In addition to the Vaultek line, Hornady also offers their RAPiD SAFE 2700 that can be accessed via RFID card, chance that someone without heavy tools or a key can access your firearms. You'll trade quick access to your loaded gun for this peace of mind.

Ultimately, deciding how you will store your firearms in the home means finding a balance between security and access. In some states and regions, local law requires that guns be stored in approved safes. This type

▶ The GunVault bedside gun safe has a finger-operated keypad that allows you to rapidly access your firearms once you learn the code. It provides both security and rapid access. Photo courtesy of GunVault.

will prevent your children from learning about guns, consult my poor mother, who swore before my birth that no child of hers would ever play with or be exposed to guns. That certainly didn't prove to be the case, but last year my mother earned her CCW and I was happy to help her learn to shoot properly.

of legislation leaves little option with regard to gun storage, but in other areas laws are less stringent or do not exist at all. Carefully consider which option is best for you and remember that safety is the primary concern.

## Speaking with Children about Firearms

There exists a taboo in this country related to teaching children about guns. While some parents deem teaching their kids about firearms a necessary and prudent step, others believe it to be irresponsible and perhaps even abusive. Somehow many parents believe that if they never discuss guns, their children will somehow be immune from the dangers of guns. This is nonsense. Their children will only be ignorant and will be immune from nothing. Guns are like nothing else in a child's life. I learned very early on that guns were very powerful and were potentially dangerous if mishandled. I was also taught (and the lesson reinforced every time I broke it) that the muzzle of any gun remains in a safe direction at all times and that the finger never touches the trigger unless you are ready to fire. These were lessons I learned at eight years old and still carry today, but children who have no exposure to real, live firearms also have no appreciation for real guns. They are more inclined to handle a firearm if they stumble upon one, and as a consequence of their ignorance, they are at higher risk. If you have any illusions that ignoring the existence of firearms

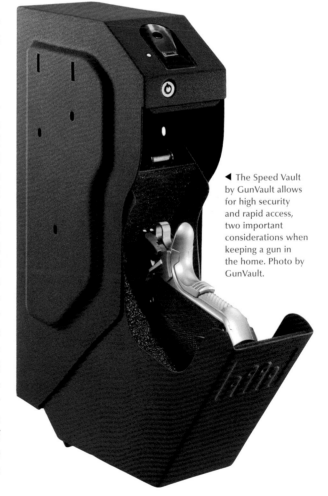

◀ The Speed Vault by GunVault allows for high security and rapid access, two important considerations when keeping a gun in the home. Photo by GunVault.

# XV. Putting It All Together

*I*n this book I've tried to cover the basics of firearms ownership and concealed carry. This certainly isn't all there is to know, and as you learn more about firearms and spend more time at the range, you may find that you are interested in learning even more about guns. You may even decide that you would like to compete someday, testing your skills at an IDPA event or another form of competitive shooting.

I hope that this book has helped you to feel more comfortable with firearms and have a better understanding of the different holsters, cartridges, finishes, sights, and a host of other choices you have to make regarding the purchase of a new gun. These choices can be overwhelming, especially if you have several different sources telling you to buy different products. Some of these choices are matters of taste or personal preference, and in the end you, the consumer, will have to be the one that makes that decision.

It is my sincere hope that you understand that there are two major components to successful concealed carry. First, you must be *safe* with your gun. In addition, you must be *comfortable* with it as well. Safety comes as a result of learning, understanding, and applying all the rules of gun safety and by understanding that, above all else, you must be absolutely certain not to put yourself or others at risk. Accomplishing this requires practicing safe gun handling procedures like keeping the action open, indexing the finger, and keeping the muzzle pointed in a safe direction. Know your target and what lies beyond it, and always protect your eyes and ears.

To become comfortable with a firearm, you must understand its basic function and mechanics and you

▼ Learning to shoot can be fun, particularly if you have a good instructor. Practicing with a firearm will also make you better prepared to defend your life in the worst of circumstances. Photo courtesy of the National Shooting Sports Foundation.

must practice often. I've tried to cover basic firearms mechanics as much as possible in the text, but since all guns are different I can't possibly cover every detail regarding every gun. This is why it will help you to have a contact who is knowledgeable about firearms and does a good job relating that information to others. Finding somebody who knows guns and knows how to teach others about guns is critical. Maybe you have a family member who is willing and capable of instructing you. If not, groups like the National Rifle Association and the National Shooting Sports Foundation have programs designed to help new shooters learn about shooting sports. In addition, the United States Concealed Carry Association has information regarding CCW reciprocity and additional information that will help you make informed decisions about concealed carry.

Many new CCW permit holders feel apprehensive about carrying their firearms. This is understandable, as most new concealed carry permit holders have never gone through their daily routines while wearing a loaded gun. It is important that you understand where you can and cannot carry and that you abide by those laws. Since concealed carry laws differ from state to state and change frequently, I've opted not to include state-by-state laws in this book because those rules would change by the time this text went to print and would continue to change virtually every year afterwards. It is important that you keep abreast of the latest changes and use the resources listed in the appendix to remain informed about the latest changes regarding concealed carry laws.

If you stay within the boundaries of the law, you are not doing anything irresponsible or foolish by exercising your rights and carrying a firearm for self-defense purposes. The best way to overcome the anxiety associated with carrying a concealed firearm is to learn the proper methods involved with carrying a gun and practice often. Sound familiar?

In many other countries around the world, citizens have been stripped of their rights to defend themselves against lethal force. Gun ownership is banned or highly restricted in many countries, leaving citizens to hope that their law enforcement and government militaries will help protect them against those that would

◀ It is important to find a firearm that you are comfortable with and to learn to shoot it well, practicing often so that you build the muscle memory necessary to be able to effectively defend yourself. Photo courtesy of Colt Manufacturing.

▲ Practice the skills that you will need in a time of crisis and learn the safety rules regarding firearms. The more you shoot the more comfortable you'll become with guns. Photo courtesy of the National Shooting Sports Foundation.

do them harm. In the United States, however, we have the liberty to protect ourselves and our families against violence. That right was not easily won, but groups like the NRA are fighting to preserve those liberties against lawmakers who would strip them away. For many Americans, guns have long been associated with violence and destruction, and this is due in part to a media that doesn't portray the truth about guns in America. By obtaining your CCW permit you are not adding to the violence but rather taking advantage of the liberties guaranteed you by the Second Amendment as well as taking steps to protect your life and the lives of those you love against the threat of violence. As long as you live within the bounds of the law, there is no reason to be apologetic or apprehensive about defending your freedom.

▶ Learning to assess a group is important to improving your shooting. Photo courtesy of the National Shooting Sports Foundation.

▲ Practice in preparation for real-life scenarios. Finding a qualified instructor that can help coach you as you learn to shoot increases your odds of success.

▲ The more you shoot the more improvement you'll see, and you'll likely come to enjoy shooting sports. Always abide by the safety rules and make sure that you keep your firearm secure in the home.

Guns aren't inherently bad, and if you learn the rules of gun safety and abide by them, shooting is one of the most exciting and rewarding pastimes available. Over the course of my life I've enjoyed target shooting with rifles, shotguns, and handguns. I still get excited when I shoot a good group and look forward to my time on the range. I've had a wonderful opportunity to meet some fantastic people who are also shooters, and I've also had the pleasure of introducing many new shooters to the sport, including my wife. She had no experience with firearms before I met her, and although she wasn't opposed to guns she simply hadn't been exposed to shooting or taught the basic principles of firearms safety. Now she enjoys shooting very much and we spend time together at the range, though she's quickly becoming a better shot than I am.

This book is filled with information about different firearms, cartridges, accessories, and other general knowledge to help you begin learning to shoot. But the

basic principles outlined in this book are very simple. If you plan to carry concealed, you must learn the rules of gun safety and proper shooting skills, find a firearm that you are comfortable shooting, and practice a lot. If you remember to focus on those criteria, then you may also find that you enjoy shooting and will become comfortable with guns.

I hope that you have the opportunity to work with someone who knows firearms and can help you become a better shooter. A good shooting coach can make you safer and much more comfortable around firearms, helping you work through the period when you are learning the basic functions of your firearm. Patience is key; when you are learning to shoot it is important that you feel comfortable with the process and that you don't rush through the important fundamental steps of shooting. I don't think that beginners necessarily need to have a loaded firearm in their hands immediately. Practice with blueguns will help you learn the basic principles without the added pressure of putting shots downrange. In addition, I believe that the newest laser shooting aids are some of the best tools for new shooters. This way you can practice all the steps of firing your own gun plenty of times before you switch to live ammunition. You will have learned the basics of gun safety, stance, grip, and trigger control before you are actually on the range with a loaded firearm.

Those are the basics of concealed carry. Be safe with your gun, be comfortable shooting, and practice as often as you can. I haven't spent very much time in this book addressing how to handle that moment of truth when you face that awful decision to shoot someone or be killed yourself. I don't imagine that I could accurately relate to you what such a terrible situation would feel like. All I know is that your conscious brain won't help you remember something you learned in a concealed carry or basic firearms class in that horrible instant. You'll have to rely on muscle memory and count on all those hours of practice to make the difference.

I hope that you are never faced with that situation. I also hope that you learn to enjoy shooting and appreciate that you can confidently defend yourself and those who mean the most to you, never forgetting how fortunate we are to have that right. Perhaps some time we'll meet in the future at a convention or seminar. If so, I hope that you've learned something valuable from this book and that your experiences with firearms are always good, as mine have been.

▲ You can learn the basics of shooting relatively quickly, but becoming a great shooter requires a lifetime of work.

# Appendix A: Shooting Associations and Organizations

### IDPA: International Defensive Pistol Association

www.idpa.com

The International Defensive Pistol Association hosts competitive events designed to simulate real-life defensive situations. IDPA competitions require "stock" or factory guns and ammunition, so unlike other shooting competitions, the sport focuses on defensive shooting using the type of pistols that one is likely to carry in real-life defense situations. IDPA matches allow shooters to use their concealed carry holsters and practice with the guns they will carry every day.

### IPSC: International Practical Shooting Confederation

www.ipsc.org

IPSC competition shoots involve a variety of different scenarios that require the shooter to be able to shoot on the move and to hit mobile targets. Targets are set up in a variety of different ways, and this sport tests the ability of the shooter to evaluate different situations and respond accordingly. There are a variety of different handguns used for IPSC competitions, from standard, off-the-shelf defense guns to customized pistols designed for competitive shooters.

### ISSF: International Shooting Sports Federation

www.issf-sports.org

The ISSF was started in 1907 and promotes competitive shooting at the highest level, including Olympic shooting. There are a wide variety of ISSF competitions, and these events showcase the very best shooters from around the world competing in a wide variety of events, from air rifle and pistol to rifle and shotgun.

### NRA: National Rifle Association

www.nra.org

The NRA was established in 1871 to help improve the shooting skills of soldiers. Today, the NRA is the largest shooting organization in the world, with millions of members around the globe from a variety of different shooting disciplines. The NRA serves to protect Americans' Second Amendment rights and works to promote shooting sports by providing classes and shooting courses across the country where new shooters can learn more about safe firearms handling and can improve their skills as shooters. The NRA has also invested millions in youth programs to help educate young people about firearms and teach them to be safe shooters. There are a variety of NRA competitions available, including pistol sports. The annual NRA conference is a fantastic place to meet with various representatives from different gun companies and to get expert advice on the firearms and gear you need to be successful.

### NSSF: National Shooting Sports Foundation

www.nssf.org

The mission statement of the NSSF is, "To promote, protect, and preserve hunting and the shooting sports," and since 1961 this organization has worked to do just that. The NSSF is a trade organization and hosts the annual SHOT Show, which introduces the latest industry products to the public. Like the NRA, the NSSF has many resources available to shooters, including information on safe gun handling and gun safety kits and updated news on legal issues facing gun owners. They also host a series of "First Shots" seminars that allow new shooters to work with qualified instructors to learn how to shoot properly and safely.

### USPSA: United States Practical Shooting Association

www.uspsa.org

The USPSA is a member organization that allows shooters to compete in practical shooting situations, and with over 400 member ranges across the country there is likely to be a USPSA shooting range not far from where you live. Membership in USPSA includes membership in the IPSC (see above) and allows shooters to compete in a host of different events.

### USCCA: United States Concealed Carry Association

www.usconcealedcarry.com

The USCCA was founded to act as a network for concealed carry enthusiasts, bringing updates on the latest equipment and editorial on concealed carry issues and products to those who carry concealed weapons for defense. The association publishes *Concealed Carry Magazine* monthly and has almost 60,000 members across the country.

# Appendix B: Ballistics Charts

The following table lists a variety of common target and defensive ammunition in different calibers from various companies. Velocities are in feet per second (fps) and energy is measured in foot-pounds (ft-lbs). Kinetic energy is a combination of bullet mass and velocity. Also listed are .410 shotshell loads. This list is certainly not a full spectrum of all companies nor all defensive loads, but it is designed to serve as a basic reference for various cartridges that are available for defensive and target shooting.

| Caliber | Manufacturer | Product | Velocity (at the muzzle) fps | Energy (at the muzzle) ft-lbs | Use |
|---|---|---|---|---|---|
| .22 Long Rifle | Winchester | Wildcat 22 40 Grain Lead Bullet | 1060 | 100 | Target |
| .22 Long Rifle | Remington | CBee 22 30 Grain Hollow Point | 740 | 40 | Target |
| .22 Long Rifle | Remington | Thunderbolt 40 Grain Lead Bullet | 1255 | 140 | Target |
| .22 WMR | Hornady | FTX Critical Defense 45 Grain Expanding | 1000 | 100 | Target/ Defense |
| .22 WMR | Winchester | Super X 40 Grain Jacketed Hollow Point | 1910 | 324 | Target/ Defense |
| .25 Auto | Federal | American Eagle 50 Grain Full Metal Jacket | 760 | 64 | Target |
| .25 Auto | Hornady | XTP 35 Grain Expanding Bullet | 900 | 63 | Target/ Defense |
| .32 Auto | Remington | UMC 71 Grain Full Metal Jacket | 905 | 129 | Target |
| .32 Auto | Federal | Hydra-Shok 65 Grain Jacketed Hollow Point | 925 | 123 | Defense |
| .32 S&W Long | Remington | 98 Grain Lead Bullet | 705 | 115 | Target |
| .32 H&R Magnum | Black Hills | 85 Grain Jacketed Hollow point | 1100 | 228 | Target/ Defense |
| .327 Federal Magnum | Federal | American Eagle 100 Grain Jacketed Soft Point | 1500 | 500 | Target |

| Caliber | Manufacturer | Product | Velocity (at the muzzle) fps | Energy (at the muzzle) ft-lbs | Use |
|---------|--------------|---------|------------------------------|-------------------------------|-----|
| .327 Federal Magnum | Federal | Hydra-Shok 85 Grain Jacketed Hollow Point | 1400 | 370 | Defense |
| .380 Auto | Winchester | PDX-1 Defender 95 Grain Bonded Jacketed Hollow Point | 1000 | 211 | Defense |
| .380 Auto | Remington | Golden Saber 102 Grain Jacketed Hollow Point | 940 | 200 | Defense |
| .380 Auto | Black Hills | 90 Grain Jacketed Hollow Point | 1000 | 200 | Defense |
| .380 Auto | Federal | American Eagle 95 Grain Full Metal Jacket | 980 | 203 | Target |
| 9mm Luger | Remington | HD Ultimate Home Defense 124 Grain Brass Jacketed Hollow Point | 1125 | 349 | Defense |
| 9mm Luger | Black Hills | 115 Grain Full Metal Jacket | 1150 | 336 | Target |
| 9mm Luger | Federal | Hydra-Shok 147 Grain Jacketed Hollow Point | 1000 | 326 | Defense |
| 9mm Luger | Winchester | 115 Grain Full Metal Jacket | 1190 | 362 | Target |
| 9mm Luger +P | Hornady | 135 Grain FlexLock Critical Duty Jacketed Hollow Point | 1110 | 369 | Defense |
| 9mm Luger +P | Black Hills | 124 Grain Jacketed Hollow Point | 1250 | 430 | Defense |
| .38 Special | Federal | 148 Grain Lead Wadcutter Match | 690 | 156 | Target |

| Caliber | Manufacturer | Product | Velocity (at the muzzle) fps | Energy (at the muzzle) ft-lbs | Use |
|---|---|---|---|---|---|
| .38 Special | Remington | 130 Grain Full Metal Jacket | 790 | 173 | Target |
| .38 Special | Hornady | 110 Grain FTX Critical Defense Jacketed Hollow Point | 1010 | 249 | Defense |
| .38 Special +P | Winchester | PDX-1 130 Grain Bonded Jacketed Hollow Point | 950 | 260 | Defense |
| .38 Special +P | Remington | Golden Saber 125 Grain Jacketed Hollow Point | 975 | 264 | Defense |
| .38 Special +P | Black Hills | 125 Grain Jacketed Hollow Point | 1050 | 306 | Defense |
| .357 SIG | Winchester | PDX-1 125 Grain Bonded Jacketed Hollow Point | 1332 | 506 | Defense |
| .357 Remington Magnum | Federal | Hydra-Shok 158 Grain Jacketed Hollow Point | 1240 | 539 | Defense |
| .357 Remington Magnum | Black Hills | 125 Grain Jacketed Hollow Point | 1500 | 625 | Defense |
| .357 Remington Magnum | Hornady | 125 Grain FTX Critical Defense Jacketed Hollow Point | 1500 | 624 | Defense |
| .38 Super Automatic +P | Winchester | 130 Grain Full Metal Jacket | 1215 | 426 | Target |
| .40 S&W | Remington | 180 Grain Full Metal Jacket | 990 | 392 | Target |
| .40 S&W | Hornady | 155 Grain XTP Jacketed Hollow Point | 1180 | 479 | Defense |

| Caliber | Manufacturer | Product | Velocity (at the muzzle) fps | Energy (at the muzzle) ft-lbs | Use |
|---|---|---|---|---|---|
| .40 S&W | Winchester | PDX-1 Defender 165 Grain Bonded Jacketed Hollow Point | 850 | 476 | Defense |
| .40 S&W | Black Hills | 155 Grain Jacketed Hollow Point | 1150 | 450 | Defense |
| .44 Special | Federal | Champion 200 Grain Semi-Wadcutter | 870 | 336 | Target |
| .44 Special | Hornady | 165 Grain FTX Critical Defense Jacketed Hollow Point | 800 | 297 | Defense |
| .44 Remington Magnum | Black Hills | 300 Grain Jacketed Hollow Point | 1150 | 840 | Defense/ Hunting |
| .45 Auto | Winchester | PDX-1 Defender 225 Grain Bonded Jacketed Hollow Point | 850 | 361 | Defense |
| .45 Auto | Winchester | 230 Grain Full Metal Jacket | 835 | 356 | Target |
| .45 Auto | Remington | HD Ultimate Home Defense 230 Grain Brass Jacketed Hollow Point | 875 | 391 | Defense |
| .45 Auto | Black Hills | 200 Grain Match Semi-Wadcutter | 875 | 340 | Target |
| .45 ACP +P | Hornady | 200 Grain XTP Jacketed Hollow Point | 1055 | 494 | Defense |
| .45 ACP +P | Remington | Golden Saber 185 Grain Jacketed Hollow Point | 1140 | 534 | Defense |

| Caliber | Manufacturer | Product | Velocity (at the muzzle) fps | Energy (at the muzzle) ft-lbs | Use |
|---|---|---|---|---|---|
| .45 Colt | Federal | Champion 225 Grain Semi-Wadcutter Hollow Point | 830 | 344 | Target |
| .45 Colt | Hornady | 185 Grain FTX Critical Defense Jacketed Hollow Point | 920 | 348 | Defense |
| .410 Shotshell (2 ½ Inches) | Winchester | 3 Defense Disc Projectiles and 12 BBs | 750 | N/A | Defense |
| .410 Shotshell (2 ½ Inches) | Federal | 7/16 Ounce #4 Shot | 950 | N/A | Defense |
| .410 Shotshell (3 Inches) | Winchester | 4 Defense Disc Projectiles and 16 BBs | 750 | N/A | Defense |

# Appendix C: Manufacturer Contact Information

## Firearms

### Beretta USA

www.berettausa.com
17601 Beretta Drive
Accokeek, MD 20607
(800) 929-2901

About Beretta: Beretta has a long history of firearms production dating back over 500 years. Today, Beretta and its holdings produce virtually every type of firearm imaginable, from rifles and shotguns to military weapons and nostalgic single action cowboy revolvers. The company's best known product may be the M9 semiautomatic pistol, which is used by the United States military and several law enforcement agencies.

Products for Concealed Carry:
Centerfire Semiautomatic Handguns
Rimfire Semiautomatic Handguns
Centerfire Revolvers
Rimfire Revolvers
Shooting Accessories

### Browning

www.browning.com
One Browning Place
Morgan, UT 84050
(800) 333-3288

About Browning: John Moses Browning was one of the greatest firearms designers of all time, and Browning Firearms began by selling his sporting guns in 1927. Though the company is best known for producing sporting guns, Browning also sells handguns, including the well-respected Hi-Power pistol.

Products for Concealed Carry:
Centerfire Semiautomatic Handguns
Rimfire Semiautomatic Handguns
Shooting Accessories

## Charter Arms

www.charterfirearms.com
18 Brewster Lane
Shelton, CT 06484
(866) 769-4867

About Charter Arms: Charter Arms was founded by Douglas McClennahan in 1964 with the intention of producing high-quality handguns at a reasonable price. Today Charter Arms continues that tradition and is best known for producing revolvers in a wide variety of configurations and finishes.

Products for Concealed Carry:
Centerfire Revolvers
Rimfire Revolvers

## Colt

www.colt.com
P.O. Box 1868
Hartford, CT 06144
(800) 962-2658

About Colt Manufacturing: Samuel Colt's original single action revolver is unquestionably one of the greatest guns of all time. Today, 160 years later, the company continues to make quality military and civilian firearms. Many of their semiautos are excellent for concealed carry purposes.

Products for Concealed Carry:
Centerfire Semiautomatic Handguns
Centerfire Revolvers

## CZ-USA

www.cz-usa.com
P.O. Box 171073
Kansas City, KS 66117-0073
(800) 955-4486

About CZ-USA: Founded in 1936 in the Czech Republic, CZ produced small arms for military and civilians. Today, CZ-USA produces a wide variety of handguns that are ideal for concealed carry. In addition, the company also owns American company Dan Wesson, which is best known for producing revolvers.

Products for Concealed Carry:
Centerfire Semiautomatic Handguns
Rimfire Semiautomatic Handguns
Centerfire Revolvers

**DoubleTap Defense**
www.doubletapdefense.com

**FNH USA**
www.fnamerica.com
P.O. Box 9424
McLean, VA 22102
(703) 288-3500

About FNH-USA: FNH has a long history of producing firearms for military and civilians. American Gun designer John M. Browning had strong ties to the company, which was originally based in Belgium. Today, FNH-USA is located in Virginia and all of their handguns are built at their state-of-the-art facility in South Carolina.

Products for Concealed Carry:
Centerfire Semiautomatic Handguns

**Glock**

http://us.glock.com/
6000 Highlands Parkway
Smyrna, GA 30082
(770) 432-1202

About Glock: Founded in Austria, Glock produces some of the most popular semiautomatic handguns for law enforcement, military, and personal defense. Gaston Glock's striker-fired pistols are known to be durable and easy to clean and maintain. They are available in a variety of calibers and configurations.

Products for Concealed Carry:
Centerfire Semiautomatic Handguns

**Kimber**

www.kimberamerica.com
30 Lower Valley Road
Kalispell, MT 59901
(888) 243-4522

About Kimber: Kimber originally began producing rimfire rifles, and later moved to the production of centerfire rifles and finally pistols. Today, Kimber is the largest producer of 1911-style pistols, and their guns have won many major shooting competitions and are carried by military, law enforcement, and civilians.

Products for Concealed Carry:
Centerfire Semiautomatic Handguns
Rimfire Semiautomatic Handguns

## Remington

www.remington.com
870 Remington Drive
P.O. Box 700
Madison, NC 27025-0700
(800) 243-9700

About Remington: Remington Arms Company was founded in 1816 in New York and has become one of the world's largest and most respected firearms companies. Although Remington is best known for producing rifles and shotguns, they also produce centerfire handguns and ammunition as well.

Products for Concealed Carry:
Centerfire Semiautomatic Handguns

## SCCY Firearms

www.sccy.com
1800 Concept Court
Daytona Beach, FL 32114
(866) 729-7599

About SCCY Firearms: Tool and die maker Joe Roebuck set out to design a semiautomatic pistol in 1998, and the result was SCCY's current line of compact concealed carry handguns. All SCCY handguns are made in the United States and carry a full lifetime warranty. The company's CPX-1 and CPX-2 handguns have received praise from the shooting media for being compact, accurate, and reliable.

Products for Concealed Carry:
Centerfire Semiautomatic Handguns

## SIG Sauer

www.sigsauer.com
72 Pease Boulevard
Newington, NH 03801
(603) 610-3000

About SIG Sauer: SIG Sauer firearms originated in Switzerland in the nineteenth century. Today, SIG Sauer is one of the world's most popular handgun makers, and military, police, and civilians around the world rely on SIG products every day. SIG Sauer offers one of the most extensive lines of semiautomatic handguns available.

Products for Concealed Carry:
Centerfire Semiautomatic Pistols
Rimfire Semiautomatic Pistols
Concealed Carry Accessories

## Smith & Wesson

www.smith-wesson.com
2100 Roosevelt Avenue
Springfield, MA 01104
(800) 331-0852

About Smith & Wesson: In Connecticut in 1852, Horace Smith and Daniel Wesson started the firearms company that would eventually grow into Smith & Wesson, one of the world's premier gun companies. Today, Smith & Wesson has one of the most extensive lines of firearms available, including centerfire and rimfire semiautos, as well as a wide variety of revolvers.

Products for Concealed Carry:
Centerfire Semiautomatic Handguns
Rimfire Automatic Handguns
Centerfire Revolvers
Rimfire Revolvers
Concealed Carry Accessories

## Springfield Armory

www.springfield-armory.com
420 West Main Street
Geneseo, IL 61254
(800) 680-6866

About Springfield Armory: The Springfield Armory dates back to 1777, and in 1794 the company began producing muskets for the United States military. In 1968 the Armory was closed, but it was reopened in 1974 and continues to produce civilian and military firearms. Today, Springfield Armory produces a wide variety of semiautomatic pistols for concealed carry.

Products for Concealed Carry:
Centerfire Semiautomatic Handguns

## Sturm, Ruger & Co.

www.ruger.com
200 Ruger Road
Prescott, AZ 86301
(336) 949-5200

About Sturm, Ruger & Co.: In 1949 Bill Ruger, one of the greatest American gun designers, began building semiautomatic pistols at a small warehouse in Connecticut. Since that time, Sturm, Ruger, & Co.

has become one of America's largest gun makers, with an extensive line of handguns for concealed carry.

Products for Concealed Carry:
Centerfire Semiautomatic Handguns
Rimfire Semiautomatic Handguns
Centerfire Revolvers
Rimfire Revolvers

## Taurus Manufacturing

www.taurususa.com
16175 NW 49 Avenue
Miami, FL 33014
(305) 624-1115

About Taurus: Brazil's *Forjas Taurus* (or Taurus Forge) began producing pistols in 1941. Today, Taurus has among the most extensive lineup of handgun offerings available, including a wide variety of revolvers and semiautomatic pistols. Many of Taurus's handguns are designed specifically for concealed carry.

Products for Concealed Carry:
Centerfire Semiautomatic Pistols
Rimfire Semiautomatic Pistols
Centerfire Revolvers
Rimfire Revolvers

## Walther Arms

www.waltherarms.com
7700 Chad Colley Boulevard
Fort Smith, AR 72916
(479) 242-8500

About Walther: German gun designer Carl Walther produced some of the most popular semiautomatic handguns of all time, including the Walther PP and the Walther PPK. Today, the company is still producing highly regarded semiautomatic pistols in a wide variety of configurations and styles.

Products for Concealed Carry:
Centerfire Semiautomatic Handguns
Rimfire Semiautomatic Handguns

## Ammunition

**Black Hills Ammunition**
www.black-hills.com
(605) 348-5150

**Federal Ammunition**
www.federalpremium.com
(800) 379-1732

**Hornady Manufacturing**
www.hornady.com
(800) 338-3220

**Nosler Ammunition**
www.nosler.com
(800) 285-3701

**Remington Ammunition**
www.remington.com
(800) 243-9700

**Winchester Ammunition**
https://winchester.com

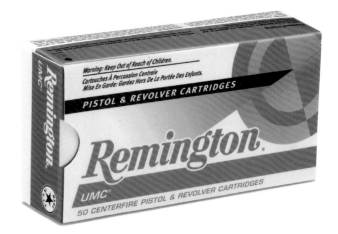

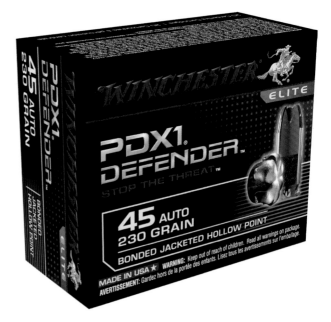

## Accessories

### Aimpoint
Optics
www.aimpoint.com
(877) 246-7646

### BLACKHAWK!
Apparel, Belts, Holsters, Other Accessories
www.blackhawk.com
(406) 284-3840

### BlueGuns
Nonfiring Practice Guns
www.blueguns.com
(321) 951-0407

### Cannon Safes
Gun Safes
www.cannonsafe.com
(800) 242-1055

### Crimson Trace Lasers
Laser Sights and Tactical Lights
www.crimsontrace.com
(800) 442-2406

▶ Tru-Spec Tactical Pants

### CrossBreed Holsters
Holsters, Belts, Other Carry
Accessories
www.crossbreedholsters.com
(888) 732-5011

### DeSantis GunHide
Holsters
www.desantisholster.com
(631) 841-6300

### Flashbang Holsters
Holsters
www.flashbangstore.com
(405) 326-6758

### Galco Gunleather
Holsters and Carry Accessories
www.galcogunleather.com
(800) 874-2526

### GunVault
Gun Safes
www.gunvault.com
(800) 222-1055

### Laser Lyte
Laser Training and Sighting Aids
www.laserlyte.com
(928) 649-3201

▶ Galco Holster

**Trijicon**
Sights
www.trijicon.com
(800) 338-0563

**Tru-Spec**
Tactical Clothing and Accessories
www.truspec.com
(800) 241-9414

**Uncle Mike's Firearm Accessories**
Holsters, Bags, Magazine Loaders, Other Shooting
Accessories
www.unclemikes.com
(800) 423-3537

**UnderTech Undercover**
Holsters, Apparel, and Accessories
www.undertechundercover.com
(800) 601-8273

**Vaultek Safes**
Gun Safes
www.vault eksafe.com
(407) 329-4164

**Versacarry**
Holsters
www.versacarry.com
(855) 278-9678

# ALSO AVAILABLE

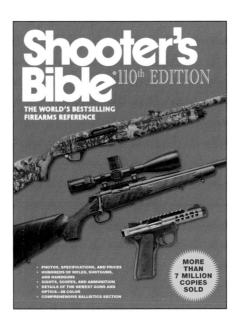

## Shooter's Bible, 110th Edition
The World's Bestselling Firearms Reference
Edited by Jay Cassell

Published annually for more than eighty years, the *Shooter's Bible* is the most comprehensive and sought-after reference guide for new firearms and their specifications, as well as for thousands of guns that have been in production and are currently on the market. The 110th edition also contains new and existing product sections on ammunition, optics, and accessories, plus up-to-date handgun and rifle ballistic tables along with extensive charts of currently available bullets and projectiles for handloading.

With a timely feature on the newest products on the market, and complete with color and black-and-white photographs featuring various makes and models of firearms and equipment, the Shooter's Bible is an essential authority for any beginner or experienced hunter, firearm collector, or gun enthusiast.

$29.99 Paperback • ISBN 978-1-5107-3838-6

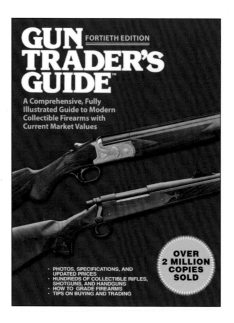